THE ART OF STEPMOTHERING

THE ART of STEP-MOTHERING

PEARL KETOVER PRILIK

Text ©1994 by Pearl Ketover Prilik

First published in the United States of America in 1994 by WRS Publishing,
A Division of WRS Group, Inc., 701 N. New Road, Waco, Texas 76710
Jacket design by Joe James

10 9 8 7 6 5 4 3 2 1

Library of Congress Cataloging-in-Publication Data

Ketover Prilik, Pearl.
    The art of stepmothering/Pearl Ketover Prilik.
        p.   cm.
    Includes bibliographical references.
    ISBN 1-56796-042-1 : $19.95
    1. Stepmothers--United States. 2. Parenting--United States.
3. Stepfamilies--United States--Psychological aspects. I. Title.
HQ759.92.K478   1994
306.874--dc20
                                                            94-5518
                                                            CIP

DEDICATION

To my husband, D.J.
Applause maker, underwriter,
soulmate, and very best friend

Table of Contents

Acknowledgments

The writing of any book may appear to be a solitary process; however, without the collective dedication, encouragement, and hard work of many others, a book remains simply a collection of unbound pages. And so, those who made this project a reality...

My publisher, Dr. Wayman Spence, who breathed life into this project with his commitment, practical assistance and infectious enthusiasm.

My agent, Harvey Klinger, for his accessibility, his quick thinking, and precise readings.

My editor Georgia Brady and copy editor Phyllis Guest, who with a steady hand cut and snipped, permitting new light to shine throughout.

My publicity editor, Sherry Claypool, who encouraged all possibilities allowing the project room to spread its wings.

My original family: mother, father, and brother, with whom my sense of family began...

My own family with whom this sense continues to unfold:

Josh, my son: all the wonder and magic of bearing him into this world has brightened with each day that followed: Loving him continues to be one of life's greatest joys—a young man, who has taken the warmth and depth of the tropical sea and colored the very definition of family and of my life with a shimmering vitality that is uniquely his own.

Cori, my stepdaughter: my love for her is refreshing, clear, and uncomplicated. Guiding her passage across the threshold from girl to womanhood provided the magic of a trip backward into my own past—a young woman who continues to soften each day with her commitment and trust and who sparkles my life with her courage and laughter.

Brett, my stepson: my deep feeling for him has taught me much about what I now know about love, trust, and dedication; about building dreams and realizing them—a young man who has enriched my understanding of the horizons of life itself, all in his own incomparable way.

Celia, ("Mother") my grandmother: upon whose green velvet carpets I, as a little girl, danced—and who continues to warm the past and fire the promise of the still unfolding future with a shimmery, silvery song that is hers alone.

And of course, my husband, D.J., for whom a proper acknowledgment would fill another volume. His confidence, forbearance, enthusiasm, love, and support have been continuous and, even more majestically, without complaint. A man who has always been grounded enough to encourage me to fly, knowing that no height can ever diminish his magnitude in my life.

Most of all, I would like to thank all of the stepmothers who participated in the study that formed the core of this project. The wonderful women who freely shared the personal pain, joy, frustration, and satisfaction that defined their lives as stepmothers. The intensity of their experiences leapt from their pages; it is their voice that resonates throughout these pages. Thank you to all the women who both opened their lives to me and entrusted me with the task of speaking for and about them. I hope that I have done them, and their stories, the justice they so richly deserve.

STEPPIE?

Approximately sixty million adults are currently involved in step situations; I, too, am one of them. Although the numbers are high, there have been few guidelines. Most stepmothers begin their stepfamily with only the vaguest of expectations.

The subject of stepmothering continues to change with each new stepmother and every new experience. When I, myself, became a stepmother many years ago, I began by feeling very confident that what I considered to be my very positive experience as a mother would translate into competence as a stepmother. I quickly discovered that this just wasn't so. Stepmothering—this new kind of mothering, mothering without the touching, the giggling, the luscious intimacy of biological motherhood—was not as natural nor as easy as I had imagined it would be.

For starters, I wasn't even sure what to be called by my stepchildren, and they certainly weren't sure what to call me. Not that we didn't try; for weeks we continued trying out different names until one of us, no one quite remembers who exactly, hit upon "Steppie." We all liked it because it named our then new and special relationship; no one else in the world had or would ever call me "Steppie." Of course there were many other issues to be worked out as we became a family. Family conferences, individual talks, letter writing— to my husband, my son, my stepchildren, and even to myself—helped us through the rough spots. By far, the greatest help in this uncharted course as a stepmother was my husband, my two stepchildren's father and a father in all ways but biologically to my son. His support for my role in all the children's lives was, and continues to be, absolute.

At the time, there was little written for, by, or about stepmothers, and so to fill this void I reached out to the real "experts" in the field; those with tried and tested experience—stepmothers themselves. To this end, stepmothers across the country answered a lengthy questionnaire of over one hundred items and addressed a wide range of stepparenting experiences. Stepmothers were far beyond generous in their replies, taking the time to add comment and personal histories that at times ran over twenty pages. Some stepmothers even designed charts and diagrams of their family constellations to help express the complicated relationships among its members. From these individual frames of reference, recurring themes began to emerge. Gradually the individual experiences of these stepmothers, added to the findings offered by existing professional research in the area, began to coalesce into a collective, normative experience of stepmothers: Shimmering and lovely, dark and light, magical and illusive—indeed, another kind of love.

Stepmothers struggled to express just what they gained from this role. I suppose it is fitting that, at this point, I, as question-poser, attempt to answer this question myself. Reflecting on my own experience as a stepmother, I'd say that for me stepmothering is a bit like driving on ice. To a novice, the task may seem either too easy or completely daunting. However, it is the ice itself that becomes the teacher. One quickly learns that quick starts, sudden stops, and jerky movements just won't work; that in fact what does work is a steady, constant, confident movement. If things seem to slide out of control, back off from both the accelerator and the brake, and always—*but always*—keep a firm and steady hand on the steering wheel. Finally, if you should skid, don't panic, just steer into the skid rather than against it, and above all remember that ice *is* navigable once one understands how to negotiate its own unique surface. So it is with driving on ice, and so it seems with stepmothering.

Stepmothering is another kind of parenting; I, too, like so many other stepmothers, sometimes miss having felt my stepchildren kick inside my womb, having held them as infants and rocked them to sleep. I miss the confidence, the validation, the sweet smiles, and conspiratorial womanliness of motherhood, present in my relationship with my son and absent from my relationship with my stepchildren. Initially, I expected an extension of the same kind of love I had felt as a mother. I found a different kind as a stepmother.

I find, too, that I am a different parent toward my stepchildren than I am toward my son—sometimes a more logical, compassionate, calmer parent. There is something both more and less inflammatory with my stepchildren; the heat that often fires the bond with my son often burns more sedately with my stepchildren. Yet there is, however faint, a distant threat of conflagration, and so I am more careful. I am proud of my role, and I know that I have been and continue to be an integral and important figure in my stepchildren's lives, and they in mine.

What have I gained from this experience of stepmothering? A new, enhanced dimension of the concept of family and relationships. Family that is not consigned from blood nor even created from desire, but that evolves through time and shared experience. Relationships that stand free from biological, legal, or other external bonds, developed from shared commitment, loyalty, respect, and common history. Such families, such relationships, may, if one is very fortunate, come to rest under the banner of love. Perhaps we stepmothers really are somewhat magical creatures, entrusted with the opportunity—and the challenge—of giving our stepchildren another chance, a different ride on the merry-go-round. And so, like that last fairy in *Sleeping Beauty*, stepmothers cannot hope to change the past; but like that well-intentioned, high-spirited fairy, we can, and do, shape our futures.

—P.K.P.
Lido Beach, N.Y., 1994

Chapter 1

THE UNKNOWN

Remember what it felt like to be a child—the brightness of snow, that sense of high expectation holding a gift wrapped in bright paper? Remember the texture of childhood —how long the summers used to be, steamy days stretching endlessly into sweet, velvet nights? Remember the incomparable coldness as the tip of your tongue met the curve of ice cream? And remember too, the scary parts of childhood—lying in bed moments after a bedtime story thinking about princes and princesses, kings and castles, evil sorcerers and wicked stepmothers—jumping as the door clicked shut too quickly, throwing the room into darkness, a darkness livened with unknown but palpable danger?

Remember the fear? How did you handle it? With a pile of stuffed animals lined up for protection along the edge of your bed? With whispered promises and pacts with a God that you were still completely certain could and would hear you. Maybe just a finger popped into the mouth, to suck away the fear.

If you were lucky, the door opened, bringing in warm light to banish the shadow-monsters and comforting voices to soothe and slow your racing heart. If not, you braved the nights alone, with bedcovers pulled up over your head, your chilled feet tucked under you, burrowing as far into the pillows as possible, and somehow you managed to get through the night—alone.

Many stepmothers don't have to return to childhood to bring back such memories. They feel this way right now. Women who marry men with children are often ill-prepared for their new life as a stepparent. Deprived of literature, support, or even a clear understanding of the role they are expected to play in their new families, such women often find stepmothering overwhelming.

Stepmothers are often isolated from one another, feeling stigmatized by society and virtually ignored by either professional or lay research. The full-time or custodial stepmother has been shunned, overlooked, forgotten, or treated with a chillingly polite distaste. This cold-shoulder treatment exacerbates the typical stress experienced by anyone trying to raise a family. Stepmothers are left to confront the challenges of their new families in a vacuum. Expected to assume primary leadership of a family that is of someone else's origin, bolstered by little or no support, too many stepmothers feel overwhelmed.

"Confused"

"Disappointed"

"Angry"

"Resentful"

"Betrayed"

These are the most common terms women use when asked how they feel about "stepmothering." But what is a "stepmother" anyway? When we look up stepmothering in the dictionary we often find that there is not even a definition reserved for stepmothers. Usually, one is referred to the more general "stepparent" for further information. But whether or not the stepmother is given her own few lines in the dictionary, stepmothering is typically defined in terms of a woman's relationship to her husband.

There seems to be a bit of a problem here; there is something particularly unsettling about describing a woman's relationship to children only in terms of the woman's tie to the children's father. There's something inadequate and unsatisfyingly chattel-like in this definition that places a distance between stepmothers and their stepchildren— especially when the stepmothers are the primary caretakers.

Although the husband is the obvious "creator" of the relationship between stepmother and stepchildren, the definition of "stepmother" cannot end there. After all, a "mother's" relationship with her children *technically* originates from her relationship with the father, but "mother" is defined in terms of the relationship between woman and child. So we return to the confusion about what a stepmother is.

We might try defining a stepmother by what she does,

but a role described in terms of its function blurs, rather than clarifies the role of stepmothers. There are drawbacks in trying to figure out who you are by what you do, since who you are sets up certain boundaries in relationships.

Perhaps the simplest way of visualizing this dilemma is with an example. What would you call: a person who rubs an unclothed body of another person?

You may have thought first of a nurse, physician, or physical therapist—or along more erotic lines, a prostitute, or along romantic lines, a lover, or more literally, a masseuse? We cannot decide who this person is unless we have information that sets boundaries of behavior and emphasizes the intent of behavior.

Many stepmothers find themselves in this quandary— faced with knowing what they do, without being able to conceptualize who they are in terms of either the intent or the dynamics of the relationship between themselves and the children they care for. Stepmothers, left to define themselves by what they do for their stepchildren may have difficulty separating their role from other domestic- and child-caretaking roles. In fact, many stepmothers describe feeling like a maid or a babysitter.

Just What Is a Stepmother?

This ambiguity is particularly stressful when it clashes with the stark realities of childcare for which most stepmothers are responsible. The enormity of such responsibility combined with the vagueness of their role creates a volatile mixture. This mixture is pressurized by the stepmothers' own expectations "to do well," "to be happy," and "to make everyone else happy." When this mixture is subjected to the unrelenting pressure of daily life, there is an increasing possibility of explosion.

To defuse the pressure and redirect the energy women bring to the role of stepmother, it is essential to take a look at stepmothering from different vantage points, starting with how and when stepmothers come into being.

Stepmothers are "made" at the altar. In this way, their new role seems linked to the romance, passion, and love they feel for their new husbands, and the promise for future happiness seems bright. This "contagion" effect has stepmothers confusing their roles as brides with their roles as stepmothers and expecting these feelings to be parallel.

However, the two roles and the prognosis for each are not interchangeable. A woman has usually given more than passing thought to marrying a man with children. Yet her attention will more than likely have been focused on the *man*; the decision to marry will more than likely have been based on considerations unrelated to her future as a stepmother. In fact, many stepmothers report that they had only the fuzziest of expectations about that role. Some even say that they "hadn't thought about the children too much at all" before their marriages.

Still, yesterday's brides, bright with romance, passion, and optimism, are the stepmothers of today. They simply don't have time to move slowly and allow their dreamy and often unformed expectations to crystalize. They must be stepmothers immediately. This conflict between the "honeymoon" expectation and the reality of stepchildren who need caring for now prompts many stepmothers to wonder just what they stepped into.

Too often, stepmothers feel they stepped front and center stage onto a set for disaster. Moreover, there is an audience: Husbands, family, in-laws, friends who have "told her so," stepchildren and children from previous marriages, and teachers... sometimes it seems that the whole world is watching.

So, the stepmother begins her role without a clear idea of who she is and is expected to assume an enormous task under watchful eyes—but that isn't the end of it! Too often, stepmothers feel that they have little control over their situation; this perceived lack of control is a significant contributor to stress. In fact, it is common knowledge that stress is high in situations in which one has a limited sense of control. "Trapped," "snared," and "caught" is the way many stepmothers describe their situations.

Poorly defined roles, unclear and unrealistic expectations, internal and external pressures, little control, and less support—too often these are the dynamics of stepmothering.

The rate of failure in second marriages is as high as sixty percent—with the predominant reason for such failures cited as children. It is suggested that it is not the children themselves who contribute to the high failure rate, but rather the stepmothers' inability to succeed in such a poorly defined role. Women who begin stepmothering enthusiastically soon feel their sails beginning to droop as their confidence flags.

The question comes down to: "Can stepmothers be successful and happy?" The answer is YES. When naiveté is countered with understanding, the stepmother can establish realistic and achievable goals—goals that allow the stepmother to clarify any dissatisfaction and confront her concerns at the source. The following pages look at the role of stepmothering from the inside out, embrace the wisdom of those who are there, and are dedicated to:

* Women who are full-time stepmothers married to fathers with custody.

* Women who are part-time stepmothers who may at any time become full-time stepmothers.

* Women who are now or who may in the future become attracted to men with children.

* Single fathers.

* Children whose mothers are or may become stepmothers.

* Children who have stepmothers or fathers who may marry.

* Family, friends, professional counselors to the men, women, and children who struggle to build families together.

Nobody Taught Us How

Let's face it: Most little girls do not spend their childhoods dreaming of becoming stepmothers. Stepmothers belong to the make-believe part of childhood. In the brightness of youth, even the most imaginative of us didn't expect to grow up and become a stepmother, yet millions of little girls do just that. I was one such child. Chances are that you, or someone close to you, is a stepmother, too. For too many of us, the reality of stepmothering is as strange as stepping into the pages of a childhood fairy tale.

A Need for Role Models

Stepmothers need role models and not those found in fiction. Although wicked-stepmother mythologies are interesting from a psychological perspective, such tales cannot guide a stepmother in the practical challenges she faces on a daily basis. Nor are the stepmothers on television helpful when applied to real-life concerns. "The Brady Bunch" and "Eight Is Enough" are simply modern-day fairy tales. Their saccharine stepmothers are as unhelpful as the story of Cinderella. Such fantasies seem to tell stepmothers "Take your choice—Crone? Or Saint?" Neither choice is viable in real-life. Stepmothers must begin to look to one another for the guidance and support they seek.

There's Comfort in Numbers—and in Each Other

Stepmothers are a very real presence in today's world. Millions of women are currently living their lives as full-time or custodial stepmothers. Sixty million adults are involved in stepfamilies in our country. Four million individuals become available for remarriage, and a possible stepfamily, each year. With such huge numbers, there is no good reason for stepmothers ever to feel alone. Certainly stepmothering has its problems—the following pages will address these concerns—but the problems are not insurmountable. Stepmothering can be, and often is, one of the most rewarding and important roles a woman can have.

In order to boost the chances for happiness and success, stepmothers need to confront the realities of modern-day stepmothering, beginning with the statistics. Although they are startling, they need to be explored without fear.

Scary Statistics

The outlook for second marriages is dismal: About half of second marriages fail. The reason most often cited is "problems with the husband's children." This figure includes both residential and nonresidential stepchildren, but these problems are obviously intensified for custodial stepmothers. Given the fact that stepmothers are often expected to assume primary parenting immediately after the wedding ceremony, and in virtual isolation, this high figure is not surprising. The pattern can only be broken by building confidence and dealing with issues directly.

First, facts must be faced: Many women are not happy as stepmothers. They feel isolated, alienated, and betrayed; they feel as though "someone changed the rules"; they feel tricked and trapped. Too often these feelings of resentment can be directly traced to the unrealistic expectations these women held going into their relationships with their stepchildren.

Ruth was one such stepmother. Even after thirteen years of caring for one stepdaughter and two stepsons, Ruth still bears a load of unattainable goals. She traces her current unhappiness to the very beginning of her stepmothering. "Naively, I did not think there would be problems in becoming a stepmother. I was confident in my mothering capabilities, my ability to nurture. I expected to be able to handle any emotional turmoil with maturity, love, and rational behavior. I also expected that the children would love me immediately, especially when they saw how wonderfully different I was from their own mother.

"When the wedding was over, the problems began—with a vengeance. It was a shock to me, and a shock to Tom, and a shock to our marriage. I'd never seen Tom red-faced with anger before. Neither of us knew how to cope. Things have gotten better over the years, but we still have flare-ups, and I still feel alone. I wish I had some sort of support group, like alcoholics and battered women have."

Like most stepmothers, Ruth began her "career" with a host of unrealistic expectations. Because she was separated from the experiences of others like herself, Ruth never did realize that her disappointment was commonplace. The failure of a stepmother's initial expectations begins a cycle of negative emotions that often destroys her sense of well-being. The failure of these unrealistic expectations causes too many stepmothers to enter a cycle of confusion—frustration—depression—anger. If left unbroken, this cycle leads directly to the divorce court.

Breaking the Pattern

In reality, stepmothers are less alone than ever before. Changing patterns of child custody and the phenomenon of late-marrying women mean that there are more stepmother marriages each year.

But despite the numbers, stepmothers continue to be threatened by feelings of disappointment and personal inadequacy. These problems can be faced and solved by sharing the information gleaned from experts in the field: stepmothers themselves.

In studying about one hundred responses to an extensive questionnaire I sent to stepmothers around the country, I found that certain common concerns emerged. Although every stepmother thought she was unique, this issue sounded increasingly familiar. I'll discuss each one in depth so that stepmothers can begin to realize that they are *not* alone: The experiences they encounter, and the challenges they face, are common to most stepmothers.

Take a look at this list, and ask yourself how many of these problems you have had to deal with:

- Lack of a clearly defined role: "Who am I?"
- Lack of a common title: "What do they call me?"
- Negative stigma of stepmothering: "Just the word itself is creepy."
- Unrealistic and/or poorly defined expectations: "What did I *think* it would be like?"
- Unfamiliarity with stages of child development: "When does he stop whining?"
- Confusion about nurturing responsibilities: "Am I supposed to do it *all?*"
- Issues relating to stepchild's biological mother: "Who has the final say?"
- Difficulty forming a family from different lifestyles: "You do it *this* way?"
- Raising two sets of children in the same household: "What do you mean, you can't share a room with him?"
- Legal blurriness regarding stepmother's rights: "What happens to my relationship with the kids if we divorce or you die?"
- Loss of personal freedom: "I never have any *time.*"
- Lack of support, feedback: "Am I all alone—or are there others like *me?*"

Who is a Stepmother?

These common concerns suggest common strategies. In order to begin to feel happy and fulfilled, stepmothers must first feel clear and confident about their role. Before you can begin to form realistic expectations and attainable goals, you must first answer this question: *Who is a stepmother?*

It is little wonder that stepmothers are confused about their roles. There is no general agreement about who is to be called "stepmother." It is difficult for stepmothers to get information, to link up with others like themselves, or even to begin to articulate common concerns when the very term "stepmother" is up for debate. This ambiguity is more than semantically troubling; the vagueness of the term is indicative of the problems faced by stepmothers today. It is hard to feel fulfilled or happy as a member of a group that has no accepted definition.

Stepmothers—in the Past and Now

It wasn't always this way. Once upon a time, the stepmother's role was fairly straightforward: The term "stepmother" referred to a woman functioning as a mother substitute for her husband's (motherless) children. In fact, the "step-" prefix comes from the Middle and Old English prefix "steop-" meaning "bereaved" or "orphaned." This term implied—as was usually the case—that the biological mother had died. In the rare case that parents had been divorced, the children typically continued to live with their father. The remarriages of these custodial fathers made stepmothers relatively commonplace.

As the nineteenth century ended, the courts began to exhibit a change in custodial preference: Mothers began to be routinely awarded custody of very young children— children the court deemed to be of "tender years." At first, the children were returned to their fathers when this period of tender years ended, but over time, the notion of tender years expanded. By the 1960s, the courts were more likely to award sole and continuous custody of children to their biological mothers.

The preference for maternal care, coupled with an ever-increasing rate of divorce, created a high number of noncustodial fathers and resulted in the blurring of the role of stepmother. Society, accustomed to referring to women married to *custodial* fathers as "stepmothers," continued to use the term when referring to women married to *noncustodial* fathers. "Stepmother," which for many years had referred to a woman assuming a primary parenting role, began to assume a very different connotation: A stepmother was seen simply as the consort of a father whose children lived somewhere else.

Custodial stepmothers now find themselves in an untenable position as a result of these blurred roles. Recognizing that the custodial nature of their relationship with their stepchildren separates them from the wives of noncustodial fathers, they often seek to identify themselves as "mothers" to their stepchildren, only to find that such attempts at replacing "mother" bring disastrous results.

The custodial stepmother straddles two worlds. Often, she lives in limbo, poised between the roles of noncustodial stepmother and biological mother.

The Bottom Line

The noncustodial stepmother may find it possible to back off from a parenting role with her stepchildren—a posture suggested by many experts in the field—but the intimacy of day-to-day living with full-time stepchildren precludes such detachment. The full-time stepmother cannot simply grit her teeth and wait for her stepchildren to go home. They *are* home. It is this unalterable fact that erases all but the most cursory similarity between her role and the role of the weekend stepmother.

The custodial stepmother's confusion grows as she seeks to define her role. Most women who care for children on a full-time, live-in basis are either mommies or nannies (now often called caregivers). The parameters of these caretaking roles are clear and familiar. Stepmothers also live with children and care for them on a full-time basis, and yet their role does not fit familiar parameters.

Stepmothers in a state of confusion seem to select a role based on what they are not. Custodial stepmothers know that they are not nannies and may assume that there is only one full-time choice left. The problem with opting for the mommy role is that it doesn't work. The stepmother who tries it will confront two problems: (1) the distinct differences between stepmothers and biological mothers, and

(2) the fact that the mommy role is already filled.

Where does this leave the custodial stepmother? Nowhere. Too many stepmothers discover only who they are not. Their alienation, coupled with the very real demands of ongoing childcare, often makes them resentful and angry. When stepmothers feel rejected, they often become angry about the implication that they are nothing to their stepchildren. Deprived of the mommy label, they feel little more than maids to their stepchildren.

To clarify the issue, it is important to understand the ways in which stepmothers and mothers are different. When the differences are clear, stepmothers can begin to define a role that is all their own. The fact that they are *stepmothers*—and not something else—is the bottom line.

A Matter of Perspective

The dilemma facing many stepmothers today is reminiscent of an episode of Rod Serling's, "Twilight Zone."

The story involves a young girl whom we meet in a hospital where she is recuperating from surgery. Her face is swathed in bandages, and she is awaiting their removal with obvious and extreme trepidation. Solicitous nurses and doctors offer their support. We quickly understand that this has been the last in a series of corrective operations to reverse the girl's horrible disfigurement. Most of the story is given over to the girl's fears of nonacceptance, her revulsion at the possibility of the surgery's failure, and her consideration of the alternatives for her life.

At the end of the episode, the bandages are slowly and ceremoniously cut away; the musical score builds as the final bandages fall—everyone gasps. The girl turns to the camera. She is beautiful, but she, too, gasps in horror as she views her reflection in a hand-held mirror. The operation is pronounced a failure; she will be ostracized, sent away. Then the camera pans, for the first time, to the faces of the doctors and nurses. It is they who are horribly disfigured.

Too often, stepmothers mirror their successes and failures by a standard that has little to do with their lives. Millions of stepmothers are doing wonderful jobs and should be filled with pride. Instead, because they lack a realistic measure of their success, they feel incompetent and not respected and begin to doubt their abilities, their marriages, and themselves.

Such doubts can lead a stepmother to one of two conclusions: either she is unworthy or her marriage was a mistake.

The Third Alternative: Becoming Confident and Happy as a Stepmother

There is a third alternative. Instead of admitting defeat and throwing in the towel, a stepmother can choose to become successful and confident in her role. Helping her to do so is the object of this book.

Connie's Message

Connie's experience is typical of the happiness a stepmother can and should attain. Connie has been a stepmother for seventeen years; her two stepdaughters are now grown women. Connie's life has not always been easy, but she never permitted outside influences to affect her feelings for her stepchildren.

Connie realized early in her marriage that she was going to be mostly on her own. Because of different religious beliefs, both Connie's family and her husband's were strongly opposed to the marriage and to her raising of her stepdaughters. Perhaps it was this isolation, although hurtful at first, that helped Connie to accept responsibility for her own happiness. By meeting all her problems head-on and insisting that her husband do so, and by maintaining open communication with both families, she weathered the prejudices of a small town and the particularly tumultuous adolescence of one stepdaughter. Connie has recently become a (step)grandmother. Looking back, she feels that she gained a great deal from her relationship with her stepchildren. "What have you got to tell us?" I asked her when we met.

"Mostly, that nothing is forever," Connie replied. "Children grow up and away. My stepdaughters gave me years of their childhoods. I have a past full of everything I experienced with these children and a future of that past locked in love forever. They gave that to me and I earned it. There seems to be a place for being a stepmother that was born into me—a place in me where these children just fit, perfectly. And when you want that to happen, you don't let anything get in the way."

Connie was able to shape a happy life for herself despite family resistance, religious differences, small-town narrowness, and her stepchildren's stormy adolescent years. Connie would like others to understand that *all* stepmothers would welcome support and respect. "Millions of children have stepmothers. Anything that can be done to give stepmothers a personhood, an identity that will build the future for these millions of children, is going to help. Stepmothers are not babysitters or substitutes or part-time help. "Stepmothers," Connie said with a smile, "step in where others have stepped out and we should be proud of the name stepmother! I am."

Note: Although many of the following pages seem to address custodial stepmothers, many of these issues apply to all stepmothers. Noncustodial stepmothers do, however, have their own special concerns (see Chapter 9). Finally, it is wise to remember that any woman married to a man with children is a stepmother and that living arrangements *are not written in stone;* they can, and often do, change.

Chapter 2

ACHIEVABLE GOALS

Stepmothers tell me they are often cautioned against unrealistic expectations. "Don't expect instant love." "Don't expect quick acceptance." "Don't expect a big happy 'Brady Bunch' family." Although these don'ts and a host of others are apt, they aren't very helpful.

I asked stepmothers to reflect on their "beginnings"— beginnings that were often turbulent. They stated with almost a single voice, "We didn't know what to expect." Stepmotherhood is probably the one personal endeavor that women enter without support, familiarity, or what the psychologists like to call "rehearsals." Girls and women generally do not discuss stepmothering. When a woman becomes a stepmother, it is often without the vaguest notion of what to expect. Fear of the unknown is perhaps the greatest fear of all. It is time to alleviate some of that fear by examining what we can expect, learning to build confidence about the stepmother role, and then forming truly realistic, achievable goals.

What to Expect:

Expect Confusion

It will take a little while for everyone to settle in. Even under the most ideal circumstances, children have to be moved, places must be found for possessions, and mealtime, bedtime, and homework schedules must be established. The business of daily living in new circumstances will create more or less chaos, depending on the individuals and situation involved.

Expect Uneasiness

Because the situation is new and everyone has not lived together before, there will be a period of awkwardness. This is normal. Try to remember that your husband will be more familiar, comfortable, and connected to you than the children will be.

Expect Wariness

Most stepchildren will be reluctant to trust anyone new. Stepchildren have already suffered the dissolution of one family. They often bring a skepticism born of fear or cynicism born of hurt to their father's new marriage. Families are built from commitment and shared experience. Stepmothers, like other good parents, will be involved in the business of "making memories." As more experiences are shared and remembered, even the most reluctant children will begin to feel and act like members of a family, and the wariness will disappear.

Expect Neediness

The notion of family wasn't just the result of some caveman's whim. The family unit evolved to ensure that biological needs, including the very perpetuation of the species, could occur safely. The timeless function of the family as a safe zone, a buffer or haven from the pressures of the outside world, continues today. People, especially children, expect and need—and demand—a lot of nurturing within the family. Stepmothers find that their stepchildren need a lot of parenting—a lot of attention. Stepmothers who attempt to assume cooler roles find that emotional distancing is both counterproductive and impractical when *living* with children.

Expect To Work Hard

The overwhelming majority of stepmothers feel that responsibility for the family rests squarely on their shoulders. Almost to a woman, they report either accepting or being given primary responsibility for the smooth functioning of the family, whether or not they work outside the home. Stepmothers are expected to create and maintain family routines including housekeeping, childcare, and negotiating with the children's biological mother.

Expect to be Tested

Stepmothers often feel as though they are sitting in a twenty-four-hour exam. Everything they do or say is scrutinized, criticized, and "graded" by their stepchildren. Such testing is a normal, rational way for children to measure the stepmother's commitment to them and the reliability of the new family.

This period of testing can be very trying. Rules, expectations, and opinions will be countered, questioned, or ignored during the stepmother's "initiation period." Dora, frazzled by the responsibility of her young stepchildren, warns other stepmothers to "expect to be hated, used, lonely, confused, cursed at, belittled, compared to others, in the middle, and exhausted." This period *does* end and, as Dora tells us, "When it's over, a stepmother can expect to be a stronger, wiser person."

Expect to Feel Left Out

Stepmothers often feel left out. When the old photo albums appear at Grandma's, when everyone is talking about holidays, trips, or times that preceded the stepmother, she may feel a pang. Such pangs are understandable, but allowing them to grow into intolerable pain is not constructive. Stepmothers may be excluded from the children's past, but they are *not* left out of the present—a present that may at times include reminiscing. Sharing family memories can spur the stepmother to share her past life, too.

Expect to Make Big Efforts

Many stepmothers operate on the mistaken notion that good families and good relationships "just happen." This is as counterproductive as the attitude of a sexually dissatisfied woman who just lies there, waiting passively for her husband to figure out how to make sex glorious for her. Many women seem to have the mistaken notion that if a person has to ask for something, it is somehow not as valuable as it would be if it had been intuited by another. Whether it's good sex or a good family, such passivity is just not practical. Refusing to get to work on making things better makes things worse. Building a new family takes work, patience, and perseverance.

Expect to Have Negative Feelings

Some stepmothers are shocked to discover that they feel resentment, anxiety, jealousy, indifference, or even downright dislike for their stepchildren. These negative feelings are perfectly normal, but they are difficult to admit and still more difficult to face. For example:

Resentment. Stepchildren alter the course of the couple's relationship. They interrupt the honeymoon phase of the marriage and introduce problems that have nothing to do with the couple's interaction with each other. Too often, stepmothers begin to feel that the marriage would be "perfect if not for the children." This feeling of lost perfection causes feelings of resentment to grow.

Anxiety. Children often do not respond to a stepmother's overtures, and this reticence can cause her to feel incompetent. Stepchildren do not come with instruction manuals. Their lack of affection, openness, or receptiveness may shake a stepmother's belief in her ability to nurture and cause her self-confidence to plummet. Lowered self-confidence makes the stepmother more susceptible to anxiety.

Jealousy. Stepmothers are often embarrassed by their jealous feelings toward their stepchildren. The sight of a twelve-year-old girl curled up on Daddy's lap may make a stepmother's stomach unpleasantly queasy. Often these feelings of jealousy have little or nothing to do with the stepchildren themselves but rather refer to the stepmother's ambivalence about her husband's former relationships and the claims of others for his attention and affection. Stepchildren also provide a constant reminder of their father's relationship with another woman—their mother.

Envy. It's normal for a stepmother to feel some envy of the biological mother, whether she is living or dead. Envy springs from a feeling that someone has (or had) something that you don't have and would like. Biological mothers have or had a relationship with their children that may threaten an insecure stepmother, and the more insecure a stepmother feels, the more intense her feelings of jealousy and envy will be. Such feelings are best met head-on: "I wish I'd known you when you were a baby" or "I wish the kids were really ours" are healthier responses than sulking or seething.

Dislike. Stepmothers often suffer from guilt stemming from unpleasant feelings about their stepchildren. They dislike their stepchildren for different reasons. Some children behave badly. Some have very different value systems from their stepmother. Some remind their stepmothers of faults in their husbands. They may also call to mind their biological mothers—whom the stepmother wants to ignore.

Annie was having a great deal of trouble relating to her sixteen-year-old stepdaughter. Although Annie had raised the child since age two, she found that she could "hardly look at the girl" as she began to mature. Annie finally was stunned to realize that a great part of this problem was that her stepdaughter had developed a striking resemblance to her biological mother. Annie stated woefully, "I don't know what to do! I knew her mother in high school and I didn't like her at all!"

Sometimes a stepchild is just not somebody a stepmother feels good about. Sometimes personalities clash. Stepmotherhood may be defined as "motherhood without the illusions." A stepmother, unlike a biological mother, is often able to acknowledge to herself that she would not, if given the choice, have chosen these particular children. Many stepmothers are plagued by guilt as a result of this acknowledgment and are reluctant to admit the glaring differences between themselves and their stepchildren. The world will not collapse from such an admission, and although stepchildren are not exchangeable, a mutual admiration society is not necessary to raise a child successfully.

But...

A warning on negative emotions. Although it is said that there is no such thing as an unacceptable feeling, feelings inappropriately shared may cause unnecessary pain. Raising kids is difficult, often frustrating, work and is an emotional business. It's okay to feel whatever you feel, but it is *never* okay to put down, hurt, or alienate your stepchildren or your husband. It *is* okay to hate your stepchildren's behavior and to share your discomfort and disapproval of that behavior with your husband—tactfully, please. Real negative feelings about stepchildren—jealousies, dislikes, anxieties—are better dealt with by an understanding professional.

If negative feelings begin to dominate your life, or if they get in the way of the care and raising of your stepchildren, it is time to get help. Sometimes simply venting these feelings in a journal or letting off steam with a trusted friend will help. If such measures don't alleviate your concerns, seek professional help in a stepmothers group, a mental health clinic, or with a private therapist.

Expect Your Life to Become Child-centered

Much of your time and energy will center on child-related concerns: Little League, Brownies, school conferences, homework, table manners, household chores, college choices, after-school or summer jobs, dating, colds, inoculations, braces, cavities, making a bow that stays tied, finding a date for the prom, scanning the shelves for just the right reference book. The list goes on and on and on. Expect compromises on your personal privacy as well.

Expect Love to Take Time... and Patience

Warm feelings may take a long time to materialize. We allow that time to our stepchildren, but we can't afford to take a long time before making a commitment to them. The needs of children and the demands of childcare are immediate and pressing. Stepmothers may find that their relationships with their stepchildren are initially lopsided. Their commitment is not reciprocated. This demands patience in large doses.

Expect to Deal With the Children's Mother Whether She's On or Off the Scene

Issues relating to the biological mother are positively volatile! (An entire chapter of this book is devoted to this issue.) Suffice it to say, at this point, that stepmothers always have difficulty coming to grips with their stepchildren's biological mother. Different issues evolve depending on the circumstances—starting with whether she is alive or dead. If the biological mother is living, the stepmother will have to deal with visits, telephone calls, and the mother's absence or involvement in her children's lives. If the mother is dead, the stepmother will confront the death in both the abstract and the specific. The stepmother may expect to deal with her stepchildrens' grief and their sense of divided loyalty between their mothers' memory and their stepmother's actuality.

Expect the Children to Resist Any Effort to Be "Made Over"

No one enjoys being made over. The very attempt at making over a stepchild presumes that there is something unacceptable about the child. Making over stepchildren, either directly as with a new wardrobe or indirectly with suggestions about hairstyles, friends, or hobbies is bound to meet with resistance. Suggesting or facilitating a makeover says that the stepmother is not pleased with the stepchildren as they are—*hold off!*

The Bottom Line (Again): Expect Stepmothering to Be Different From Any Other Type of Child-rearing

Although stepmothering shares certain similarities with other child-rearing roles—mother, noncustodial stepmother, adoptive mother, or foster mother—the stepmother is different from all of these. For a:

Biological Mother: There is a period of bonding and nurturing that is socially approved and supported.

Stepmother: There is a finiteness to the relationship, a time limit to the physical interaction proscribed by legal agreements between the biological parents.

Adoptive Mother: The adoptive mother has *chosen* to accept full parenting responsibility for a child whose biological mother has relinquished all rights and responsibilities through legal surrender or death. In either case, great pains are taken to protect the adoptive mother from the intrusion of the biological mother.

Foster Mother: The foster mother recognizes that her relationship with her foster children is temporary and that the long-term goal of the foster relationship is to return the child to the parent(s).

Stepmothering shares characteristics of all other types of mothering, but it is a way of life all its own.

Building Confidence

Once stepmothers have a general idea of what to expect, they need to begin to learn about their own families. They need to understand as much as they possibly can about their individual situations. No family is exactly like another. Each stepfamily is different from every other one. In order to begin building confidence and enhancing the possibility for success and happiness, stepmothers need to assess the particular characteristics of their situation and their children.

Stepmothers who understand the unique dynamics of their own families will minimize surprises and find that they are more confident and comfortable. Ideally, stepmothers will find out the facts about their new situations before they marry and/or begin to live with their stepchildren, but those who did not can benefit from reflecting about their family's characteristics.

Confidence Builder #1: Assess Your Situation

In order to begin formulating concrete goals, stepmothers might use the following questions to put their situations into perspective.

1. Where Will You Live?

Husband's house? Stepmother's house? New house? If you're moving into or living in your husband's house, how do you feel about the furnishings? Will there be opportunities for you to redecorate or personalize the house to your taste? If you are planning to live in your own house or apartment, will your husband expect you to make changes? How do you feel about any such proposed changes?

Fran is a middle-aged stepmother of two teenage girls. A state of "decorative warfare" developed between Fran and the girls and nearly drove her mad. Fran had married a widower and moved into her husband's house after their marriage. The house was decorated in a taste that was generally pleasing to Fran. Indeed, in an odd twist of fate, Fran had been a friend of the girls' mother and had actually helped her shop for some of the furnishings! Sensitive to her stepdaughters' loving memories of their mother, Fran planned no major redecorating; she was happy with the house the way it was. However, she was unprepared for her stepdaughters' insistence that everything in the home remain *exactly* as it had always been. Fran found that her stepdaughters "permitted" not the slightest change.

If she moved a coffee table or rearranged a lamp, the

moved articles reverted mysteriously to their former place. Finally, Fran confronted her stepdaughters, only to be told sweetly but adamantly that they had "just put things back where they belonged."

2. Will You Be Working Outside the Home?

If you continue your present job, how will your new responsibilities fit into your daily life? If you will be leaving your job, have you planned your transition from the work world to work at home? Will it be a sacrifice—or a relief—to give up your life in the workplace?

3. Will There Be Time and Money for Fun?

Will money be available for the family, for you, for your husband, and for you and your husband as a couple to have fun? What activities can you enjoy as a family? As a couple? Individually? Will your own financial picture change, and is that change acceptable to you?

4. How Will You and Your Husband Share Responsibilities?

Most stepmothers report that they assume the overwhelming proportion of child and domestic duties after their marriages, whether or not they work outside the home. How much responsibility do you really want to assume? Do you need to feel in control of the family? Do you want your husband to share the chores? Do you expect your stepchildren to help? Does your husband concur?

5. How Do You Feel About Marriage and Stepmotherhood?

If you've been married before, have you worked through any residual feelings from that former relationship? If divorced, have you resolved what went wrong with your previous marriage? If widowed, have you finished grieving for your late husband? What do you want from this marriage? How are you prepared to get it? How will your personal life change as a result of marriage and stepmotherhood? How will you choose to handle any problems that you can foresee? Do you know any other stepmothers?

Stepmothering calls many emotional issues into play.

Stepmothers need to be more self-confident and self-assured than typical "brides." Stepmothers need to think carefully about personal issues, to "get their act together." It is very important that stepmothers know themselves well enough to understand how their own personal issues affect their feelings about marriage and the role of stepmother.

6. What Will "They" Call You?

Stepmothers are often unhappy about what their stepchildren choose to call them. If you expect to be called "Mom" or "Mother" by your stepchildren, you may be severely disappointed when the children insist upon calling you by your given name. On the other hand, you may find yourself uncomfortable being called "Mom" by a child you don't even know. What would you like to be called? You decide. The unique relationship between you and your stepchild calls for a unique name as well—a derivative of stepmother such as "Steppie," or a nickname that is used only by your stepchildren, highlights the special and exclusive quality of your relationship to these children—one that is different from all the other relationships in your life.

7. Will You Have Support? How Do Family and Friends Feel About Your Becoming a Stepmother?

Stepmothers need support outside the family. Will you have a strong support system? Do you have friends or family who feel positive about your becoming a stepmother? Too many stepmothers, during times of stress, hear only "You knew what you were getting into." Stepmothers need others who will be there for them. Do you have someone who will help you through the rough spots? Do you have people who are eager to share in your family's joys?

8. How Does Your Husband Feel About Living With His Children?

Did your husband actively choose to have his children live with him? Did the children begin to live with your husband by default? Would your husband really prefer another living situation for the children if circumstances were different? What are your feelings about the suitability of fathers raising children? How suitable do you feel your husband is to raise his children, either without assistance or with you beside him? Will you make a good parenting team?

Confidence Builder Number 2: Focus on Your Stepchildren

Another important step in the building of confidence is getting to know your stepchildren. It is nothing short of amazing that many women attempt to begin relationships with children based on little or no personal contact, to marry without thinking in depth about the individual personalities of their stepchildren. Some brides, swept away in the honeymoon phase of their marriages, dismiss their stepchildren as minor characters in a romantic play or items in a "package deal." If they think about their stepchildren at all (and many do not), they consider them merely as extensions of their husbands.

Some stepmothers go to the opposite extreme: Infatuated and excited by the prospect of a new family, they romanticize their stepchildren. Little children are gushed over as if they were cuddly cherubs. Older children are giggled with as friends or helpmates. Dismissing children either as extensions of their fathers or as willing characters in some vague soap opera of instant family bliss is a dangerous mistake. Stepchildren of any age will have tremendous impact upon a marriage. The unique personalities, personal histories, and individual perspectives of the children will change every day life. Remember: Relationships are not forged with strangers. The wise stepmother will get to know her stepchildren as well and as quickly as she can.

Getting to Know Them

Any relationship is based on an exchange of personal information. Women certainly realize this in other areas of their lives. However, in the rush of infatuation for their husbands, or in the case of later-arriving stepchildren, many stepmothers don't take the time to find out who their stepchildren are. This is an occupational hazard for biological parents as well. Many adults are simply not in the habit of thinking about children as individuals; they refer to "their" children, implying both ownership and a sense of children as extensions of themselves.

Learn about your stepchild's view of the world. Ask questions. Listen carefully to responses. Watch reactions to various situations. Aim for sensitivity. Stepchildren do not, it is true, come with instruction manuals; however, their daily behavior will be your guide.

What are these children like when they are relaxed and "themselves"? Is the child who acts out during initial meetings with the stepmother really a shy child under less pressured circumstances? Is the little child sulking in the depths of that movie seat a chatterbox at Grandma's house? The more aware you are of your stepchildren's personalities, the more comfortable and confident you will feel with them.

Stepmothers usually aren't given any choice about how they will view their stepchildren. When the initial expectations of "instant love" and "instant family" dissipate, as they usually do with startling speed, stepmothers often panic: They realize that they don't "know" their stepchildren at all. Stepmothers do not possess that maternal selective blindness that familiarity and love often bring with the passage of time. However, the stepmother's ability to see the individuality of her stepchildren can actually become an advantage rather than a liability. Her objectivity permits her to understand her stepchildren in a way that others, who are too close to the situation, may overlook. One of the stepmother's most important contributions to the family is her new and fresh perspective. This permits her to recognize when the children are unhappy, frustrated, or distressed. It also allows stepmothers to tune into talents, strengths, and interests that the children's father or other family members might have missed.

What Are Your Stepchildren Really Like?

The following questions may be helpful in focusing on the children in your new family.

1. How Old Are They?

Children of different ages will have different needs that must be addressed. Various stages of child development will call for different parenting skills. For many women with limited, or rusty, child-rearing experience, a good childcare guide is essential. You'll find a shelf filled with such books at your library or bookstore. Children develop physically, emotionally, and intellectually at different stages of their lives. Familiarity with typical stages will help stepmothers frame age-appropriate expectations.

Chapter 5 is devoted to a more detailed examination of stages of child development.

2. Boys or Girls or a Combination?

Youngsters today live in a world where all options are theoretically open to them regardless of their sex. However, gender-related differences, be they emotional, physical, or cultural, have certainly not been eliminated. It is very important for stepmothers to explore their own personal feelings as they relate to the differences between boys and girls. What are your feelings about any innate differences? Do you expect or accept different types of behavior from boys and girls? Do you anticipate that boys and girls will have different interests and/or abilities? Do your feelings mesh with your husband's?

3. How Do the Children get Along With Their Father?

It is important to understand the type of relationship the children had with their father prior to your arrival on the scene. Did the children live in a single-parent situation with their father? Did the father have assistance raising the children? From a housekeeper? A grandparent? Has the father just recently assumed physical and/or legal custody? Will the children need time to adjust to their father, as well as to their stepmother, as a primary caregiver?

4. What Circumstances Resulted in Father Custody?

The circumstances that lead to children living apart from their biological mother will affect the stepmother's relationship with them. The facts surrounding the children's separation from their mother will have contributed to their receptivity to new relationships and the speed with which they can be expected to develop trust in you. Are you prepared to handle the special problems these children may bring? (fear about death, fear about critical illness or disability, and familiarity with drug or other substance abuse) Are you prepared to cope with the effects of real or perceived abandonment? Neglect? Abuse? Many children, living apart from their biological mother, have suffered through a variety of traumatic experiences. The more you know about the history of their past, the better prepared you will be to cope with their future problems.

5. How Do the Children Feel About Their Mother?

Children's feelings about their biological mothers run the gamut. Do yours feel abandoned? Resentful? Defensive? Confused? The children's relationship with their mother will affect their ability to trust their feelings about themselves and will impact their relationship with you.

6. Any Special Problems You Should Know About?

Special problems that might confront a stepmother range from a physical, emotional, or learning disability to unacceptable social behavior. Stepmothers may have to cope with social, school, mental, or physical problems. Any identifiable problems should be explained clearly to you. You may have to ask your husband for this information.

7. What Are the Children's Interests?

Taking the time to learn about children's interests is a lovely way to begin a relationship. Many children are uncomfortable with their father's marriage; they are not quite sure what this relationship really involves. Stepchildren are often pleased by evidence of their stepmother's interest in their lives. A note of warning: As with all other beginning relationships, stepmothers should exercise caution and not push. Stepchildren may have mixed feelings about their fathers and stepmothers "talking about them"; they may feel flattered by the attention but threatened by their loss of exclusivity with their father.

8. What Have the Children Been Told About You?

It is important to understand what, if anything, the children already know about you. What do they know about your relationship with their father? Do they know that you plan to marry? Do they know that they will be living with you? Have you been "bad-mouthed" by anyone? Do the children fear the title "stepmother"? Have they accepted the fact that you will be their stepmother?

9. How Will the Children React to Surprises?

Keep surprises to a minimum. Children do not enjoy major life changes posed as surprises. "Surprise! We just got married, and we're all moving tomorrow!" is unlikely to prompt happy reactions. Ask as many questions of your fiancé/husband as possible. Ideally, most of these questions will be posed and answered before you meet or begin living with your stepchildren. However, learning about each other is a lifetime process!

Stepmothers who have a clear sense about general expectations, and who have taken the time to learn about and think about their individual situations, will have a far easier time creating a role for themselves in their new lives.

Until now, the stepmother has concentrated on learning about others. Now it's time for her to answer the question "Where do I fit in?" In the next chapter, we will examine the various aspects of the stepmother's role and offer practical guidelines for stepmothers who are struggling to find their new family identity.

A ROLE OF YOUR OWN

Stepmothers are often treated as so many Alices at a "mad tea party." Although people are usually polite, the expectations of stepmotherhood are sometimes difficult to understand. The mixed messages they relay are always confusing and sometimes maddening.

Stepmothers who try to fulfill the expectations of others find that such expectations often clash and nobody is satisfied. As I spoke with stepmothers about what they felt others expected from them, the following three consistent and clashing expectations emerged:

1. Stepmothers should care for their stepchildren as their own, BUT stepmothers should never attempt to replace the biological mother.
2. Stepmothers should never identify themselves as stepmothers, BUT stepmothers should never identify themselves as "mother" either.
3. Stepmothers should forget about fairy-tale nonsense, BUT stepmothers should laugh (cheerfully) at allusions to wicked stepmothers.

Failure is built in for a stepmother who attempts to meet any of these expectations because each contradicts itself. The resulting confusion makes us feel off-balance and unsure.

What can a stepmother hope to "be" for her stepchildren? Can she be a "mother"? Should she just forget about being a parent and define herself as "Dad's wife" or "friend" to her stepchildren? How can she create a role that reflects her responsibilities and expresses her commitment to her stepchildren?

Why "Mommy" Won't Work

The majority of stepmothers at some point attempt to define themselves as "mother" to their stepchildren. Most are uncomfortable about being referred to as "stepmother"; they prefer to be referred to, acknowledged, and treated as their stepchildren's "mothers." And why not?

Certainly stepmothers perform the duties of "Mom"! When asked to define their role as stepmothers they offered a litany of child-care responsibilities:

"I'm the same as Mother," states a young stepmother of an eight-year-old. "He is treated exactly the same as my two sons."

"I'm the MOM!" proudly claims a particularly bubbly stepmom. "I perform the same duties for my stepsons as for my biological boys: cooking, cleaning, laundry, attendance at school conferences and functions, Scout leader, etc., etc., etc...."

"I do everything the 'lady of the house' (sometimes known as Mother) would do, and I'm in the Football Mother Club for my stepson. I make homemade goodies and send care packages to my stepdaughter at college. I carry out all the responsibilities a real mother would."

And so it went: Stepmother after stepmother defined herself as "mother" and validated the definition by reciting her responsibilities—lists at times daunting in scope. But despite their litanies, stepmothers are *not* replacements for their stepchildren's biological mothers. This misdefinition is at the root of much of the dissatisfaction plaguing stepmothers today.

What is all this fuss about anyway? A woman raising a child is a mother. Right? Stepmothers are on the scene every day. Stepmothers sit in those uncomfortable little chairs on conference night; they pace the floor when a child is late. Stepmothers stuff their pockets with soggy tissues. Stepmothers clean up after a sick child. Stepmothers swallow their meals while trying to ignore table manners that drive them up a wall. Stepmothers advise little children about bullies and bigger ones about pregnancy. They worry about scraped knees, monsters under beds, coughs that linger, and kids that are too noisy or too quiet. If a stepmother isn't a mother, who is? After all, as one stepmother quipped, why should the term be reserved for some woman who "just happened to be there at the moment of birth"? *Why isn't a stepmother a mother?*

The Role Is Filled

The primary answer to this question is that the role is already filled. Stepmothers who try to be "mother" open themselves up to unnecessary disappointment and pain. Engaging in "motherhood" competitions diminishes the importance of their role.

A Different (Not Less Important) Role

The stepmother can and most often does function in a nurturing capacity, offering emotional support as well as care for her stepchildren. Her responsibilities may replicate or even surpass those of custodial biological mothers. However, the stepmother's role is *different*. Because it is so important to stepmothers that their role be defined with dignity, it is essential to spend some time examining those specific features that differentiate biological mothers from stepmothers.

Dedication and time cannot erase these differences. The inability to accept them is often the cause of the dissatisfaction many stepmothers feel. Such feelings are absolutely avoidable if stepmothers will stop pretending or striving to be something they are not. Stepmothers who claim or strive to be mothers indicate their own ambivalence about their role. Only by refusing to compete for someone else's role can you begin to shape your own.

What's the Difference?

Remember *Sleeping Beauty?* In this tale a wicked fairy places a curse upon a baby princess, condemning the infant to an early death. A protective fairy is powerless to lift the curse, but she *can* modify it, softening the sentence of death into a lengthy and peaceful slumber. So it is with stepmothers. Stepmothers cannot erase the past, but they can and often do determine the course of their stepchildren's future.

A biological mother and her infant begin their relationship free from any personal history. The infant has neither the ability and experience nor the language to pass judgment. The infant learns about the world from the daily interaction with the mother. The biological mother and child have the luxury of a period of bonding. During this time the baby comes to expect certain reactions to the signals that he sends and begins to form expectations that will be enlarged to apply to the world. The stepmother, however, meets a child who is usually able to talk and whose personal history has already helped to formulate expectations about the world. The child's personal history excludes the stepmother.

The biological mother creates expectations, whereas the stepmother must modify, or coexist with, the child's previously set expectations *before* she can even begin to create a relationship with that child.

The "Ideal" Mother

"Mother" is perhaps the most basic of all human roles. Mother may be the figure who sets the emotional tone for the rest of our lives, either supplying us with a nurturance we seek to replicate or depriving us of the nurturance which we seek to find. The search for recovery or discovery of that early nurturing may last a lifetime. Mothers have been examined at length by sociologists, psychologists, and poets. Motherhood is perhaps one of the *only* roles that is clear in its idealized state.

The ideal mother is the consummate nurturer. She is perceived as "all-giving," offering a sort of extended coverage plan of sustenance and support. Hers is a socially acceptable role. Greeting cards, comic strips, plays, novels, art, social sciences, humor, all reflect the common acknowledgment of the primacy of the "mother" role. Mothers are always available, uncomplaining, loving, nonjudgmental, supportive, unselfish. So ingrained is our familiarity with this idealized role that stating that a woman is, or is not, "acting like a mother" is culturally defined and needs no further explanation.

Bad Press for Stepmothers

On the other hand, the expected behavior of a stepmother springs from the fear of abandonment and rejection by the mother. Fairy tales and myths made the "bad mother" synonymous with the stepmother. Stepmothers are portrayed as the antithesis of ideal mothers: unavailable, complaining, unloving, judgmental, critical, and selfish as perfect witches.

Although stepmothers may in fact supply stepchildren with the bulk of nurturance and support, their very presence testifies to the reality of another deep-seated fear. The daily *presence* of a stepmother suggests the *absence* of the birth mother.

More Differences

The birth of a planned child creates or intensifies a deep emotional bond between a man and a woman. A woman who marries a previously married man has to make certain adjustments in her romantic vision; she has to come to terms with her predecessor. She must "rewrite history," employing a form of selective amnesia. In this way, the new couple chooses to forget certain specifics of a past marriage or relationship. They "forget" that the husband has loved another woman and was loved in return. The new couple does not often discuss former relationships and, in the course of time, the past recedes naturally. As time progresses, the couple's shared experiences assume a primacy and validity that erase the power of the previous relationship. So complete is this rewriting of history that many such couples come to think about their present marriage as their only "true marriage."

No such illusions for stepmothers! It is difficult to forget about the past when its products are sitting at the breakfast table each morning! It's difficult to rewrite history in the presence of firsthand witnesses. The stepmother, unlike the biological mother, must create a relationship with children that includes another woman, a woman who is, unlike an adoptive mother, known to the children as their "birth" mother and who is often actively involved in their lives. In addition to this competition for the primary nurturing role, the stepmother must acknowledge the ongoing existence of the woman who once shared her husband's life.

It is not often that you hear "I hope this baby loves me" from a biological mother. The expectation of biological mothers is that their children will love them simply because they *are* mothers. There is something almost mystical in the expectation and acceptance of the love between child and mother. The taboo against voicing negative thoughts against one's mother is primal and generally universal. Biological mothers may typically demand and be accorded "love" despite apparent contradictions in their behavior toward and concern for their offspring; nowhere else do we find a nine-month investment expected to pay such long-range and continuous dividends.

Stepmothers long for this unconditional love and fear they will never receive it; they probably won't. Stepmothers continually describe situations where biological mothers are granted love and loyalty despite the quality or quantity of their involvement with their children. Stepmothers often feel that no matter how much they labor they must continue to earn each and every "I love you"—if they earn any at all.

Given the differences between biological motherhood and stepmotherhood, it is easy to understand why many women simply opt to "become" mothers to their stepchildren. Given the choice, who would choose to be a "witchy, wicked, evil" stepmother? But choosing to try to be a mother to her stepchildren is probably the greatest error a stepmother can make. Women may choose to nurture, to love, and to commit to their stepchildren in varying capacities, but if they wait for a shower of unconditional love and acceptance, they are in for a long wait—ending, most likely, in painful disappointment.

What Is "Unconditional Love"?

Unconditional love. Everyone seems to want it, everyone mourns its absence; yet what *is* it? The very notion of love given without any conditions suggests a relationship plagued by irrationality. The notion of one person giving without hope of reciprocity suggests the possibility for huge abuse and disappointment. Who needs it? Stepmothers may be confused when they stumble upon a troubling discovery: Unconditional "love" is not very loving, nor is it real love! In fact, the unconditional love that is so coveted by stepmothers and so easily awarded to biological mothers is often a catchall label for otherwise unacceptable emotions. Unconditional love is often little more than another way of saying, "You have to." Unconditional love is an acceptable repository for unfulfilled needs, guilt, unexpressed rage, and fears of abandonment.

Real love has little or nothing in common with unconditional love. Love that is granted despite mistreatment, despite abandonment or reciprocity, is something the stepmother will not receive. Looked at in this light, it's hardly worth having. The love that a stepmother will ultimately find will be firmly rooted in shared commitment and respect.

Developing Inner Strength

The stepmother's search for "mother-love," although painful, causes a surge of personal growth and understanding. She may discover that her relationship with her stepchildren causes them to review and adjust their views of their relationships with their own mother. Such analysis causes many stepmothers to begin thinking about themselves in ways that they may never have gotten around to. Over and over again, stepmothers reported that their relationships with their stepchildren ultimately resulted in their becoming stronger. One of the ways they built that inner strength was by examining and adjusting personal myths about mothers in general and in particular. How many individuals truly have the nurturing, mutually satisfying, supportive relationships of the idealized biological mother? Most people have difficulty with their mothers. In exploding the myth of the ideal mother, stepmothers begin to realize that they are capable of building a healthy and workable relationship with their stepchildren—on their own terms.

Many custodial stepmothers distance themselves from the role of stepmother and protest that they act as mothers to their stepchildren. An overwhelming percentage were quick to point out that their stepchildren called them "Mom." Many other stepmothers added that people didn't even know that their family was a stepfamily. Their vehemence was loud and clear.

But Is It Real?

Although stepmothers seemed clear about their need to be acknowledged as mothers, a truer sense of their self-image emerged when they were asked, "Where would the children go in the case of your husband's death?" Almost every stepmother assumed that her stepchildren would return to their biological mother (if she was living). This assumption held despite the past or current relationship with the mother. More revealing of the stepmother's acknowledgment of the tenuousness of her role was the fact that in cases where the biological mother was no longer living, most stepmothers assumed that the children would go to live with another blood-related family member. Obviously, the majority of stepmothers considered that their "motherhood" relationship with their stepchildren was dependent upon an intact marriage. Scratching the surface, one finds that many stepmothers seemed to regard their relationships as subject to control by outside forces: the family courts, the wishes of biological mothers, grandparents. This is not real motherhood!

Given these differences and the likelihood that stepmothers accept them, at least surreptitiously, why do stepmothers continue to insist upon motherhood as the definition of their role?

Does It Seem the Obvious Choice?

Stepmothers may opt for motherhood simply because it's more familiar. When my son was about three years old, he was particularly fascinated by pregnant women. He asked lots of questions, which I tried to answer as simply and factually as possible. One day in the park he stared with rapt attention as an obviously pregnant young woman strolled past. "Mommy," he said, "I can't wait to grow up and have a baby inside me." I explained that only women grew babies inside them and hastened to add that he would play a very important part in the creation of a baby some day. I watched his little face darken as he took in this disappointing news. After a quiet moment he brightened and announced, "Mommy, when I grow up, I'm going to change and be a woman!" He had worked through a solution to his problem; because he couldn't understand the nature of his future role, he opted for a choice that was familiar and comprehensible. It made sense to him and it seemed to settle the problem; *but the choice wasn't his to make.* Changing into a woman was not possible.

Changing and becoming a biological mother is not possible for stepmothers, either.

Danger Signs: The Opposite Extreme

A small percentage of stepmothers do not attempt to function as mothers to their stepchildren: They go to the opposite extreme. These stepmothers described their relationships with their stepchildren as nonnurturing. They attempted to distance themselves from their stepchildren as a result perceived rejection or an inability to compromise with their husbands about different child-rearing styles. They tried to assume the various roles of "housekeeper," "Dad's wife," or "friend." None of these roles brought happiness; indeed, this group was generally dissatisfied both with their marriages and with stepmothering.

The Housekeeper

Some stepmothers described situations where they felt like interlopers or intruders in their own homes. They felt caught in relationships between their husbands and stepchildren that were strong and exclusive. They couldn't find their place—their role.

Even after seven years of marriage, Gretta still felt like the housekeeper she had replaced. After the wedding, the housekeeper was dismissed, and Gretta assumed total care for her two young stepsons until six o'clock, when her husband came home. When "Papa" arrived, Gretta was excluded from all involvement and interaction with the children. Her husband went so far as to speak Hungarian to his sons, a language Gretta did not know and which her husband refused to teach her. Her hurt and resentment at being shut out of discussions, confidences, and family decisions mounted. Like many stepmothers in this position, Gretta found her resentment shifting from her stepchildren to her husband. A stepmother who is consistently banned from involvement with the family unit will often withdraw not only from her stepfamily but from the marriage as well.

Dad's Wife

A tiny percentage of stepmothers described themselves as having no responsibility for their stepchildren. This small group totally removed themselves from emotional interaction with their stepchildren; their husbands continued to assume all responsibility for the care of the children. These women regarded themselves as their "husbands' wives" and not as stepmothers. They simply acted as though their stepchildren were not part of their daily lives. Such unhappy situations almost invariably resulted in the stepchildren's eventually leaving the stepmother's home to live elsewhere.

Friend

Some stepmothers tried to act as friends to their stepchildren, particularly in cases where stepmother and stepchildren were close in age. Stepmothers who are only a few years older than their stepchildren or who live with adult stepchildren frequently experience confusion about their roles. Extending the hand of friendship may seem like the only possibility. But the role of friend doesn't work very well. There are definite and observable differences between the friends and stepmothers:

• Friends don't generally instruct; stepmothers do.

• Friends have shared interests and/or perspectives about the world; a stepmother and her family may not.

• Friends come together as individuals who have chosen, and enjoy, each other's company; stepmothers and their stepchildren come together in a pseudo-familial manner through a third party, and may or may not enjoy each other's company.

• Friends don't usually live together and are not required to integrate each other's personal habits into their lifestyles; stepmothers and stepchildren must confront and cope with each other's most intimate habits.

• Friendships are voluntary and may be canceled at any point by either or both friends; stepmothers and stepchildren, although they may feel like canceling out, do not have this option.

Suggesting to a stepchild that you be friends allows the child to decline and provides the opportunity for hurt feelings all around.

Attempting friendship with adult children who still live at home may set up some very strange family dynamics. A stepmother seeking friendship runs the risk of overidentifying with the "children." She may find herself *becoming* one of the children. Although this alignment with the younger generation may seem like fun at first, the stepmother will eventually discover that her self-esteem, as well as her identity in her marriage, will suffer. Friendship is an unworkable as well as inappropriate role. Most adult stepchildren will be uncomfortable discussing marital issues that concern their father. Stepchildren, despite their age or level of sophistication, generally become uneasy when trying to think about and relate to their father as their "friend's husband."

Further complications arise for the stepmother-as-friend if she and her husband decide to add their own children to the family. These complications are discussed in more detail in Chapter 12.

Stepmothers are not mommies, housekeepers, Dad's wives, or friends. They are stepmothers. Yet they may avoid the obvious, choosing to remain locked in ambiguity rather than focused and satisfied. Why have they rejected the role of stepmother? Perhaps because they have not confronted and banished the negative image of stepmothering.

Understanding the Negative Stigma

Stepmothers have received bad press for a long time. The historical tradition of cruel stepmothers transcends cultural boundaries. Greek mythology is replete with cruel stepmothers, women who plotted elaborate schemes to assassinate their stepchildren. Wicked stepmothers can be found in the folk literature of every country in the world. The Grimm brothers, who are generally held accountable for inventing the wicked-stepmother stories, really should be let off the hook; they did nothing more than collect and dispense about two hundred old folk tales. In fact, the familiar "Cinderella" story can be traced to ninth-century China.

Both the printing press and an increase in literacy led to the wide circulation of these tales in the Western world. But these factors alone don't explain this *acceptability*.

Why did the wicked stepmother tales catch on? Why is history so much harder on the stepmother than on the stepfather? Why do women always get the blame?

If you had asked my grandmother this question, she'd have answered with another: "So what else is new?" Maybe she'd have had a point. Motherhood and fatherhood are different.

Motherhood is more clear and certifiable than fatherhood. In fact, many cultures use maternal lines for determining legacies, names and, in the Jewish tradition, religious affinity. Such cultures assert that whereas fatherhood may be questioned, motherhood is a certainty.

Most children and adults find it uncomfortable to voice anger or hatred against their biological mothers. Mother is perceived as a life-giver and life-sustainer. She functions as primary caretaker and is responsible for her child's survival and individual identity. To reject the mother is to reject the source of one's own identity. To be abandoned by the mother is to lose part of that identity.

The "wicked stepmother" offers a safe outlet for the natural anger and hatred that children may feel toward their biological mothers from time to time. One psychological explanation for the acceptance of the cruel stepmother myth is that it allows children to safely ventilate negative feelings about mothers while leaving the "good mother" image intact.

This is all very interesting when discussing literature. However, when a woman is trying to foster a real relationship with real stepchildren, the implications of stepmothers as evil and biological mothers as saintly are chilling. Stepmothers will discover that the best way to deal with the negative connotations is directly: If the "wicked" stepmother was created to answer a fear, then a "kind" stepmother can be created to answer a fear as well.

Easier Said Than Done?

Stepmothers may indeed appear cruel from a child's perspective. Many of the tasks involved in childcare are restrictive and unpleasant by definition. The stepmother will be involved with limit-setting, correcting, and reprimanding. This unpleasant side to nurturing is balanced, for the biological mother, by love, affection, and close ties to the child that started long before the child's conscious memory. The child accepts, as a given, that the mother has only the best interests of her child at heart. The stepmother begins her relationship with the child as a virtual stranger. Although she carries out many of the same duties as a biological mother, she lacks the affection and bonding that are needed to balance her demands. Trying to "raise a child" without this balance may cause the stepmother to appear cold and, at times, even cruel. The more a stepmother attempts to nurture her stepchildren, the more demanding and cruel she may appear.

In addition to the worn stereotypes of children's tales, stepmothers must deal with very real slights, ranging from insensitivity to out-and-out bigotry. Detractors may be next-door neighbors, teachers, family, and friends. But the stepmother's worst enemy is her own ambivalence about her role. Stepmothers share the same prejudices and cultural discomfort with stepmotherhood as the rest of the population.

To be happy in their role, stepmothers must refuse to perpetuate the negative mythology and the unflattering prototypes.

Rules and Tips for the Confident Stepmother

Stepmothers who described themselves as being very satisfied with their role shared a pattern of success. They shared three simple rules and a few not-so-simple patterns of behavior:

- Assume a great deal of control within the family.
- Assume a role as primary parent to stepchildren.
- Do not compete with *anyone* for stepchildren's loyalty.

Stepmothers Are Advisers

Stepmothers who functioned in the capacity of adviser or guide to their stepchildren report that they felt a special sense of fulfillment and happiness. These stepmothers often built their relationships with their stepchildren around activities they could teach or share. Because the goals were concrete and measurable, such stepmothers were able to gauge their success and to take pride in the special reward found in "making a difference" in their stepchildren's lives.

Stepmothers Are "Trusted Adults"

Stepmothers are also delighted when they become the recipients of a child's trust. Stepchildren, as a group, have suffered a severe blow to their ability to trust. Divorce or death and the resultant upheaval of the original family shake even the most sanguine child's sense of security and can severely damage the child's ability to trust the world and himself. One of the most important and rewarding components of a stepmother's role is the rebuilding of her stepchildren's often shattered or damaged ability to trust. Such trust is built over time by stepmothers who are consistent, honest, and discreet.

The Confident Stepmother: What She Does

Confident stepmothers, who describe themselves as happy and satisfied with their role, point out strategies that have worked for them as they strive to strengthen the solidarity of their new families. A good stepmother, they maintain:

Remains in the Present

The confident stepmother is not threatened by the past. She realizes that discussions of the past are the product of her stepchildren's personal history. The confident stepmother acknowledges, without insecurity, that her stepchildren were not born on the day she became their stepmother; this knowledge may prompt some regret, but it is not threatening.

Plans for the Future

The confident stepmother is always making plans, whether for next year's holiday dinner or her relationship with her stepchildren's babies. Confident stepmothers look forward; this forward-looking approach renews their personal confidence and extends a feeling of optimism and confidence to their stepchildren.

Respects Herself

Confidence and self-respect go hand in hand. The confident stepmother does not expect abuse and does not demean herself by allowing inappropriate or hurtful behavior. She realizes that she is a person worthy of respect and love and is wise enough to acknowledge the difference. She expects respect but does not demand love.

Commits Herself to Her Stepchildren

The confident stepmother does not wait for her stepchildren to love or accept her before she makes her commitment to them. She knows that her role occurred with or without their consent. She realizes that there is a tremendous imbalance in family power and that she now holds that power. As the feminine head of the household, she commits herself to caring for and about her stepchildren.

Recognizes Limitations

The confident stepmother realizes that she is capable of *sustaining* a meaningful relationship with her stepchildren. She plans goals and sets her expectations logically rather than emotionally. She learns all that she can about any situation, projects alternatives, and acts with an awareness of any inherent limitations.

Accepts Responsibility for Her Own Actions

The confident stepmother judges only her *own* actions. She comes to realize that any individual can only be held accountable for her own behavior. She accepts that no one "makes" anyone else do anything. She is responsible only for her half of any relationship.

Is Active Rather Than Passive

The successful stepmother functions from a position of energy and confidence. She takes action rather than languishing about, waiting for things to fall into place. Stepmotherhood often forces a passive woman into a more active stance; this new assertiveness can have positive effects throughout her life.

Accepts the Rewards Gracefully

Through her relationship with her stepchildren, the confident stepmother comes to know the reward of a deep interaction with another human being that is different from any other parenting role, *a relationship free from the psychological entanglements that often complicate biologically determined relationships.* Stepmothers enjoy relationships that are ultimately the products of mutual choice rather than obligation.

Chapter 4

GETTING STARTED

If You're Already a Mother

Does being a mother help a woman in her role as a stepmother? No, said stepmothers with children from previous marriages. Although they were familiar with the stages of child development and had plenty of experience with the mechanics and responsibilities for daily childcare, they found themselves totally unprepared for the differences between mothering and stepmothering. Nothing prepared them for the confusion and resentment they felt as they witnessed changes in their relationships with their biological children. Expecting that their "mothering" would simply be extended to include their stepchildren, they were often surprised to discover in themselves a differences in expectations, tolerance, and feelings for their step and biological children—differences that seriously affected the new family's chances for success and their own chances for personal happiness. What were these differences?

Stepmothers found, often to their surprise, that they were stricter with their "own" children—and more demanding. They found that they were quicker to set rules and to enforce infractions with their children than with their stepchildren. They were also quicker to flare up in anger at their biological children. They wondered why. Some speculated that their anger might spring from frustration over child-rearing attempts in their new, combined family, and embarrassment over their unexpected failure. A stepmother tends to see her "own" children's behavior as a reflection of her mothering ability, whereas a stepchild's misbehavior, though frustrating, does not make her feel personally responsible.

Stepmothers found that they had vastly different expectations for their biological children and their stepchildren. They found themselves often turning to their biological children to provide emotional support and personal validation when the going got rough, when instant love and an instant family didn't materialize. Stepmothers with children of their "own" were surprised and distressed to find themselves expecting their children to take up the slack in the family, thereby subjecting them to tremendous and unfair pressure.

Barbara, a stepmother of one and mother of two, admits to this pattern of unfair expectations. "If my stepdaughter's room is a mess," she said, "I find myself screaming at my *own* daughter for something as minor as a bath towel draped over her chair." She realizes this causes resentment among the children in the family and between herself and the children. "Sometimes it just seems easier to ask your own kid to do something," Barbara concluded.

Over and over, stepmothers voiced this feeling. But why is it easier to ask your "own" son to take out the garbage rather than your stepson? "Oh," claims Debby, "he just knows what I want him to do." "I don't have to go through all those explanations when I ask my daughter to do something," Ann admits.

It doesn't require a Sherlock Holmes to detect that something else is going on behind such statements. When stepmothers don't feel secure with their stepchildren, they turn to their biological children. It's easy to ask someone whom you know and love, and who also loves you, to do favors for you; it's hard to ask someone who doesn't trust you yet. The reasoning behind this is simple: The stepchild's love is conditional; it's still to be earned. On the other hand, the biological child's love is perceived as unconditional. Stepmothers seem to revel in the fact that love and respect do not have to be earned or maintained from biological children. This feeling of the immutability of their love serves as a basis for assuming that all sorts of chores and favors may be demanded, thanks to this reciprocal love between mother and child.

When a stepmother falls into this trap, she runs the risk of expecting her children to demonstrate far more compassion, maturity, and altruism than they are capable of. She runs the risk of viewing her biological children as "ideal" and her stepchildren as "real"—and therefore subject to more realistic, lower expectations.

What can a stepmother/mother do about these unequal feelings? How can she equalize the pressure on both biological and stepchildren and prevent herself from perpetuating a pattern of behavior that can only harm the new family?

Acknowledge Those Different Expectations

First, it is best to acknowledge your feelings and discuss your expectations with the children. Biological children will have their feelings of worth confirmed; they *are* being asked to do more, but this is a natural result of their already secure relationship with their mother. Stepchildren will similarly feel validated. They will be delighted that more is being asked of the biological child, whom they have probably perceived as favored.

Sharing these feelings isn't always easy. Stepmothers are often uncomfortable when they realize that they don't feel the same way about their step and biological children. Over and over, stepmothers described how they treated both sets of children the same; how they acted the same toward both sets of children; how the rules were the same; and how their responsibilities for both sets of children were the same, too. Yet despite such repeated protestations, most stepmothers agreed that there was an intangible "something" that separated their feelings for their step and biological children. This "something"—an effort to show affection and forgiveness toward the stepchild—softened reprimands, criticisms, and anger. This "something" was a strong biological identification and empathy for a mother's "own" child. Once admitted and brought out into the open, this distinction was easier to deal with.

The single mother who marries and becomes a stepmother finds that both she and her children face a number of practical and emotional changes that will affect the ways in which they interact with one another. Facing and discussing each aspect of family life—as it comes up—will help pave the way to a smooth transition.

Mothers who become stepmothers will need to help their children adjust to new homes, neighborhoods, and schools. Any change for a child is a BIG change. Practical changes, such as financial ones, cannot compare in intensity to the emotional changes children confront when they are required to accept their mother's new role as a stepmother.

Loss of Status

Single mothers often relate to their children in different ways than mothers who are married; there's often a "friendship" component; single mothers tend to *talk* to their children in more sharing ways than married mothers do. The absence of another adult in the home promotes the child to an almost adult level in the realm of receiving the mother's confidences. When a mother marries, she then turns to her husband for adult confidence—leaving the child behind. When that mother also becomes a stepmother, her children are even more likely to resent their apparent "demotion" to one of the mere "children" in the new family.

Less Individual Time With Mother

Single mothers usually have random chunks of time to spend with their children; mother and child may share a bathroom mirror in the morning, chat while getting ready for work and school or for a date in the evening, and spend time shopping for dinner together, or grabbing a quick meal at a fast-food place. Children often substitute for adult companionship; single mothers spend a good deal of their leisure time with their children. When they marry and become stepmothers, that intimate lifestyle changes, and those precious chunks of shared time disappear. Doors are now closed; time and confidences are shared with the new husband. Leisure time includes mother, stepfather and stepsiblings as well.

Many new stepmothers become edgy and uncomfortable when this happens. They miss the lost intimacy and the ease of the mother-child relationship as keenly as their children do.

While Joan was a single parent, her life revolved around her twelve-year-old daughter. Joan took each day as it came; caring for only one child was simple and pleasant. Indeed, virtually all of her time, aside from her work as a commercial artist, was centered on Jessica: taking her to ballet class, helping her with homework, shopping with her for the dinners they'd share. Then Joan married and this intimacy changed; Jessica moved from the center of Joan's life to a satellite position. Joan found herself dropping Jessica off at ballet to continue on to her stepson's hockey practice. She did not enjoy hockey; she felt out of place and unappreciated. Her stepsons did not seem to notice her presence, and Jessica began to show less interest in ballet. Joan grew increasingly edgy.

The stepmother who was a single mother to an *only* child may face a rocky adjustment for herself and her child. The only child has to accommodate to another adult, other children, *and* the sharing of his/her mother in a way that is totally foreign. The mother has to learn how to divide her childcare responsibilities among several children and how to cope with jealousies, bickering and boisterous play, all absent issues in a single-parent, only-child household. Sometimes, however, a mother's remarriage can signal positive changes for her child or children.

Dorothy was a young single mother who, like many young divorcees, was surviving at just above the poverty level. Her marriage to Don radically affected her children's standard of living. Dorothy and her three children were, as she claims, "pretty good at pinching pennies" before she married. She remembers her children's amazement when they all moved into Don's home in the suburbs. While she and Don busied themselves moving in, the children stared at a large bowl of fruit on the dining room table. The children had never seen a big bowl of fruit like that; in their household there had never been any money for dessert. When Dorothy and her children had wanted a special treat, they would walk up and down the hall of their apartment building and "get fat on their neighbors' fumes"; the children weren't sure that the bowl of fruit was real, and when they found it was, they weren't sure it was for eating. When Dorothy and Don assured the children that it was theirs to eat, they pounced on the bowl and ate every piece. Dorothy, like many single mothers, found that her marriage greatly improved her financial situation.

Of course not all single mothers find that their marriages bring financial advantages. Some new stepmothers, like Hannah, find that they have less money to spend. Hannah had been a single mother with one young son for seven years before her marriage to Rex and had been in the habit of spending money quite freely. She and her young son had lived with relatives, and although Hannah paid a nominal rent and shared household expenses, the remainder of her salary as a high school music teacher was hers to spend—without accountability. Hannah spent most of her salary on her son. Hannah's marriage increased the *amount* of cash on hand, but the *way* in which money was spent changed drastically. Like scores of other stepmothers, Hannah found that handling money in the new family involved new disciplines and a sharing of control: Planning and sharing were the rule, instant gratification the exception. Family living involves more expenses than the single-parent lifestyle—higher food bills, additional expenses for clothing, higher rent or mortgage payments, and insurance bills. Again, stepmothers like Hannah found that adjustment was easier when they faced, and discussed, the changes marriage would bring to them and to their children. They didn't always find this process easy, however, and most of them felt the need for guidance in taking the first steps toward creating a new family.

Beginning Steps

1. Don't Rush!

Going overboard in an attempt to treat stepchildren in the same way as your biological children is just unworkable. Although the new stepmother may have good intentions, she just won't *feel* the same about all children in the family. To expect to feel the same way about children you've just met as you do about those with whom you share a biological and historical connection serves no one! Your "own" children will feel confused and betrayed by protestations of instant-equal love and stepchildren will see such dishonesty for what it is. There is nothing wrong with acknowledging truth.

2. Share Your Time

Sharing is difficult for all children—and most adults, too! Your children are being asked to share their mother with other children and with another adult. It is also a well-kept secret that stepmothers often resent time spent with stepchildren if they perceive that it detracts from time spent with their "own" children. Even the most well-adjusted stepchild will need extra time and affection from the new stepmother. If the stepmother does not feel that she is getting anything in return, she may resent even more keenly the time spent away from her own children.

3. Keep Talking

Encourage children to speak freely, about their feelings. Each child must have an arena where negative as well as positive feelings can be safely expressed. Harriet, a widow, was very much in love when she married Vincent; she was thrilled that her son, John, would have a "father" and two brothers. Despite Harriet's happiness, John deteriorated during the first five years of her marriage, changing from a smiling ten-year-old who loved school and Little League to a sullen fifteen-year-old who was frequently a truant and more than occasionally high on marijuana; he was unhappy and out of control. Harriet took John to a therapist, who learned, during the first sessions, that John had hated the idea of his mother's marriage from the beginning and still hated his "brothers"! Harriet was shocked; John had always said everything was fine with the family.

4. Maintain as Many Routines as Possible

Children are fearful that they will lose their mothers. This is a deep emotional fear that cuts across age lines. Whether you are dealing with a two-year-old who suddenly attaches himself to your leg or a teenager who plants herself on the sofa for a month like a silent couch potato, the fear is the same. Any change in routine may exacerbate a child's fear that *Mother* is changing!

Sarah tried to be a superstepmommy—and discovered that changing all the routines for her young son and trying to be a perfect mommy, wife, and stepmother backfired! Sarah had been a single mother for most of her son's ten years. She had worked as a nurse from the time Jason was nine months old, and as he matured he had assumed many household chores. At the time of his mother's marriage, Jason was a responsible and independent fourth-grader. Sarah was proud of his competence in domestic areas. Sarah's new stepchildren were older than Jason and had no desire or flair for domestic chores. Sarah worried that perhaps she had overburdened her son during her single years and determined to do more for Jason now that she was married and had the opportunity to cut back on her working hours. One evening shortly after her marriage, Sarah tiptoed into her sleeping son's room to put away some laundry. It was 1:00 a.m. and everyone was asleep. Jason sat up in bed, wide awake, and asked, "What are you doing?"

To Sarah's surprise, her independent, respectful, previously calm little boy began to yell, "STOP IT!!! WHAT ARE YOU DOING? I'M SUPPOSED TO PUT AWAY MY CLOTHES! I ALWAYS PUT AWAY MY CLOTHES! I ALWAYS CLEAN UP MY ROOM! WHY ARE YOU CHANGING?" As Sarah held her sobbing son she realized that even positive changes can be very threatening for children.

5. Make Time for Yourself—Alone

It is especially important for a new stepmother to find time to be alone. Too often, in the haste to create a family, the stepmother rushes everyone into an idealized level of intimacy. Stepmothers must remember that they married primarily for *themselves.* Children may or may not be absolutely delighted with their mother's marriage; children may or may not be delighted to be part of this new family. Children shouldn't ever be given cause to feel that they have lost their relationship with their mother, but she, too, must have time for herself.

6. Help Children Understand Your New Commitment

A stepmother must clarify and recommit herself over and over again to all the children in the house. Biological children will need to understand that they are still loved and are still irreplaceable. Some stepmothers perversely try to "prove" their love for their stepchildren by minimizing or disguising their loving behavior toward their biological children. They may stop showing affection to their biological children if they are uncomfortable showing affection for their stepchildren; everyone loses with this approach!

Children will understand their mother's commitment to their new stepsiblings if this commitment is discussed. Talk about fears, get them out in the open; children need support at this time. They need to be told that their mother's new commitment does not diminish her feelings for them. A stepmother should not minimize her expression of loving feelings for her children; such demonstrations set a positive example of closeness for stepchildren and reinforce her own children's self-confidence.

7. A Different Kind of Love

Most stepmothers feel so guilty about not feeling the *same* love for their stepchildren and their biological children that they overlook the obvious: *People love in different ways.* Mothers certainly do not expect to feel the same kind of love for their children that they feel for their own mothers; stepmothers don't expect to feel the same kind of love for their children as they do for their husbands. Stepmothers easily acknowledge different kinds of love in other aspects of their lives. So, too, they can feel different kinds of love for their stepchildren and their biological children.

If You've Never Had Children

Stepmothers who have never had children of their own are most prone to disaster in their marriages. Inexperience with children often causes stepmothers to be totally unprepared for the impact children have on their marriages and their personal life. Inexperience prompts them to underestimate—or overestimate—the stepchild's contribution to the new family and either to overlook the richness that children bring to any couple's life or to lean too heavily on children to "make the marriage work." These misapprehensions must be exploded before a stepmother can begin.

Common False Expectations

"I'll Have 'Nice' Stepchildren"

Children are, by nature, self-centered creatures. Children are also, by nature of their immaturity, often not "nice." Children are dependent, self-centered, emotionally and intellectually immature, and overly concerned with their own comfort. Feelings for others must be taught and are not usually felt automatically.

"The More I Give the More I'll Get"

Giving is not usually reciprocated in direct ways by children. Many stepmothers who are inexperienced with child-rearing believe that the more they try, the more they will get in return. Often, such women have been active in the work force and apply inappropriate criteria to child-rearing only to find that strategies which worked beautifully in the office simply bomb out in the home. Children tend to take a lot more than they give. Parenting, by definition, implies that the parent will help "socialize" the child so that the child learns the skills of reciprocating, sharing, and exchanging good feelings.

Not only will children often fail to be "nice," but it will probably fall to the stepmother to teach her stepchildren about "niceness."

"Only 'Real' Mothers Have Power"

Stepmothers often feel that they don't have the right to any authority over their stepchildren. Stepmothers are the adults in the family. Children and adults are not on equal footing. The stepmother, although inexperienced in mothering, possesses a wealth of adult experience and skills that she will share with her stepchildren. This sense of adulthood should encourage stepmothers to become more confident.

"I'll Rescue My Husband and His Children"

Children and husbands are not social-work projects. Many stepmothers enter their marriages as rescue workers. Like so many Wendys in the children's tale of *Peter Pan*, they fly off to rescue their husbands and stepchildren, only to learn a scary truth: Husbands and stepchildren generally do not feel the need to be rescued by anyone.

"I'll Be Their Real Mother"

Some stepmothers assume that a child is a child is a child; they anticipate that their stepchildren will fill their need to be a mother. It doesn't work that way. Stepmothers with that expectation are susceptible to tremendous hurt. Eager to shower their new children with a love they have been saving up for years, they are often desperately disappointed when they are met with coolness, hostility—anything short of adoring, open-armed love.

"I'll Be a Better Mother Than Their Own"

Stepmothers must refrain from competing with biological mothers. The stepmother who perceives her relationship with her stepchildren as a competition with an adversarial mother is setting herself up for anguish and defeat. Raising children is a commitment and a responsibility, not a competition.

"This New Family Will Replace the Original Family"

There really are no replacements in life; there are only *new relationships*. No one feels this more keenly than a child. Think about a child whose puppy has just been run over. Well-meaning adults tend to rush in and offer a replacement. Their good intentions are usually rejected with wails of "I don't want a new puppy, I want my puppy." No loving adult would remind such a child of all the complaints he or she used to have about the departed puppy. Certainly no one would blame the new puppy for the child's rejection. Most people faced with this situation would understand the child's grief: One puppy cannot replace another. Families and mothers are not interchangeable or replaceable, either. Only when the child has completed his grieving for the previous family, and for the absent mother, will he be ready to accept a new family or a new parent.

"They Will Have to Love Me"

Love cannot be legislated. Children cannot be told to love their stepmothers any more than stepmothers can be forced to love their stepchildren. Children will *not* automatically love you because you are married to their father; respect in the form of polite behavior can be required; love cannot. Love must grow on its own.

"Love Will Conquer All"

A woman actually becomes a stepmother at the altar. Caught up in the romance of the moment, she tends to sweep the children along with her prevailing mood. Alas, the wash of romanticism inherent in the new marriage is not the most ideal atmosphere for logic. Love for stepchildren is not conferred with the exchange of marriage vows.

"This Marriage Has Nothing to Do With the Kids; They're His"

Although many stepmothers begin their relationships with starry-eyed expectations of motherhood, others start out assuming that their stepchildren will not affect their lives. Such women begin their marriages with the assumption that they will be able to distance themselves from their stepchildren's lives, leaving their care and responsibility totally to the father. Many such stepmothers have remained childless by design and have conveyed their preference for a childless life to their husbands. They somehow imagine that marriage will in no way change their husband's previous arrangements for childcare: They assume that the husband will continue to manage childcare the same way he did before the marriage. There is no way this can work. Stepmothers who plan on excluding themselves from their stepchildren's lives while living under the same roof are simply kidding themselves. Living with children without any interaction is, at the very least, "cold." It is also unrealistic.

What Can a Stepmother Expect?

Becoming a stepmother *will* change your life; it *will* link you intimately with the lives of one or more children. It will *not* automatically ensure your husband's love, imbue you with respectability, or provide you with an instant family. All of *that* is up to you. In the next chapters, we'll talk about how to do it. We'll ask and answer a lot of practical questions, and a few philosophical ones:

• What are some typical behavior patterns that an inexperienced stepmother may discover?
• What common problems impede the beginning of a smooth relationship between stepmother and stepchildren?
• How can she cope with these problems?

Chapter 5

LEARNING ABOUT CHILD DEVELOPMENT

The age of a child will greatly influence that child's readiness, ability, and desire to begin a new relationship; each age group presents a different set of concerns, issues, and joys for stepmothers.

The Infant and Preschool Child

Stepmothers are often upset to find themselves in charge of little cherubs who are anything but cherubic. The dream of an adorable child slumbering peacefully in one's arms is often shattered by the reality of a sobbing, sullen, frightened child clinging tearfully to its father's trouser leg.

It will help the stepmother to understand the world of a little child—a world that is limited by thought processes that aren't capable of dealing with abstractions. It will help to understand that the world of a little child is truly a scary place, a place without clear borders—where a new stepmother may represent a threat to the fragile order the child is only beginning to construct. It will help stepmothers to understand that the sometimes rejecting, hostile, or pitiful behavior of the child is not personally directed at her; it's a sign of confusion and lack of comprehension.

The very real pain of the new stepmother must be addressed, too. Most women assume the care of young children with extraordinarily high hopes. It is easy to "fall in love" with a little child and it is all too easy to expect that love to be immediately returned. It is hard not to be hurt when a child rejects those early advances; it is hard to know how to approach a child who so obviously wants someone else. However, it is possible for a stepmother to form a close and loving relationship with a baby or a very young child if she understands the child's world and the ways she can become part of that world.

How Do Babies Think?

There's obviously little point in handing a baby a how-to book or writing a baby a letter. There are lots of other communication techniques that won't work with babies, either. Stepmothers of very young children will have to shoulder the bulk of all reasoning and thinking simply because little children are developmentally unprepared to reason and think on their own.

Babies don't make plans; they have no understanding of cause and effect. In fact, they're just beginning to figure out that they are separate from the world around them. Babies are entirely dependent upon adults for their most basic physical survival; the extent and richness of their lives, and the way they will grow and perceive the world, is in the hands of those who care for them.

As babies grow into toddlerhood between eighteen months and three years, they are almost entirely involved with the business of exploring their world and the people who inhabit it. Toddlers and preschoolers are naturally wary and skeptical. Language skills improve at this stage and communication with the child becomes a little easier.

Little children will not be able to give detailed explanations either of their feelings or their experiences. They spend much of their time trying to make sense out of their world, deeply engrossed in the effort to meet their own needs. It's not realistic to expect a child to deal with the abstractions of a stepfamily when he or she is struggling with mastery of the fork! Understanding the way little children begin to think may help stepmothers as they begin their new family lives.

Toddlers Lump Things Together

Toddlers will group things together without any apparent pattern; for example, a "daddy" may become any person who scratches his nose in a way that the toddler's father does.

Words Have an Individual Meaning

You may be saying "Honey," and that means something

totally different to your little stepchild. "Honey" may mean something that a child desires, a catchall word for feeling good or perhaps for feeling deprived or sad.

They're Inconsistent

The world is "magical" to a little child; people change identities with their clothing. Toddlers don't "see" each adult in a consistent way. They don't see events consistently, either.

Toddlers adopt one opinion after the other. Don't expect them to like ripe bananas today just because they liked them yesterday!

Between the ages of three and five, children begin to give "reasons" for their behavior and try to interpret their experiences; however, their "reasons" may not have much to do with an adult's reasoning. The ways in which children reason at this age sometimes lead adults to believe that they are lying or being obstinate when in fact they are simply thinking things through to the best of their limited ability.

They Lack Direction

Little children often mix up unrelated explanations when trying to work through the causes of an event; they don't really know what is relevant to their reasoning. When a little child is asked how a car works, he may respond by naming off all the parts of a car.

Children Lack a Sense of Sequence

Children may reverse the order in which things happened. A child may announce that he lost his fork because he's not eating, for example, instead of the other way around.

Children Don't "Think About Thinking"

If a child is asked, "Where did you learn that?" the response may be "I always knew it"—or a surprised stare.

Children Have Trouble with Relationships

Children have difficulty understanding family relationships, age relationships, spatial relationships. They are just learning how to name individual objects; they haven't mastered the skill of fitting things or people together.

Children Give Meaning to Chance Happenings

Children believe that things happen because they are caused by someone; objects can act on behalf of people or in obedience to them. A little child of this age might wail over a missed plane, then ask, "But didn't it see we were here?" If he tells you about a dream, and you don't remember how it turned out, he'll protest, "But you were there!"

A cork might be "reasoned" to float not because of any scientific principle but because it is simply "smarter" than the rock, which sinks.

The Adjustment Period—What to Expect?

Little children may not be ready to think about the changes in their lives, but they certainly do feel them. They don't have the vocabulary, the experience, or the developmental ability to deal with change. Because of these limitations, they let their actions speak for them. What can a new stepmother expect?

The Angry Child

Three-year-olds angry about the changes in their lives may turn the anger inward; they may whine, complain, or chronically boss other children around. They may become self-destructive, pulling their hair, biting their nails, or picking their skin. They may turn the anger outward, alternating between being bullies and crybabies, acting out the pattern of pain over and over again by lashing out and then seeking comfort. Such acted-out behavior is easy to spot; however, just as important for the stepmother and stepchild's adjustment are those "too quiet" kinds of behavior.

The Timid Child

Many stepchildren, especially little ones, have been overprotected by their fathers and other loving relatives. Overprotected children may be timid and reluctant to accept their stepmother into their lives. Children need to explore, to grow, and to view the world as a safe place. Overprotection gives children the message that the world is a frightening, dangerous place and that they are not competent to deal with these dangers. The child raised in an overprotected setting will commonly be fearful and will resist trying new experiences. Some children have such a strange view of the world that they may choose to play the "victim" rather than the "hero" in their pretend games.

The Perfect Child

Such children are "little angels." On first glance they seem to have adjusted perfectly to their new stepmothers. However, the child who never misbehaves is usually a very frightened child. Having experienced disorder, he or she is fearful of creating any further chaos.

The Denying Child

Young children often feel that they possess power over situations; their normal egocentricity causes them to believe that their perception or desire can alter the reality of a situation. Denying the presence of the stepmother and the fact that "Mommy" is not coming home may become the young child's reality.

The Fearful Child

Three-year-olds see parents as a concept—a single unit comprising two people. The three-year-old who accepts the fact that her biological mother will no longer be living with her may begin to fear losing other important people as well—and may be particularly fearful of losing her father or new stepmother.

The Self-Blaming Child

Three-year-olds are often convinced that their behavior causes events to occur. A child of this age may believe that breaking a plate has caused it to rain on the day of a planned picnic. Children of this age may assume that their behavior has caused the death or divorce of their mothers or the remarriage of their fathers.

The Babyish Child

When children of this age become very insecure, they seek security by reverting back to a safer time in their young lives. Three-year-olds derive much of their courage from the security provided by their families. Any disruption in this security may cause them to become fearful, shy, and cautious. Thumb-sucking, blankets, bottles, and the need for diapers may reappear.

The Manipulating Child

Little children prefer to have the adults' attention all to themselves; this is a normal phase of young childhood. They may cry and cling to whoever was taking care of them before their father's marriage; they may wail pitifully for Daddy to stay home or for Grandma to come back and live with them. This behavior may be very upsetting for the stepmother.

It is best to realize that a little child takes the stepmother's measure by such attempts. A stepmother must address these fears and not permit the child to manipulate her by crying, screaming, clinging, or sulking. Little children don't have many tools to get what they want. A two-year-old who figures out that separation fears can be used to attain whatever she wants when she wants it may quickly come to use such "fears" as a tool. The fears may be real, but if left unaddressed they can become manipulative.

How to Cope

Stepmothers need to be calm and consistent and to understand that acting-out behavior stems from the very real fears of the young child. The calm, confident handling of little children will allay the child's fears and quiet the acting-out or regressive behavior.

Distract Babies and Young Children

Babies try to understand situations that are hard for them to comprehend in ways that are familiar to them; sometimes these actions just don't work. A little child may try, for example, to turn on a light by blinking her eyes open and shut, mimicking the light. The same baby may run back and forth to the door calling "Mama" in an attempt to recapture the former home. One-year-olds are into everything; they often attempt things that are way outside their current competence and become easily frustrated. Fortunately, they are easily distractible. Saying "No" won't work with an infant or a very young child, but "No" followed by a distraction—something to take the baby's attention elsewhere—is very effective.

Two-year-olds, asserting their newly discovered independence, dislike being told what to do. Couple this negativity with the clinging and separation anxiety typical of most two-year-olds, and you've produced disaster for a stepmother. Try to avoid confrontations with two-year-olds. They function best when their world is arranged so that they may attempt to do the things they wish to try as independently and with as much of a chance of success as possible.

Learn By Watching Them Play

Stepmothers can learn a lot about children by observing them at play. Very young children use play as a way of making sense of their world. Children talk to—and through—their toys; as they get older, they enjoy imitating, role-playing, and pretending games.

Reality and fantasy are still confused for most three-year-olds. Children of this age mix things up, sometimes imagining that people are living inside the TV set, for instance. Little children may need help separating real stepmothers from stepmothers in their storybooks!

Children of this age confront a host of fears, all of which seem very real. In addition, they idealize the adults in their lives and want to be like them. They believe that adults are very powerful; they have no inkling of their parents' limitations. The world, to a young child, is magical. Children believe that inanimate objects have feelings; children believe in retributive justice; and children are confused as to just how their desires interact with what actually happens. Complicating things even further is the child's sudden awareness of sexual differences and the beginning of questioning about birth, sickness, and death. Children typically struggle with severe guilt around age three; Freudians explain such guilt by pointing to the child's romantic attachment to the opposite-sex parent. Others explain this guilt as the beginning of the child's formation of a sense of right and wrong. If you observe the child at play, you will discover which common fears plague him. Then you will be able to calm those fears and help the child to feel safe in the world and secure in his new relationship with you.

Common Fears and Concerns

Fear of Unfamiliarity, Separation, Being Startled

A baby's fears center on sudden noises, being startled. As they get older, babies fear separation, the new, and anything unfamiliar.

Fear of New Experiences

A young child's way of coping with his fear of new experiences is to make the new experience a part of his fantasy world. There are problems in this strategy for the little child who really can't differentiate between fantasy and reality in the first place. The child at play is trying to learn about the world, to assimilate reality. New situations and new relationships only complicate this task.

The Scary World of the Three-to-Five-Year-Old

As children begin to mature, their world expands, prompting many young children to begin to see the world as a potentially dangerous place. As the child begins to see the enormity of the world, he begins to have a sense of powerlessness. Beginning at about age three the child becomes curious about birth, life, and death; this curiosity often leads to a litany of worries as the child tries to gain a hold over a world that at times seems filled with danger These childhood worries include a fear of monsters, the dark, dogs, fire engines, illness, death, injury, and handicapped people.

Signs of Stress

Any good childcare book, or any experience with young children, will reassure a new stepmother that a measure of fearfulness is normal for young children. How, then, can stepmothers tell if a child is unduly tense, fearful, or angry?

Children, like adults, show certain symptoms of tension: Nail-biting, hair-pulling or twirling, wetting the bed, and stuttering are common at this age. Stuttering is often tied to tension; some experts believe that this tension simply springs from the child working hard at language formation, while others contend that stuttering indicates some sort of psychological tension. Nevertheless, most children outgrow stuttering within a few months. Don't try to correct the child's speech or worry about speech training. Try to remove the tension. If there has been too much of a push for talking or correct speech, relax the pressure.

With any of these stress indicators, leave the child alone. Give the child and yourself some time to settle in. If the indicators of stress continue or intensify, seek the help of a family counselor, social work psychotherapist, child psychologist, or psychiatrist.

Comforters

Even if the children are behaving in ways that are personally unpleasant or undesirable to you, the adjustment period will go along more smoothly if children are permitted to retain their "comforters." Babies and young children use comforters to help themselves deal with the stresses of their lives. Comforters such as blankets, thumb-sucking, masturbation, rocking, singing, etc., are a child's way of trying to meet its own needs. Stepmothers should be encouraging about the child's eventual giving up of the comforter but should not force the issue. Permit the child to sleep with the stuffed animal, toy, or old baby blanket. Remember that children's fears are especially acute until they develop a strong sense of the difference between real and make-believe. Telling a frightened child that the monster is make-believe is not helpful. Helping a child to hold onto a favorite toy and compare that toy to the monster is more helpful in assisting differentiation between fantasy and reality.

Dragging a fearful child over to a dog will probably not do to much to end the fear; however, desensitizing the child to his fear of dogs by incorporating such fears into stories, games, or other play may help.

Role-playing

Children around the ages of three, four, and five delight in role-playing. Such play-acting, in addition to being fun, gives the stepmother a way of understanding a child's point of view quickly, vividly, and with a depth that often outdistances the child's verbal abilities. Role-playing allows even a very young child to reveal his version of reality, which may or not reflect actual events or circumstances.

The little girl who "plays" stepmother by frowning and yelling is conveying her perception of the world. The arrival of a new stepmother is an earthshaking event for a little child; it is a grave error to assume that young children will easily accept their stepmothers. The child's inexperience and natural wariness of strangers is bound to prompt initial resistance. Fortunately, young children respond well and quickly to regular routines, consistent behavior, and cheerful attitudes.

Your Love Is Vital

Children desperately need loving caregivers. You will be such a caregiver. Children who are deprived of constant, supportive, loving care become timid, withdrawn, and depressed; these children are often not very lovable. They may not fit the idealized picture of the open, loving, little nursery school cherub.

Children who have been ignored, neglected, or mistreated in their young years especially need the loving care of their stepmothers. Too often, children who have been abused grow into adults with skewed perceptions of the world and recreate abusive situations in their adult relationships as victims or perpetrators. The stepmother who provides loving support and attentive, consistent caregiving can change the course of her stepchildren's futures. Children count on their parents for leadership, love, and security. They watch their parents and pattern themselves after them. Personalities are formed in this way. Dr. Spock goes so far as to say, "The greatest gift from parents is love, which they express in countless ways: a fond facial expression, spontaneous demonstrations of physical affection, pleasure in their children's accomplishments, comforting them when they are hurt or frightened, controlling them to keep them safe and to help them become responsible people, giving them high ideals." Stepmothers can begin to provide the loving care that young children so desperately crave—and will find, in the process, that loving a little child feels good.

A small child may be a bit problematic at first for a new stepmother. The little girl has "lost" her biological mother upon whom she has modeled herself. The little boy has lost his first love and is left with his psychological rival—his father. The stepmother may not be particularly welcomed by either boys or girls. A little girl may feel guilty over the departure or death of her biological mother and may resist a stepmother's attentions, resenting the way she has "usurped" the little girl's next-in-line position with Daddy.

Children between the ages of three and five need constant reassurance. How can a stepmother begin to build a meaningful relationship with her young stepchildren?

Commitment

Little children are responsive by nature. Stepmothers must take the first step in beginning a relationship; a little child just can't. The need may be present, but the ability to begin a relationship has not been developed yet. It's up to you.

Build Trust by Being Consistent

Stepmothers will play a great part in a child's ability to trust others and the way in which a child comes to view itself and the world. Children gain trust in themselves by being respected as human beings. The self-assurance built during the first five years of life will help the child become comfortable with itself and with other people for the rest of its life.

Provide Security to Encourage Independence

In order for babies to feel safe enough to explore the world, they must feel that they can return to a "safe harbor." Babies who feel secure will explore, reach out to discover new people, places, and situations. However, these adventuresome babies will want to return to people who are safe. We have all seen the baby who smiles at the stranger and then hides its face in Daddy's shoulder.

Build Love and Respect

The love that a child receives creates an ability to give love in return. Stepmothers can help children learn to love by loving them. The love a child begins to feel will affect that child's ability to form and sustain positive relationships throughout life.

How to Begin

A Gradual Approach Is Best

Young children respond best to a gradual approach; they will cling to familiar, trusted individuals and be suspicious, frightened, or hostile to newcomers—stepmothers included! Suspiciousness and wariness are normal for little children. The support of your stepchild's father is a very important factor. Fathers should try very hard not to hover, and to be cheerful, confident, and unafraid to leave the child with the stepmother. The attitude of those the child already trusts will help or hinder the young child's relationship with the stepmother; the attitude of those trusted adults is perhaps the most powerful initial factor in helping the child into the new relationship.

Spend Time Alone

Spend lots of time alone with the child. You'll know that you have become important in your stepchild's life when the child seeks you out in times of stress or misses your presence when you're out of sight.

The Years from Six to Twelve

School-age children can reason and think, give explanations, and form relationships. However, their thinking and emotions remain very much tied to the "here and now"; their way of thinking is concrete. School-aged children enjoy classifying things. They like to make collections.

Children of school age are typically very active, enjoying a wide variety of games and sports. Peers become very important; the grade school years are the time for best friends and buddies, for clubhouses and secrets from the adult world. There is a rigidity to childhood in thought and in emotion; things are right or wrong; there are no mitigating circumstances. Children require "proof," tangible examples, in order to learn effectively or wholeheartedly to accept anything new. Children tend to take each experience as it comes rather than think about a sequence of events in general terms; they use a trial-and-error method in most areas of their lives. This is the age of fun for children and parents alike: games, hobbies, outings, friends, sports, and a wide range of activities.

The rigidity of childhood, the need to see evidence as proof of fact, will preclude abstract conversation and analysis between you and your stepchildren. Children of school age are not yet capable of drawing generalizations from their experience. The world is composed of good guys and bad guys; everything must fit into a neat category. The child will spend a good deal of time trying to classify the people and things of his world; the new stepmother may seem to defy classification. A stepmother can help her child override certain limitations in reasoning skills and emotional maturity by taking the time to enter the magical world of childhood.

How to Understand a Child's Thinking

They Don't Generalize

Young children have difficulty making generalizations; in fact a great many adults also have trouble with these higher-order thinking skills. Children are usually incapable of accepting a premise and reasoning from it; they see only a special case without appreciating the need to express a general law.

They Don't See Contradictions in Thinking

Children cannot perceive contradictions; they have difficulty seeing a situation from another's point of view and do not see any reason to relinquish their own point of view.

They Don't "Get" Hidden Meanings

In a proverb, for instance, or a fable, the child will fail to see a hidden meaning but instead will relate some familiar aspects of the story to an experience he already understands. Children do not readily understand sarcasm, analogies, or abstract examples. They are very literal-minded.

They Have Difficulty with Definitions

Children will define something by its use ("a spoon is to eat with"); later on, they begin to be able to generalize by noting an object's use and its relationship to other objects. A stepmother may prove indefinable for children.

Stepmothers "act" like mothers, but they aren't. The simple frustration of the child struggling to define the indefinable prompts the common cry of "You're not my mother." Although this disclaimer is especially hurtful for the stepmother, perhaps it should be viewed as the child's attempt to define what is in terms of what is not!

Names Retain Mystical Significance

Until late in childhood names (like rules) are graven in stone. Few children realize that names were conferred by people and can be altered; children will often assert that names were God-given and as such are unchangeable. A mother is a mother is a mother...

Children Explain Every Coincidence

The child's mystical attitude toward rules and names extends to his general feeling about the world. Until late in childhood, a child will attempt to explain every occurrence, not really believing that there is such a thing as a chance occurrence or a coincidence.

They Learn by Doing—Not by Listening

Children find it very difficult to learn from verbal teaching. A new skill or concept will be better learned when connected to an activity that has meaning for the child.

How To Help Children Think

Adults can help children move from one level of reasoning to another. New concepts and difficult relationships need to be explained. Children need frequent opportunities to discuss their actions and opinions in their own words. Helping children to understand their world is an ongoing process— a job that you'll do every day. You can help children give definitions, solve problems, or state propositions verbally by asking them to perform tasks and then to discuss the way those tasks have been carried out. Verbal expressions should be linked to tangible action until it becomes possible for children to make generalizations from similar experiences or to recognize situations similar to those they have already learned to solve and describe in terms that are meaningful to them. Everyday chores and events around the house—doing the laundry, walking the dog, mowing the lawn—are gold mines of experience for the child.

Children Need to Try Things Out for Themselves

Children find it difficult to go beyond the specific information they are given and to imagine new possibilities or explanations for events. They have an almost mystical attitude about authority. Until they are about ten years old, they often believe that the rules of games are created by their parents. Violating rules at this age is seen as almost impossible. After the age of ten, there is a change in a child's thinking about rules; the child may accept that the "rule" still has a lot of authority, but no longer feels that "everything was arranged for the best" and that the established order must be respected. Children at this age begin to believe in the value of experimenting, though they will still seek the approval of their peer group.

Children Are Very Concerned With Fairness and Concepts of Good and Bad

Children now begin to explore motives and the concept of cause and effect. They learn to distinguish "mistakes" from deliberate wrongdoing and are very concerned with the fairness of punishments.

Children try to sort through why they don't live with their mother—why she died or why she left. The need to see one "mother" as good and one "mother" as bad may cause the child's loyalty to leap from stepmother to biological mother and back again.

A caring adult to listen to the day's happenings is essential—someone to be there when a child comes home from school or at least in telephone contact. Be aware of the "push-me-pull-me" quality of children's independence: They need to be autonomous, but they also need constant love, validation, and support.

Around age six, children begin to fall out of love with the other sex parent as they begin to identify more strongly with peers of their own sex. Stepmothers may find that they have a more difficult time with their stepdaughters than their stepsons because of these psychological and emotional changes. Experts have long claimed that boys have a harder adjustment after divorce because, living with their mothers and "losing" their fathers, they find themselves in flux; if this is true, then probably girls who live with their fathers and "lose" their mothers will suffer similar conflicts. Stepmothers simply add another complication. You'll need a lot of patience.

A Few Tips

• Children often shove their feelings underground because they don't want to rock the boat. They may fear antagonizing anyone and, like their younger siblings, may just decide to be "very, very good." Be aware of this "false goodness" and encourage the child to express its real feelings.

• Beginning at about age six, children begin to "cool off" toward their parents. They still enjoy being silly on occasion, or even cuddled for a brief period, but they begin to look to people outside the family for information and amusement. At this stage, children tend to dislike displays of affection. Go easy on the cuddling and be aware of their desire for privacy.

• Children are hugely interested in what other kids say and do. From the age of six on, there's a fascination with secret clubs, cliques, and complicated rules and strategies. The six-year-old may not be permitted membership in the clubs of older children, but he enjoys their attention and is happy to become a gofer for older children, cheerfully running errands, retrieving balls, or doing chores. Do not minimize these activities; try to show interest in the day-to-day details, if the child is willing to share these with you.

• Children are beginning to pull away from parents; they need support but they will be naturally suspicious of motives and distrustful. Try to be patient and let the child come to you.

• You may have to cultivate a thick-skinned toughness. Children are rigidly moralistic; much of their "cruelty" springs from a need to define relationships and concepts in terms that are familiar to them. When Sandy, a stepson of eight, announced at Christmas dinner that he, his father, stepmother, and two stepsisters were not a "real" family, the assembled guests gasped with embarrassment. Sandy, however, continued to eat his Christmas turkey, unaware of the pain he had inflicted. When he was given a chance to explain his statement later, he claimed that families were one mother, one father, and one child, and that he lived in a stepfamily!

• Be a resource person. Children are fascinated by adults; the adult world is seen as powerful and mysterious. Children like to concoct tales to explain the inexplicable doings of the adult world. A stepmother can provide a key to this world. The fact that she is not blood-related may serve as a boon to her relationship to her stepchild, who is trying to gain independence from parents. A stepmother may be "cool" if she doesn't try too hard to be "Mommy." The children can have their cake and eat it, too: They complete their cooling-off period with their parents and attach to this new person—a trusted adult who is around the house all the time.

• Children don't want to be different. It is helpful for them to realize that they are not the only ones with a stepmother. Often children go to great lengths to disguise their stepfamily status. Some children begin to refer to stepmothers as "Mom" and pretend to be nuclear families; other children ignore the existence of their stepmothers and any stepsiblings. Ten-year-old Maryann simply chose to ignore everyone's existence. When her stepmother visited her school during open school week, the teacher was amazed at her existence. Maryann had "forgotten" to tell her teacher that her widowed father had married; she had similarly forgotten to deliver the notes her stepmother had written to her teacher. Maryann had explained away her two stepsisters as her "friends."

You'll find lots of opportunities to be part of your stepchildren's lives. School-age children are great joiners. There are Cub Scouts, Brownies, Little League, "the gang." You can satisfy your own need for closeness and provide real help to your stepchildren simply by being around— going to games, being a den mother or troop leader, supplying the cookies or driving in the car pool.

Adolescence

Adolescence is a time of flux. Teenagers are engaged in a struggle for personal identity and independence from their families. Conflict between a stepmother who is seeking to build a relationship and a teenager seeking independence is resolvable. Adolescents, because of their sophisticated reasoning abilities and their increased maturity, may not be as difficult as they first may appear to be.

Adolescence is a time of exclamation points. It is a time for experiencing and testing life. Adolescents tend to analyze and judge everything, including their parents. Much of the adolescent's energy is directed toward moving away from childhood and getting ready to assume a place in the adult world.

The adolescent struggles with new physical, cognitive, and emotional skills in a state of heightened self-consciousness. Everything seems suddenly different to the adolescent. Trying to fit a "strange body" into a world grown suddenly unfamiliar can be scary; for the adolescent with a new stepmother, it can be overwhelming. Some adolescents express their stress by acting out, while others withdraw and become depressed. More commonly, they swing from one mood to another.

It is helpful to remember that adolescence is a time of searching for values: Adolescents struggle to arrive at their own unique point of view about everything. They are constantly involved in this struggle to weigh, measure, and decide from the experiences that bombard them. The adolescent is also in the process of developing a recognizable adult personality; he has not yet chosen the primary face he will wear for the world. Adolescents try on great varieties of personalities; additionally, they try on the gamut of emotions. Adolescents, as we used to say, "let it all hang out."

This can be very confusing for the new stepmother who is trying to get to know her adolescent stepchildren—particularly if she is not accustomed to teenagers. A few tips about how teenagers think, act, and react will help the novice stepmother as she approaches her new "job."

How Adolescents Think

Many adults are fooled and frustrated by the seeming sophistication of adolescent thinking. They now are capable of a wide range of new and highly developed thinking skills, but because these new cognitive skills are used in conjunction with a lack of world experience and social and emotional immaturity, they may actually impede interaction with others and understanding of events.

The constant exchange and discussion of points of view with their peers leads adolescents to a greater understanding of themselves and of the world. Their constant probing curiosity often causes them to seem intrusive as they seek to find out exactly how others think and feel. Ironically, they bristle when asked the same kinds of questions by an adult.

The consideration of many viewpoints gives adolescent thinking new flexibility, but this very quality often leads to indecisiveness. The adolescent seems to consider every possibility for every decision. Again, if the adult seems indecisive, the teenager is quick to call her a "wimp." The typical adolescent has a predilection for gossiping and for heightening simple events into grand dramas. Let the adult "overreact" in return, however, and she's making a "big deal out of nothing."

Adolescents tend to be argumentative about anything and everything. The stepmother who exclaims, "They just want to argue for the sake of argument" may be more correct than she realizes. She had better gird her loins for battle—there's no way to avoid an occasional argument with a teenager. Arguing comes with the territory.

Adolescents can give exhaustive definitions, state hypotheses as general laws which they then go on to test, consider every possibility, and then state the result as a law—a law which will hold good in all similar cases. This new ability to create "laws" may also make the adolescent a rigid and unyielding "world critic." The adolescent is increasingly interested in various social systems, including the ones that operate within his own family. He is critical of his own standards and of the assumptions of the various groups of which he is a member—family, school, the world.

Perhaps it is this capacity to expect to create immutable laws that enables the adolescent to recognize a chance event—one that takes place where no law is operating. Then what? Adolescents become unduly fatalistic and reluctant to accept responsibility for their own actions.

A Passion for Justice

The newfound ability to think things through gives the adolescent the idea that it is very important to justify the judgments he makes, and he expects others to do the same. It may be very hard for an adolescent to accept another's point of view if he can't follow the reasoning that led to the conclusion. Whereas a younger child may answer, "I don't know," an adolescent will test various hypotheses and assert that something "is not possible." Often, only a time-consuming and perhaps stressful explaining process can assure the teenager that the adults thinking is "justified."

The Beginnings of Empathy

Adolescents can now begin to understand analogies and to apply examples that they have not directly experienced to their own lives.

The adolescent's new ability to see different viewpoints may initially lead her to "overidentify": An adolescent who watches a soap opera may fall in love, while one who takes a first-aid course may suddenly suffer from a score of self-diagnosed maladies. New abilities to think abstractly, compare viewpoints, and empathize with the feelings of others carry with them a sense of confusion and, often, a wariness and suspiciousness of adults. Now, more than ever, communication is important. We can begin helping teenagers over the bridge to adulthood by helping them to clarify their thinking.

Helping Adolescents Think Better

Many adults never attain the level of abstract thinking that most teenagers today attain. Many adults continue to think as children, or to revert to thinking as children, failing to analyze their experiences and to perceive and create general laws in the world around them. One of the greatest gifts a stepmother can offer to her stepchildren is the ability to develop the habit of thinking clearly.

Providing Concrete Examples

Adults often talk in abstractions; they speak about loyalty and love, respect and responsibility, without relating these qualities to the events of everyday life. Adolescents need definite and clearly understood examples in order to begin to understand what you mean when you use abstract terms. Provide adolescents with ample opportunity to discuss and solve problems that refer to their own concrete experience. Above all, don't be in a hurry to arrive at a "solution." With adolescents, the route from A to B includes a trip through the entire alphabet.

What to Expect

Adolescents cope with life in strange ways, many of them unattractive and unappealing. It helps if you can understand that these common behavior types, while unpleasant to deal with, are necessary coping strategies.

The Challenger

Some adolescents challenge everything; their vocabulary is charged with antagonism. They compulsively rebut everything and everyone. These teenagers need a combination of patience and limit-setting.

The Self-Defeater

Other adolescents deal with their fears by becoming passive; those who have enjoyed especially close and loving homes may fear competing within the new family. They seek to avoid competition and loss by "withdrawing from the race." Such adolescents may suddenly fail tests, forget appointments, and act in ways that short-circuit their progress and sabotage their success. They need bolstering and support. They need to hear that they are lovable and are capable of succeeding and that they will not be abandoned or ignored as they grow more capable and independent.

The Rebel

Many adolescents cope with life by rebelling, often fixating on a career, professional goal, or lifestyle that is diametrically opposed to their parents' way of life. These young people seek to find their identity by initially deciding what they are not; in most cases the initial decision is to be not like their parents. These rebels need to be helped to realize that they actually have the latitude to develop individually without parental disapproval. Often they'll drop the "rebellion for rebellion's sake" pace and seek true independence—but sometimes it takes a while. Again, patience and a certain amount of teeth-gritting may be the stepmother's best strategy.

Setting Limits

What about rules? What about punishment? What about just getting teenagers to behave? Most parents have a difficult time with adolescents and compliance. Adolescents need to test and challenge rules; rules are usually perceived as impediments to the adolescent's natural drive toward independence and autonomy.

Setting limits is difficult for the new stepmother; she has no history to refer to, no background of support and coping through the years of childhood. New stepmothers need the support of their husbands and others who are already trusted and loved by the stepchildren.

The transition to adolescence can be stormy for "old" stepmothers as well. An adolescent who has been parented by a stepmother throughout childhood may, in the way of adoptees, suddenly express a desire to learn about his own mother or in some way change the nature of the relationship.

The relationship between stepmother and stepchild during childhood is not an accurate measure of their life together during adolescence. Sweet, compliant children may go through tumultuous adolescence, whereas mischievous children may settle into a relatively uneventful teenage period.

Rules: A Delicate Balance

Unlike children who believe rules to be unalterable, adolescents realize that these rules have been decided by adults; adults are fallible; therefore, the rules are subject to change. The discovery that their parents are fallible beings combined with the adolescent's natural self-centeredness and lack of experience (or tact), can cause a child to constantly question a stepmother's authority.

Rules Should Encourage Independence

The purpose of rules should be twofold: to shield adolescents from danger and to enable all members of the household to live together amiably. Rules should be designed to help adolescents negotiate difficult situations and to encourage the development of independence. Parents who are willing to be tough guys may actually help adolescents through sticky situations; the adolescent with strict parents can maintain his or her dignity when rejecting a forbidden adventure.

Stepmothers need to balance support and empathy with firm, flexible guidelines. It is wise to avoid placing yourself in confrontational situations. One way of minimizing confrontation and power struggles is by initiating "house rules." And remember to change the rules as the child grows older. Guidelines appropriate to a twelve-year-old can serve only as rebellion fodder to a teenager.

House Rules

"House rules" refer to the way the stepmother and father have chosen to live. As a member of the household, the adolescent is expected to comply. House rules must be reasonable and should be based on mutual courtesy. Adolescents can, and will, understand that even bunkmates in camp and roommates in college agree upon certain ways of living.

Common Courtesy

If you want to know where your stepchild is, be sure that all members of the household are in the habit of informing each other, via note or phone call, of their whereabouts. If adults as well as children and adolescents do this, the rule will be seen as a common courtesy—not spying.

Keep rules to a minimum, and make them flexible enough to permit the adolescent to exercise his own judgment in specific situations. Stepmothers can help their adolescents exercise good judgment by supplying the criteria necessary for making wise judgments. Adolescents can be helped to weigh variables, think about possible alternatives and consequences, and enjoy the rewards when a good decision is made.

Katherine strongly objected to her stepchildren attending parties that were unsupervised or where alcohol or drugs would be available. She did not wish to police her stepchildren or have to naysay each of the inappropriate invitations that came to her stepchildren. Katherine learned that the simple way out of this situation was to put the responsibility upon the adolescents' shoulders in a positive way. She told them they could attend any party that is supervised and alcohol/drug free. Telling them what is acceptable, rather than what is forbidden, set a friendlier tone. When you make them responsible for compliance, you teach them to see rules as examples of common courtesy rather than as punitive restrictions.

Changing the Parental Role

Parents of adolescents often notice that their role shifts drastically during this period: A redefinition is in order. Adolescents no longer delight in the attention they enjoyed during childhood. Family dinners, outings, and "togetherness" are often abruptly shunned in favor of "hanging out" with the guys or the girls. Parents are often confused and hurt; they resent this rejection. Stepmothers may be especially distressed, feeling that such behavior is directed against them. Such distancing, moodiness, or strangeness around families is the norm for adolescent children. It's a tough lesson to learn, but a necessary one. A few hints may be helpful.

Tips for Living With the Adolescent

Remain Calm

Remember that adolescence is a time of incredible highs and lows. Mood swings are so pronounced that some have even claimed that adolescence mimics the symptoms of the manic-depressive. Adolescents are trying to fit a body and a mind into a world that has suddenly grown too large and too unfamiliar. Adolescence is a scary time. Make allowances for tempestuous moods, and don't overreact.

Help Adolescents Find Acceptable Methods of Letting Off Steam

Rebelliousness is a normal part of adolescence. However, as with the exploring two-year-old, parameters of acceptable and safe behavior must be maintained. An adolescent may feel like smashing all the lamps in the living room, but obviously such behavior is not tolerable. The adolescent should have the family's permission to feel—to be angry, sulky, whatever, in a way that will not cause family upheaval—but not to do destructive things.

Respect the Adolescent's Feelings

Too many adults keep repeating to troubled teenagers that these are "the best years of your lives." This is not true, except in adult nostalgia. Adolescence is tough. As they try to find a place for themselves in the world, adolescents must come to grips with plans for their future and at the same time struggle with strong sexual urges and pressures to socialize. It's not easy. Be prepared to listen and to sympathize. Take confidences seriously and never ridicule an adolescent's feelings.

Understand the Need to Separate From the Family

Adolescents need to separate from their parents in all ways: physically, by going to college or an apartment of their own as soon as they can; intellectually, by trying on ideas and ways of thinking that are often exactly opposite to the parental point of view; and emotionally, by distancing themselves from the parents. This moving away is normal and necessary.

The greatest conflict between parent and child usually comes in early adolescence. As teenagers actually assume and accept their increasing competence and ability to move into the adult world, the need for conflict with parents decreases. Parents need to limit dangerous or unattractive behavior, avoid oversensitivity, and continue to serve as role models for their own personal value systems.

Don't Criticize Their Friends

Having ruled out most of the adult world, adolescents seek the company of their peers. In their haste to find a place for themselves, they may try to create an entirely new environment, conforming to faddish styles and behaviors. You may not like their music, clothing, hairstyles, or values, but it's best not to criticize.

Be a Parent, Not a Friend

Too many stepmothers make the mistake of trying to be a buddy to a teenager. Adolescents do not need stepmothers who are buddies. Too often, stepmothers fear that they will lose their closeness to the child and so are reluctant to set or enforce rules. Stepmothers who seek to avoid their stepchildren's disapproval by rejecting the parenting role will incur scorn and rejection. There is nothing more ridiculous to an adolescent than an adult trying to "act like a kid." One stepmother went out of her way to revamp her businesslike wardrobe. Hoping to move closer to her stepdaughters' sense of style, she bought a closet full of designer jeans and name-brand shirts, only to be greeted by giggles that turned into out-and-out hoots. The girls did not want a forty-year-old friend; they were comfortable with their stepmother as her old-fashioned self. The typical adolescent has quite enough friends, thank you. Parents, on the other hand, are in short supply.

Be Honest

Adolescents are constantly on the lookout for hypocrisy. Stepmothers who are honest about their feelings and opinions may not win a popularity contest, but they will be trusted and ultimately respected.

Be Flexible

Adolescents cannot be expected to remain static. Rules and expectations must be modified as the adolescent grows toward adulthood and circumstances change.

Solicit Their Opinions

Adolescents who feel that they have a say in the workings of the house, be it a change in curfew or a change in chores, will be more communicative and more likely to comply with rules.

Be Available

Stepmothers should never put off a teen who needs to talk. Personal issues and concerns are often difficult for the adolescent to frame and convey. An adolescent who approaches a stepmother may have spent weeks garnering the courage to do so.

Listen

If you have adolescents who are talking to you, you are halfway home: Listen carefully. What they present as other kids' problems may be theirs as well.

Don't Give Hasty Answers: Take Time to Think

Adults often assume that every question must have an instant answer. Not true! Many questions that adolescents ask concern complex issues or problems that the stepmother is not prepared to deal with. If in doubt, wait. There is nothing wrong with putting off decisions; it's okay to listen without giving an immediate response. Adolescents may be delighted to realize that when time passes between a question and its response, the answer is more satisfying.

Respect Their Privacy

Privacy is a paramount issue for adolescents. Because they are so deeply engaged in figuring out their own identities, privacy becomes almost an obsession for them. Snooping through personal belongings is taboo, as is betraying confidences, listening in on phone calls, or "grilling" them about their friends.

Relax Control

Just when adolescents seem to need the most control—when grades are critical for future success, when rooms and laundry and chores seem to balloon, when nothing seems to get done on time or competently—that's the time to BACK OFF. Adolescents build self-esteem by assuming responsibility for their own lives. Permit real consequences to teach responsibility. Adolescents who are permitted to taste the consequences of their actions learn to be responsible faster than those who are lectured; if an adolescent "forgets" to take care of her clothing, let her wear a wrinkled blouse—or iron it herself. A stepmother can then change her role from nag to commiserator.

Encourage Independence: Part-time Jobs Are Wonderful

Part-time jobs provide financial independence and a role in the adult world. Adolescents need confirmation of their emerging independence; part-time jobs give them a way to feel less dependent on their parents.

Find Something Positive To Say Each Day

Everyone needs to hear positive things. No one needs this support as much, and as often, as a self-conscious adolescent. Find something, no matter how small, to praise each day.

Share Their Interests and Concerns

Whether it involves sitting at a sporting event that you couldn't care less about or defending your stepchild's point of view in a neighborhood confrontation, devote time to your stepchildren. Taking a genuine interest in their lives will create a real and lasting relationship. You needn't be personally interested in the things that interest your stepchildren; you need only be interested in them. All parents would love to have children who shared their interests and avocations, but that rarely happens. Support sports, clubs, and hobbies; read the books they like. You may get lucky and find yourself really sharing those interests.

Be Willing To Negotiate

Rather than playing policewoman, negotiate; ask teens what they will be willing to give up, or do, for something they want. Don't listen to aimless complaining and whining; ask teens to list specifics. Asking them to list what they would like to change helps them to focus their discomfort on something that is concrete and attainable and to accept their share in the responsibility for the changes they seek.

Have Courage!

Adolescence is tough; so is being a stepmother. Although stepchildren and stepmothers may seem at cross-purposes, with the stepmother wanting a family and the adolescent wanting to leave, they may actually have more in common than either can imagine.

The new stepmother seeks to order her new life and develop an identity within the family. The veteran stepmother questions exactly where she will fit into her stepchildren's increasingly independent lifestyle. Whether novice or veteran, stepmothers may be surprised to discover that they are engaged in many of the same struggles as their adolescent stepchildren. The stepmother who recognizes these parallel identity crises may be a breath of fresh air to the teen who really does need adult guidance and a listening ear. In turn, stepmothers may be delighted to find compassion from a most unexpected source—their adolescent stepchild.

By now you know a great deal about children in general and your stepchildren in particular. The time for living together is approaching. It is time to begin thinking about building your family. What will you need to think about before you actually move in? Will there be a wedding? A honeymoon? Where will you live? What will you be called? An exciting time is ahead.

PREPARING TO LIVE TOGETHER

A stepmother's relationship with her stepchildren begins long before she actually lives with them. Many stepmothers miss the opportunity to get off to a good start because the first meetings with their stepchildren come at the wrong time: either too soon—before there's a plan to become a family—or too late. First impressions do matter.

It's not always possible for a potential stepmother to plan a first meeting with her stepchildren-to-be. Often these first meetings occur spontaneously. Some women become stepmothers to children they've known for years in other contexts, perhaps as students, neighbors, or friends of their own children.

First Impressions: Setting the Stage for Success

When I asked stepmothers about their first meetings with their stepchildren, most reported that the meetings were successful. Their generally casual nature contributed to their success. It was the later meetings—those that occurred after the children had been told of the impending marriage—that needed more careful handling. In order to begin a relationship on the best possible footing, it is important not to dismiss those first successful meetings but to use them as a key to later successes.

Reduce Pressure

The first "real" meeting between a stepmother and her stepchildren occurs when the decision to marry and create a new family has been made. At this point, you begin to become a stepmother. Often it is a painful process. In order to enhance the chances for a relaxed and happy beginning, take some hints from your successes at those earlier chance meetings. Although the stepmothers I spoke with met their stepchildren in a variety of settings, they all agreed that first meetings must be unpressured. Reduce the chances of pressure and tension to as low a level as possible. This means no formal dinners, no grilling, no spilling of too-personal information.

If possible, plan a real activity of some sort for your initial meetings. Nothing is more uncomfortable for children than to be subjected to examination and interrogation or "long boring discussions." Early meetings are best treated in the manner of a "blind date." In order to reduce everyone's nervousness, plan an activity that allows for possible escape!

The Importance of Spectator Events

Spectator events are particularly appropriate for early meetings. No one has to *do* anything at a movie or a ball game except be there. A spectator event gives the stepmother and her stepchildren a chance to be together without anyone feeling threatened. Even the most hostile teenager or fidgety toddler will eventually relax if not pressured to perform or take part in some required activity or conversation. Aim for an activity that permits, but does not require, some limited interaction. Movies, a television show, a sporting event, a fireworks exhibition—anything that can be watched (or politely ignored) together. It is impossible to fail when nothing is required.

Check Your Progress

After several casual outings, you and your future husband will be able to gauge the direction in which you are moving. You may discover that you and the children are more and more comfortable together, often chatting away, or you may find that you are returning home in tears, frustrated and weary of trying without response, tired of watching your soon-to-be stepchildren stare silently at movie screens, pick at their uneaten meals, and pointedly ignore you.

Begin to Visit Each Other's Homes

After several outings, it is important for each to see the other in territory where they can "be themselves." *Take it slowly.* Being in someone else's territory can be uncomfortable and threatening. Everyone should have some time to take in the bombardment of personality that is evident in the home. A short visit, maybe a stopover on the way to or from an activity, is appropriate and nonthreatening.

What About Sleepovers?

Sleepovers between father and future stepmother complicate an already complex situation. Early sleepovers turn the getting-to-know-each-other process inside out. Although the stepmother may hope to speed up the process by this intimacy, it may be counterproductive. If sleepovers occur in the child's home, the child is forced to accept the stepmother into his or her territory too soon. If the sleepover occurs in the stepmother's home, the child will probably feel displaced. Generally speaking, sleepovers before marriage or formal moving-in are as emotionally unsatisfying to the developing family as one-night stands are to most single women.

What if Nothing Works?

What should you do if nothing seems to work? The baby still shrieks in fear behind her father? The teenager is still scowling? The nine-year-old is whining? If things have not improved over the course of several nonpressured outings, the time has come to talk. Talking out tension will set the stage for the future. Frightened children don't need lectures, but they do need to know that their displeasure is not being ignored. They need to be assured that their unhappiness has been noted and that the soon-to-be-stepmother hopes that they will be able to have more fun next time.

Whatever the words, remember that a stepchild's cool or hostile behavior usually indicates fear rather than hate. Stepchildren need to know that you are aware of their feelings—and that you care.

Early resistance by stepchildren boils down, simply, to what used to be called testing. Stepchildren have already been abandoned, either by death or divorce. They may or may not have been exposed to other women in their father's lives; often, they have. Many children initially give a potential stepmother a hard time because they have been burned and are often simply afraid to be hurt again. Such children need time.

If Things Are Going Well

After several meetings that involve activities, you are ready for outings with a more personal touch. What you do will depend upon the ages and interests of all involved. This is the time for you and your stepchildren to begin to build your relationship by sharing interests that you really care about. If the relationship seems to be moving along well, you might ask them to help plan the next activity. A good way to get everyone talking is to begin sharing their likes and dislikes. A good rule for these early outings is that each child gets to choose one activity and then to accompany the others on their choices.

Be Yourself

In order for any relationship to have a chance at success, all parties must be accepted for themselves. This is particularly true for stepmothers and stepchildren whose relationship is that of a parent and child but with a built-in contradiction: The stepmother and her stepchild begin as strangers! In order to begin to feel comfortable, let your stepchildren get to know you and try to really get to know them—be sensitive to clues about their interests and supply the information they need to get to know you. Don't climb onto a horse if you've always hated horses or expect your stepchildren to be thrilled about the opera when you've already seen the rock posters in their rooms. Don't expect them to be mind readers. They need real information to make up their minds about you, too!

Let them know your likes and dislikes—the kinds of things that make your eyes mist with joy or with hurt. Let them know what kinds of things really drive you up a wall. Nothing hurts or confuses or angers a child more than a phony. Don't smile at muddy footprints on your white carpeting when you really want to scream. Don't pretend an avid interest in football if you're bored to tears by the game.

Be friendly, flexible, and understanding, but most important, *be honest*. *You* will be living with these children; pretenses you begin today will remain between you and your stepchildren for years to come!

Common Problems

According to the National Census Bureau, about half of second marriages fail. No one likes to think about the possibility of a marriage failing but the statistics can't be ignored. The best way to weather any storms that blow into your marriage is by facing the most common problem areas head-on.

Conflicts between stepmothers and their husbands revolve around these major areas:

- Unequal treatment of children in the family.
- The husband's lack of involvement in childcare.
- Unrealistic expectations.
- Intrusion of the biological mother (See Chapter 11).
- Loss of romance in the marriage.

Let's discuss these problems one by one.

Unequal Treatment of All Children in the Family

Stepmothers who had children from previous marriages often felt that their husbands treated the children in the family unequally. Most stepmothers also felt that they were trying much harder with their stepchildren than their husbands were trying with *their* stepchildren.

Fran put it this way: "Most of our conflicts are about fairness in treating the children. For example, sometimes my husband is quick to ask Maureen, his daughter, to assist him by handing her a screwdriver and showing her how to use it when my little son is standing right there and could just as easily be taught how to use tools." Fran found herself getting increasingly upset over such inequities. Obviously there was more going on than who got to wield the screwdriver.

When a stepmother feels that she is "bending over backwards" to be fair and equal, such small inequities may quickly escalate.

Many stepmothers reported that they were resentful or disappointed by their husbands' lukewarm reception of their children from previous marriages. These same stepmothers, however, were even *more* upset when their husbands showed a lack of involvement with their *own* children—leaving a double burden of caring and responsibility on the shoulders of the new stepmother.

Husband's Lack of Involvement

Many a stepmother is shocked by her husband's lack of involvement with his children. Although these daddies were perceived, during courtship, as actively involved with their children, much of the caring seems to disappear after the vows are exchanged The gap between the stepmother's anticipation and the reality may be huge. Most women who married men with children thought they were marrying into a "new breed of men"— thoroughly modern fathers who had a deeply ingrained sense of commitment to their children. The discovery that such men were not as "maternal" as they'd anticipated comes as a tremendous shock to most stepmothers. This disappointment often translates into a feeling of being duped or betrayed, of being "snookered" into a situation where the father takes the credit while the stepmother takes the responsibility.

Unrealistic Expectations

Most stepmothers assumed, before their marriages, that their husbands would continue to function as both mother and father to their children. These women were disappointed to discover that the husband's interaction with his children did *not* replicate a mother's feeling and responsibilities. If the stepmother was a biological mother as well, this resentment sharpened. Stepmothers discovered that mothering and fathering are different—that a father's sense of commitment and responsibility for his children translated into a far different kind of behavior from what they had anticipated.

This difference between expectation and reality was perhaps the most difficult aspect of a new marriage for stepmothers to accept. Most found that they were expected to have a much higher level of involvement with their stepchildren than their husbands had—just as a matter of course. These stepmothers did not always resent the amount of responsibility that they were expected to assume, but all were stunned by the lack of appreciation for their efforts.

Most stepmothers were amazed at the casualness with

which family members—grandparents, aunts, uncles, friends, husbands, and stepchildren—expected that they would assume the care and maintenance of the family as a natural part of their new marriage. The disappointment they felt in the husband's lack of responsibility for the stepchildren, her own and others' unrealistic expectations of her role, and a lack of appreciation caused many stepmothers to feel resentful and unhappy. If left uninterrupted, this cycle of resentment can spiral a stepmother directly to the divorce court.

A new stepmother can begin the cycle at any point. Most often it starts because she feels unloved by her stepchildren. She seeks support and is criticized by her husband either for being "insecure" or for "complaining." Her anxiety escalates. She increases her childcare efforts. To decrease her anxiety she draws closer to her stepchildren. At the same time, she tries to prove to her husband that she is not insecure. If her efforts are rebuffed, her anxiety mounts. She takes desperate measures in an attempt to win love, appreciation, and respect. If, her husband then criticizes her as being obsessive, her anxiety and frustration may become intolerable.

Cycle Of Resentment

- Feels unloved
- Seeks support
- Is criticized
- Increases involvement
- Is rejected
- Takes desperate measures
- Is criticized as obsessive
- Anxiety mounts
- Depression and/or explosion
- Feels unloved

Breaking the Resentment Cycle

Take some time alone to figure out just what is bothering you. *Be specific.* Take paper and pen and list your specific goals and specific problems.

When you've clearly defined your problem, attempt a solution. You might ask yourself, "What do I need to do to make this better?" Once you've pinpointed a problem and begun to think about what will really make you feel better, you *will* feel better. The very process of sitting down and thinking about feelings in specific, concrete terms may even end the problem.

More often than not, a stepmother will discover that the "who" in her question, "Who can make this better?" is... "Me!" If the solution does lie within the stepmother herself, the process ends with her feeling of relief and of being much more in control. Her heightened sense of control will help her through the next crisis. If she realizes that her husband is part of the problem, or part of the solution, she will tell him so. Too many wives expect their husbands to intuit their needs. Don't expect acts of clairvoyance outside of a nightclub routine. Husbands are not particularly psychic—they must be told specifically what the problem is and what you need from them.

Intrusion of the Biological Mother

A stepmother must understand and come to grips with the fact that her stepchildren's biological mother will be a presence in all their lives—whether she is living or dead. There are practical issues that must be addressed: in the case of the absentee mother, questions of visitation, telephone contact, school conferences, sharing children's activities, and special events. If the mother has died, discussions of death, visits to the cemetery, and maintaining contact with the mother's relatives are important tasks. In addition to these and many other practical issues, children must ultimately reconcile a host of complicated emotions in order to come to terms with their relationship (or lack of relationship) with their mothers. The task of helping children sort out these difficult issues often falls to the stepmother.

Loss of Romance

One of the primary killers of romance is children. Children make privacy difficult; children bring out conflicting viewpoints; children change a family's priorities. Keeping romance alive is vital for the happiness of both husband and wife. The stepmother who feels that romance has gone out of the marriage will more than likely blame her husband; the husband will more than likely blame her; both may blame their stepchildren. The best way to prevent the loss of romance—*or* to nip it in the bud—is to function as a team with your husband from the very beginning.

Forming a United Front With Your Husband

Unequivocally, the relationship between you and your husband is the most important factor in the success and happiness of your new stepfamily. Stress, unhappiness, tension, and ultimate failures of stepmother/stepchild interaction are usually directly traceable to a nonsupportive husband. The stepmother, plagued by insecurity, often stung and confused by the seeming rejection by her stepchildren, needs the daily support of her husband to survive. Often, she has to ask for this support and demonstrate her need for it.

The high percentage of marriages that break up due to "problems with the husband's children" actually break up due to problems between the wife and the husband with *regard* to the children! Too often, stepmothers find themselves expected on the one hand to accept responsibility and act as "mothers," while at the same time refrain from overreacting to inappropriate or hurtful behavior. They find themselves accepting responsibility for problems they did not create in order to please their husbands. Such behavior reflects a dangerous lack of communication and cooperation between the new couple.

The happiest and most successful stepmothers are those who enjoy mutually supportive relationships with their husbands. Stepchildren behave better and are eventually happier and more secure when the family is headed by a securely coupled pair.

Putting the Marriage First

You can't "rescue" the family; you can't replace or erase the memories of the original biological family; you can't become the children's "mother." You *can* deepen and enrich your new marriage by assuming responsibility for sharing the care of your stepchildren and all the problems and joys that arise. You *can* share your life with a man who has chosen to accept the responsibility for raising his children despite the trying circumstances of his life. His marriage to you is a testament to his belief in the institution of marriage despite the frustrations, hurts, or tragedies of his previous relationships.

Separate Child-Related Problems from Marriage Problems

Stepmothers sometimes react to problems with their stepchildren as though they were marriage problems. For example, a stepmother who can't stand her stepdaughter popping her chewing gum at the dinner table may lash out at her husband for his lack of support rather than telling her stepdaughter to get rid of the gum.

Don't be reluctant to approach your husband with problems or be afraid to discuss problems for fear of seeming incompetent, complaining, or nagging. Many stepmothers reported that they were loath to spoil the honeymoon phase of their marriages with complaints, or that they were reluctant to discuss any problems with their husbands for fear of damaging a good relationship.

Too many stepmothers do not really talk to their husbands until they are ready to explode. They bottle up irritations, slights, annoyances, and major hurts until they are at the breaking point.

Why do so many women wait until it is too late? Stepmothers are afraid of being compared. Their husbands have already suffered one or more losses; they have survived marriages that ended in divorce or death. No stepmother wants to be compared unfavorably with an absent mother who is perceived as incompetent or with a deceased mother whose memory is idealized by the family.

These fears are easily put to rest by communicating. Stepmothers who enjoy a strong and mutually directed couple relationship will not fear comparisons. You can sidestep such comparison by emphasizing your own relationship with your husband.

Share Goals and Responsibilities

In order for a stepmother to have a united front with her husband, there has to be a strong sense of partnership. You and your husband should share the same short- and long-term goals and enjoy heading toward them together. The successful marriage has a plan—sometimes a specific one, such as, "In five years we will change our careers and open a flower shop"; sometimes one as philosophical as, "We will simplify our life and surround ourselves with only loving and friendly people." A strong couple will agree on their goals. This unified perception of the world will help the couple to remain focused on each other during any stressful periods.

Stepmothers rarely complain about the breadth or depth of their household responsibilities, but they do, almost with a single voice, complain about their lack of validation, appreciation, and pats on the back. They need recognition for what they do. Take the time and make the effort to agree about who is responsible for what. Do this early on in the relationship and modify these responsibilities when necessary. When stepmothers assess what they are responsible for and what their husbands are responsible for, they may see that the real issue is not the number of chores (although these can seem overwhelming) but rather their feeling about carrying out some of these responsibilities. Again, paper and pen are helpful. List all your responsibilities in one column; list your husband's in another. Talk to him about trade-offs if you feel overwhelmed or particularly uncomfortable or resentful about some of "your" tasks. And don't forget to include some responsibilities that you and he will do *together*.

Set Aside Time for Romance and Fun

We've been discussing the importance of sharing family concerns, problems, and issues; these are undeniably important. However, it is equally important to *stop* talking and thinking about problems each day. Some stepmothers, in a misguided attempt at being "good mommies," become little more than drones: They turn *too much* of their attention toward family problems. Such women find, to their ultimate confusion, despair, and anger, that this over-involvement with family issues is rejected by their husbands. When issues of child-raising eclipse the couple's marriage, everyone in the family will suffer.

In order to keep the marriage alive and viable, the couple must have some time alone. Time alone means just that: adults only. The focus of this time alone may be romantic, sexual, or recreational, but it *must* be characterized by the sharing of adult interests. (Remember dating?) Discussion of children or family concerns should *not* take place during such times. Alone time does not have to be exotic or expensive. Alone time may consist of nothing more than sitting in a room that has a door that can be shut behind you and your husband.

One couple got into the habit of "parking" each day. They sat in the car in their garage, tuned the radio to their favorite station, and just talked for a half-hour. Another couple had late lunches together. Still another had a cup of tea together each day when they came home from work. Time alone may be as simple as walking the dog or sitting on the front stoop or as luxurious as a weekend getaway. Short periods alone each day are vital to keeping the couple intimate, connected, and in touch.

Some couples like to plan activities together: skiing, fishing, bowling, cards, hiking, dog-training classes, an opera series, or season tickets to a particular sport or series of plays. *What* you do together is inconsequential— enjoying regular planned time together is *critical*. Stepmothers have found that planning something for the kids to do during these times helps erase resentment. During the times that the couple is doing "their thing" together, the children might be doing something they enjoy, whether it's their own activity or something as simple as having pizza on the evening when their parents go out for a romantic dinner *a deux*.

Three Simple Rules for Creating a United Front

1. The couple comes first.

If possible, the couple should have time to see and/or speak to each other alone before dealing with the crises of the day.

2. No unilateral decisions.

The husband or wife will make no decision without talking it over first. Crisis situations that call for immediate decisions are subject to review. This prevents the children from finding the "softer" touch or playing off father and stepmother against each other. (In our house, the children referred to us as "the Congress.")

3. Allow children to strengthen your marriage.

The presence of live-in children actually solidifies a good marriage. Stepmothers and their husbands find that children give a marriage a permanence and an increased sense of time that childless marriages do not have. Stepmothers and their husbands often feel that they have been together far longer than the calendar reflects.

Consider Sandy and her husband, Al. Al brought two children to the marriage—a girl of ten and a boy of twelve. Sandy brought an eleven-year-old boy. After five years of marriage, Sandy and Al had been through their own *two* weddings (one a private ceremony and one with a large reception), two Bar Mitzvahs and one Bat Mitzvah, a Sweet-Sixteen party, five school graduation ceremonies (two elementary graduations, two junior high school graduations, and one high school graduation), and had seen their oldest boy through the college admissions process from applications to acceptance to settling in.

Sharing the experience of watching the children grow from childhood through these various rituals gave Sandy and Al the feeling that they had been together since the beginning of the children's lives. As couples begin to share a family history with their children, their actual time together begins to blur. Although others often treat them as newlyweds, Sandy and Al feel as if they could be celebrating their twenty-fifth rather than their fifth anniversary.

Children and the experiences they bring to a family are tremendously enriching, but remember that the marriage comes first. In order to keep a family healthy, the family members must retain their individuality. A family must not become defined by its problems.

The Good News

Most husbands want to be supportive, but they need to be shown how. Most husbands want their marriages to work, so they often find it difficult to look below the surface of a stepmother's complaint. Most men are more direct than abstract; they seem to function more effectively in the here-and-now. In order to have a united front and good communication with your husband with respect to child-rearing, you need to be *specific*. "Modern" men try to be understanding, empathetic, and analytical, but most of them haven't had the years of conditioning and practice at communicating at an emotional level that women have. *Be patient.* And *always* remember to separate a problem with a child from a problem with the marriage. By defining the problem correctly at the outset, you'll prevent your husband's going on the defensive.

A fresh, sullen, withdrawn, hostile, depressed, hyperactive, silly, giggling, rude, mischievous, spiteful, horrible, and/or manic stepchild is everyone's concern. But what happens when Grandma or Daddy or Auntie comments, "But they're such sweethearts with us. They never..."

The confident stepmother does not accept inappropriate behavior as "her" problem. Children who are acting out or unhappy in any situation are both the father's and the stepmother's problem. In the same way that the stepmother would acknowledge that a child who was acting out in school was in trouble, a father will acknowledge that a child who is acting out or unhappy with his stepmother is in trouble! When the problem is defined (by you) as "our" problem—not "his"—it's much easier to solve it as a team.

In order to create a united feeling, use the word "we" whenever possible. It is amazing how such a simple tactic can turn around a couple's perspective. Let's imagine that Andrea, a young stepmother, has been having a terrible time handling her two-year-old twin stepsons. Most of her day is spent running around cleaning up after the toddlers' tantrums.

See the difference in presentation:

1. Vincent, I can't take this anymore. Your sons are destroying our house. I can't have anything nice! WHAT ARE YOU GOING TO DO?

or:

2. Vincent, we have a problem. The boys broke our flower pot. Remember the one that Aunt Jane and Uncle Elmer gave us for a wedding present? What can we do?

Husbands are not unique; no one enjoys being criticized. Criticisms only serve to alienate your husband: They make him feel attacked. As an unpleasant side effect, the constant repeating of "your" son, "your" daughter, "your" children only serves to separate you from your stepchildren and further diminishes both your sense of connection with the children and your power and authority in the house. Problems properly defined can be solved by thought or by additional information. Ask yourself: Why are you posing this problem to your husband? What do you want him to do?

Ask for His Help

Rather than criticizing, try asking for your husband's help in understanding, analyzing, or figuring out a solution. This is the time for "I" to come out of the closet. You are not criticizing. You are asking for help with something that bothers you. Again, be specific both in stating the annoyance and in soliciting help. What do you want from your husband? A kiss? A word of encouragement? Actual intervention? *Be clear:* "I need a hug" is friendlier and more productive than "You don't love me."

Support Him

Do not criticize, demean, put down, or in any other way diminish your husband in the eyes of the children. Unfortunately, many stepmothers seem to try to exercise power over their husbands when they feel a *lack* of power over their stepchildren. It is important for children to see mutual respect between their father and stepmother. Subjecting your husband to criticism or to anything less than unflagging support in front of the children will lead him to resent you. He may retaliate by being disrespectful and unsupportive, or he may withdraw. Dissension between stepmother and father will cause stepchildren to escalate their struggle for family power. In a word, if you want support, give it!

Accentuate the Positive

Keep the fun in your marriage! Find something to smile about each day. Share something silly or happy. Say something pleasant to your husband. Compliment his clothes, his hair, his after-shave, or the good way he smells after a shower. Drop him a note; remember silly anniversaries of personal importance. Surprise him with a night of uninterrupted sports-watching or a back rub. Buy him a silly card.

Shared interests, mutual goals, good communication, time

alone for romance and fun, mutual support in a noncritical atmosphere: These are building blocks of a united front with your husband. Keeping them alive in your marriage is fun and exciting.

A Success Story

Jane and Jonathan are a professional couple in their late forties, a happy stepfamily with a combined group of six children for the past seventeen years. In speaking with the couple individually and in tandem, I learned something interesting: Their conception of success was based on the *achievements* of the members of their family rather than on the way everyone felt about everyone else. I heard about one boy who was in law school, another who had won a swimming tournament, a daughter who was on the honor roll. As our talk continued, Jane and Jonathan casually alluded to problems that would have knocked the socks off other stepmothers: One of the boys had returned to his biological mother for a semester; one of the girls had spent her adolescence sulking that she didn't have a "real" mother. I marveled that such emotional stress did not have an impact on Jane's perception of herself as a successful stepmother and her family as a happy stepfamily.

Jane and Jonathan have an important lesson to share: Family success can be gauged in nonemotional terms. Obviously a warm greeting card or a bouquet of red roses will mist the eyes of all stepmothers. However, "mushiness," hugs and kisses, I-love-you's and you're-wonderful's are not the only indications of success!

One of the best ways of gauging success is by setting specific goals and time frames, and reviewing them later. When the goal has been met, celebrate! If the goal is still outstanding, renew it! Is this goal still important? If not, revise your time frame and your approach.

Some women become stepmothers at the altar; others become stepmothers by design, or by surprise, sometime after their marriage. Still others find that after years of marriage, situations or circumstances change and they become responsible for older children, adolescents, or even adult stepchildren. Whatever the timing of the event, *all* stepmothers will need to think through their feelings and to find ways to announce their new family to their friends and relatives.

Chapter 7

THE WEDDING: ANNOUNCING THE NEW FAMILY

Weddings call up all sorts of romantic illusions. The public proclamation of love and commitment is one of the most cherished of human rituals. When a woman marries a man with children, this ritual often embraces a large cast of characters, some of whom may respond in negative ways.

Stepchildren as Participants

Stepmother brides may find that they confront many other problems along with wedding-day jitters. The most common are stepchildren who refuse to attend the wedding; stepchildren who you wish would have stayed home because they choose the wedding as a stage for acting out or otherwise inappropriate behavior; and stepchildren who choose to refuse to participate.

The Resisters

Many stepchildren resist the idea of their father's remarriage. This disapproval is more likely to reflect the children's conflict about the remarriage than any personal dislike of the stepmother. Such resistance is found in children of all ages and may appear in a variety of forms: crying toddlers, sulking nine-year-olds, teenagers who refuse to dress up, college students who can't find the time to come home for the wedding.

The Panickers

Some children suddenly panic over their place in the soon-to-be formed family. Panic appears most commonly in children who seem to have been welcoming the new marriage and have not really shown any evidence of problems. Their panic seems to drop from the skies; it strikes both the stepmother and her new stepchild.

Such panic is not unlike that of the vaudeville virginal bride of yesteryear, who locked herself in the bathroom on the eve of the marriage. Stepchildren may be suddenly overwhelmed with the changes their lives are about to undergo and become immobilized by fear. Or they may seek to stop the proceedings by refusing to cooperate.

Carolyn describes a typical example of this panic. Michael had been a happy and relaxed eight-year-old in the months that preceded Carolyn's marriage to his father. In fact, so enthusiastic was Michael that Carolyn had dubbed him her "assistant." Michael helped select the color scheme for his dad's attendants, helped Carolyn plan the wedding reception menu, and chose special desserts for guests under age ten. The entire planning process had given Carolyn an especially warm and tender feeling about her soon-to-be-stepson. So when Michael panicked at the ceremony, Carolyn was both upset and confused.

"We had a beautiful and elegant wedding and luncheon. The only negative was Michael. He didn't want all the pictures taken. He began to cry and refused to sit still. Out of the fifty or so pictures that were taken, his teary face ruined all but one!"

Michael, like many stepchildren, just panicked. Unsure about how his life would change, unsure about his new role in the family, feeling suddenly pressured and insecure, Michael simply dug in his heels and refused to be photographed.

Jealousy

Weddings are typically the "bride's day." Some stepchildren have difficulty accepting this special attention graciously. So do some stepmothers, who are embarrassed to admit that they had a little trouble sharing their special day with their stepchildren.

Most stepchildren will naturally feel anxious about the possibility of losing their father and about their place in their family amid all this romance. The wedding, and the limelight shining on their new stepmother, may be enough to exacerbate their jealous feelings.

Stepmothers may be embarrassed to admit their jealousy about sharing their wedding day with their stepchildren. These feelings are common—and easy to overcome when you face them head-on.

Tracy told me that her wedding was just about ruined because her stepchildren "were always around their father. They even opened most of our presents," she said.

Diane added that her stepdaughter almost ruined her wedding with her pouting because she wasn't part of the wedding ceremony. As Diane put it, she "really was too old to be a flower girl, and besides it was OUR day."

Martha asserted that her actual wedding day had no particular problems, but she did add that she was annoyed with her husband because they had only one day to themselves for a honeymoon—and he insisted on calling home to check on his young son several times during that one day!

And then there was Laura, who began her honeymoon with the screams of her stepdaughter ringing in her ears. The six-year-old had been a lovely flower girl, had danced with her father and her new stepmother in a "family dance," and had fully expected to go on the honeymoon; this little girl had to be taken away forcibly in tears from the reception by a family friend.

Stepchildren in the Wedding Party

Most stepmothers reported that their stepchildren, regardless of age, were included in the wedding party. Stepchildren functioned as ushers, attendants, flower girls, best men, and bridesmaids. Even the youngest children often participated.

Some stepmothers incorporated the stepchildren in the wedding vows; Marge and Larry, Marge's daughter from a previous marriage, and Larry's son all had the judge ask them to hold hands as they accepted one another as a family.

Still other stepmothers used the wedding as an occasion for the clergyman or judge to ask the guests to accept, bless, or welcome the new family.

Enjoy Your Wedding

Minimize Conflict by Careful Planning

Everyone has heard tales of family feuds that began with a wedding "slight." Hurt feelings in families are painful; hurt feelings among family members living under the same roof can be intolerable! Obviously everyone will not be able to be accommodated; however, stepchildren should be given preference.

How to avoid problems? *Lots of talking and meticulous planning are essential.* Most people become uncomfortable around weddings because they simply don't know what is expected of them. The size of the wedding or the ages of the stepchildren are fairly irrelevant to this issue of preparation. Rehearsals, either actual or talk-throughs, are absolutely necessary for ironing out potential problem areas. Stepmothers need to have backups and alternate plans for everything!

Marie's wedding day was ruined by poor preparation. Her two young stepchildren, both under age five, were seated in the front of the church. As the organ began to play, the children started sobbing and continued to cry quietly until the ceremony ended. On reflection, Marie realized that her little stepchildren had not been prepared adequately for her wedding to their father. Two months prior to Marie's wedding, the children's mother had remarried and almost literally dumped them on their father's doorstep; they hadn't seen her yet and were still very confused about *why* they couldn't live with her any longer. It's hard even to speculate about the fears these little children had about their future after *this* wedding.

You will find that your wedding day is much smoother if you discuss and resolve the following issues:

- What is expected of the children?
- Will there be an exchange of vows?
- Are the wedding-day outfits purchased, fitted, laid out, and agreed to be worn? (Be sure everything is tried on—an itchy shirt, a too-starched dress, or shoes that pinch may create havoc when the big day arrives!)

• Have the children a ride to the wedding, either with you, their father, or a trusted relative or friend? (Many stepchildren do not make it to the wedding when mothers of maternal relatives are depended on.)

• If there will be a honeymoon without the children, do they have a place to stay with a person who is supportive of the new marriage?

Stepchildren shouldn't be bullied or manipulated into participating more than they wish. On the other hand, if a stepchild wants to participate, create a role if need be. The key is to anticipate and avoid problems before the wedding day.

The Stepchild Who Doesn't Wish to Attend

Participation may be optional, but it's difficult to see how the same child who refuses to attend a wedding will be able to live with a stepmother and father after the ceremony. All children will probably experience some sort of discomfort and/or nervousness as the wedding day approaches, but the child who actually refuses to attend the wedding should receive professional counseling *before* moving in with his or her new stepmother.

Outside Interference

Many stepmothers report sabotage attempts by the mothers of their stepchildren, who refuse to permit the children to attend. This refusal to grant permission is an odd but common feature of the stepmother's wedding— especially odd when the biological mother is aware that the children will be living with the stepmother. Despite this awareness, mothers frequently go out of their way to try to keep the children from the wedding, either directly, by not returning them from a visit or through psychological pressure.

Gina spent the early hours of her wedding day pacing her wedding suite as her fiancé, Tony, consulted with his attorney; Gina's soon-to-be stepchildren were being prevented from attending the afternoon wedding by their mother, who had decided to take them for an unapproved overnight visit. The attorney intervened, and the children finally made it to the ceremony.

Unfortunately, a wedding sabotaged by the biological mother seems to serve as the kick-off for a game that will play itself out over a long period of time. In order to minimize this unpleasantness and tension, it is best to ensure the presence of stepchildren by having the children spend the night before the wedding at home with their father or with a trusted friend or relative.

Have a Good Time

Weddings cannot be "done over." At some future point, the individuals who have been thrown together *will* coalesce and become a family, and for the sake of that future family, *all parties* who will be members of the family should be present. For the sake of the family they will become, make every attempt to share a wedding that you'll all look back on fondly.

Telling the World

Some stepmothers elope. Perhaps they do not wish to use their wedding as a "family" affair, believing that a couple gets married, not a family. Some women become stepmothers several years *after* their marriage. *All* stepmothers need to announce their new family at some point.

There are no stepmother showers, no fanfares, none of the pleasant rituals that attend a birth or even an adoption. Of all the stepmothers interviewed, not one remembered that becoming a stepmother was celebrated or acknowledged in any way. Stepmothering is probably the only life event that the general public chooses to acknowledge by ignoring it.

Do Stepmothers Really Need Rituals?

Do we need public acknowledgment of our new responsibilities? Do we need a line of greeting cards? Do we need "Steppie Showers"?

In a word—yes.

There is a good reason for rituals. They help us to move from one stage of life to another. They assure us that many others have passed through these same experiences. And they help to soothe our fears and give us strength and confidence.

Becoming a stepmother is a life-changing event. Stepmotherhood affects a woman's personal lifestyle in a far more profound and dramatic way than marriage itself. Rituals imply acceptance and public acknowledgment. Acceptance, support, and validation for stepmothers provide a sure way to address the complexity of the stepmothering role.

Rituals can also help others in their relationship to the stepfamily. Too often family and friends aren't quite sure how they are supposed to react to the new family. Rituals can help establish the existence of the family and clarify the depth of the stepmother-stepchild relationship.

Many people are uncomfortable with stepmothers. Friends, family, and community may be unsure about what the new stepmother should be called, what titles are used within the family, and how the new family functions. Even people who are close to the new couple are unsure about their relationship to the new family. This discomfort and unfamiliarity may actually prevent a good relationship from blossoming.

Announce the New Family

People are accustomed to being notified of various life changes: engagements, marriages, births, graduations, professional practices, and the like. Stepfamilies need announcements as well. Announcing the family members and their new relationship is an excellent way of stabilizing the family.

Creating an announcement for your new family will help you and your husband confront new family roles in a practical way. One stepmother questioned me about announcing these roles "so early" in the formation of the new family. "What happens," she asked, "if those roles change?" The question implies a lot about what is wrong about stepfamilies. Stepfamilies seem to want to adopt a wait-and-see attitude when it comes to thinking about "who" they are in the new family, rather than identifying specific roles and goals and committing themselves to doing the best job they can. Waiting won't work. When a woman gives birth she doesn't decide what her role will be, depending on "how it goes" with the new infant; she is a *mother*. When a woman assumes responsibility for her husband's children, she is a *stepmother*. Since the world can't figure that out, you'll have to tell it.

You won't find printed announcements at your local stationery store. Your announcements may be handwritten or designed and printed professionally. Style is a matter of personal preference; the purpose of the announcement is of primary importance. Announcements will include the names of the couple and the names of the children—but more important, the titles and relationships of all the members of the new family. Because the husband and wife in this new family will, by definition, have different relationships to the children—either step or biological—a general announcement will have to clarify whose children are whose.

Let's consider the mythical Hamilton family consisting of Jonathan Hamilton and his two children, Brett Scott and Cori Hope Hamilton, and Samantha Smith Hamilton and her two children, Joshua Seth Smith and Jessica Lynne Smith. The following announcement would be appropriate:

Samantha (Smith) and Jonathan Hamilton
announce our marriage and
are proud to introduce our new family:

Brett Scott Hamilton (November 6, 1984)
Cori Hope Hamilton (January 19, 1982)
Joshua Seth Smith (December 26, 1981)
Jessica Lynne Smith (May 3, 1983)

Have a Party

Celebrate the occasion! Have a party! The nature of the party will be as individual as your particular family, whether you choose a catered affair complete with printed invitations and a six-piece band, or take-out chicken. Have a party that introduces the children to your family and friends, and your family and friends to your new husband and stepchildren. This gathering should be totally separate from the wedding. Invitations may be as informal as a telephone call or conveniently included as part of your wedding announcement or invitation.

Introduce the Children to Family "Secrets"

Tell your stepchildren anecdotes. Describe family members they have not met because of circumstance, distance, or death. Bring your stepchildren up to date on their new extended family. Extended families can be great disappointments or joys for you and your stepchildren.

The day does arrive when you and your stepchildren will begin living together. Together you will confront a host of practical and emotional issues. Recognizing and coping with nervousness, unrealistic expectations, and hopes for the future are exciting challenges. Setting up house, coping with privacy issues, integrating different lifestyles, and accepting and delineating house rules and consequences for misbehavior all have to be accomplished without damaging anyone's self-respect or enthusiasm for the new "family." A tall order? Absolutely.

Chapter 8

MOVING IN

Setting Up House

Okay, so the day has arrived. The moving trucks have come and gone, or you've simply packed up your suitcases and arrived. The day everyone has been thinking about is here; the family begins. The first few days—even the first few moments—are important; they set the tone. Start at the very threshold, and take each step carefully.

Unpacking

Depending on the age and interest of the children, unpacking can be a family adventure or a disaster. It is important that children do not feel overcontrolled or overwhelmed. Everyone should be responsible for finding and putting away his own possessions. Even the younger members of the family will enjoy "finding" their toys. Definite chores give everyone something to do and help children feel less uncomfortable. Participating in the moving-in process helps everyone feel a real stake in the creation of the new home.

There are no awards for quick unpacking, but to listen to many stepmothers you would think they were involved in an Olympic competition. The first day together, spent unpacking, sorting, and trying to establish some sense of order, should be as relaxed as possible. First impressions are created that first day and the frazzled stepmother who seeks to get everything looking picture perfect will more likely be remembered for her short temper than for her quickly arranged rooms. RELAX! The goal for the day should be easily attainable and should set the stage for further successes. Plan on readying a place for everyone to sleep that night, and make sure there's food for breakfast the next morning. Anything more that gets accomplished is icing on the cake.

Celebrate the First Day as a Family

Remember that this is the day stepchildren will remember as the beginning of their life with you. Make it as pleasant for yourself, your husband, and your stepchildren as possible. Don't set impossible standards that can only fail. Set a time limit and then stop working and celebrate. Eat dinner out, or order in a pizza. Be creative. Think of something fun. Have little surprises—housewarming gifts. Take pictures (even of the mess!). Have fun that first evening. Try to think of something memorable to do. If you must put away the pots and pans, try to have fun. Play geography while you work, or sing, or toast marshmallows in the fireplace or on the kitchen stove. It's not hard to have fun with children. Enjoy the evening and try to smooth over problems or fears that you may have overlooked.

Keep Away From Rules/Make Only Necessary Decisions

The moving-in night is not the time for rules, regulations, and long-term decisions. School-aged children should be aware that this is a "special night" and that there will be plenty of time later for deciding exactly how everyone will live together.

Who Sleeps Where? Making a Place for Everyone

The best way to handle critical decisions, such as who gets the bedroom nearest the bathroom, is to take time with them. It is difficult to make decisions before everyone has really settled in and gotten to know one another. It's important to understand that little is permanent during the first months together. If possible, and if the ages and temperaments of children permit, allow the children to have a voice in where they sleep. Don't assume they want to remain in their old rooms; don't assume that children want to move into new ones. Don't assume anything. If the child is old enough to speak, ask for his or her opinion; shoulder shrugs and "I don't know" get no vote. Room changes may be made temporarily, say for one week, then the family can reconvene and decide whether they want to switch again. Be especially sensitive about suggesting that children double up and room together!

What to Expect

Stepmothers will find that their stepchildren's ages affect the way they react to moving in.

Small children may be totally confused and frightened by their new surroundings; the hustle and bustle may simply be overwhelming. If there has been a change in custody and the children are not used to sleeping at Daddy's, there will probably be a sleepless night or two. Be very careful about events of the first night. If the children are restless, they should be comforted in their own room. Avoid like the plague taking a little child into your room or your bed. The concession of the first night will become the pattern of the first month!

Little children are very fearful about any sort of change. To calm their fears be sure that their comforters and familiar toys are beside them. School-aged children may actually have fun moving. Being treated as grown-up and given special tasks may help the school-aged child feel that he or she has a real stake in the new family.

Adolescents will be more concerned with their own interests. Allowing an adolescent the personal time to settle in by providing telephone time, privacy, and perhaps the freedom to listen to his "own" music will help calm everyone's nerves. Permitting adolescents free rein that first day is a gift.

Stepsiblings

Stepmothers who are biological mothers as well often find that juggling the needs and well-being of two "sets" of children is initially unsettling.

Almost all the stepmothers I talked to reported that their children were negative at first about their potential stepsiblings. It seems to be easier for children to accept the idea of their parents marrying than it is for them to accept the fact that there will be additional children in the family.

Mothers and fathers who have fallen in love hope their children will also love each other and will help create a happy family for everyone. Because children are by nature self-centered, they are often unwilling or unable to suspend their own interests for the sake of others' happiness. Stepsiblings do not usually dislike each other inherently as individuals, but they are bound to be wary, at least at first.

Don't Expect Instant Love or Instant "Family Feelings"

Family feeling grows as children live together. At first, they have no commitment to one another. They are committed only to their respective parents and biological siblings. Stepsibling relationships will grow and deepen based upon many contributing factors, including the ages of the children involved and the opportunities for growing together through shared experience. Many parents try to do everything together in an attempt to create a feeling of family. Don't forget that in a typical family, children form a subgroup apart from their parents.

Bite Your Tongue...

Many parents, while proclaiming a desire for a "normal" family, really aspire to some mythical, fairy-tale family life where all the children play happily and quietly under the benevolent smiles of their parents. Real families are colored with a bit more human emotion; they are often noisy, subject to rapid changes, and involved in power struggles and identity crises. Real families exhibit jealousy and competition as well as quicksilver flashes of rage and unexpected shimmers of kindness. Real families, when defined in real terms, begin to sound a lot more like—stepfamilies.

In order for children to grow together, they must be permitted to develop their own relationships without parental interference. Children need to understand that short of dangerous physical violence, their altercations will not gain the sympathy or intervention of either or both parents. Children need to be given the opportunity to experience things together, whether it's walking to school united in their "status" as the new kids or being shipped off to the same summer camp. Parents need to find ways to ensure that their children share experiences apart from parental intervention.

Sally and Robert decided to send their four children to the same school for the first year of their marriage. Because the children were in different grades, they needed a school that would include grades two through high school. The only convenient institution meeting this criterion was a parochial school noted for its academic excellence and unrelenting strictness. Sally and Robert debated the advantages and disadvantages of such a rigorous academic climate for their children, finally deciding that they favored letting the children meet the challenge of the parochial school together rather than splitting them up into different schools.

The decision proved to be wise. As expected, the children, accustomed to the more relaxed atmosphere of public school, were not happy. However, this dislike actually turned out to be a plus: "Suffering" through the experience together gave the children something to complain about to one another that had nothing to do with their parents. United in their common hatred of the school rules and dress code, they quickly became close. Years later, they still reminisce about what they fondly remember as the "School of Horrors." The experiences stepsiblings share apart from their parents tend to promote quick bonding.

Will They Get Along?

Whether or not all the children will get along with one another is probably the biggest question on any potential stepmother's mind. If by "getting along" you mean happy children playing together before the fireplace, exchanging whispered secrets and shared giggles, the answer will most likely be "No," at least not for a long while. However, if you want to know whether a real family will develop, a family based on the give-and-take of shared values, interests, and occasional disagreement, the answer is a resounding "Yes." Stepsiblings do get along as well or in some cases markedly better than children who are biologically or legally related.

After an initial period of adjustment, most stepmothers find that the children settle down to typical sibling difficulties revolving around the issues of sharing, competition, and jealousy. Many stepmothers were greatly warmed by signs of closeness among the children, and spoke lovingly of times when children defended one another against a school bully or stuck together during a family crisis.

Common Problems

Sharing

The most prevalent problem for stepsiblings is sharing— sharing possessions, sharing rooms, sometimes sharing friends. Underlying all the hundreds of items to be shared is one that is hardest of all to share: parents! Sibling rivalry is nothing new to any family with more than one child; stepsiblings just use different ammunition. A blood-related brother might shout, "I wish you weren't my brother!" whereas a stepsister will shout, "You aren't my sister!" Such statements grate on a parent's ears, but a wise parent will simply wait for the minor tempest to blow over.

Different Parental Styles

Children now have to adjust to different ways of doing things and witness different interactions among family members. If the stepmother is less than thrilled with the way her husband and his children interact, she'd better discuss it before she decides to move in. Behavior that the stepmother finds unacceptable may prove intolerable if she believes her own children will be affected adversely.

Visitation

If both sets of children have living, noncustodial parents, they will all have to deal with visitation. The different patterns of visitation will affect the entire family. Stepmothers with children from a previous marriage reported that their children visited their fathers on a regular basis and enjoyed a good relationship. Most children spent frequent weekends and holidays with their biological fathers. Most stepchildren did not visit with their noncustodial mothers, however. This disparity left stepmothers in a strange predicament: their "own" children were leaving for a visit with "Dad" while their stepchildren would remain at home. These stepmothers lost out on the breaks from childcare they had enjoyed as single parents. This lack of relief, combined with existence of an uncooperative biological mother, was responsible for a good deal of resentment and stress.

Stepmothers whose children continued to enjoy good-to-excellent relationships with their noncustodial fathers seemed particularly stressed when their stepchildren could not enjoy the same relationship with their noncustodial mothers. Claire was such a stepmother. She saw no comparison between the children's relationships with their respective biological parents. "My ex is genuinely involved with his children. There are never excuses why he can't see them.

'She' does her best not to include her children on holidays. She has never even seen them during a vacation."

"Late-arriving" Children

It is very difficult for children who have been "visiting" to be incorporated into daily family life. "Late-arriving" stepchildren—those who come to live with the family because of a change in circumstance—usually are uncomfortable and unsure about their role. Stepchildren who have previously visited their fathers, stepmothers, and stepmother's children may need to redefine their attitudes and feelings about the family before they can adjust to living with the family on a full-time basis.

Visiting a home is vastly different from living there. The stepmother needs to demarcate carefully the difference in the new routines and responsibilities and the difference between "visits" and living at home. Additionally, most "late-arriving" children are already adolescents, often angry ones. Such teenagers seem determined to break rules. Late changes in custody are often prompted by some sort of problem: drugs or truancy, for example, or an inability to get along with their mother's new husband. The stepmother may then fear and resent the influence her troubled stepchildren will have upon her children. Sometimes the mother's situation changes; she becomes unable or unwilling to care for the children on a full-time basis. Whatever the circumstances, children who move in later feel strange and unsure, and stepsiblings may exacerbate these feelings. If the late-arriving children are older or younger than the residential children, age-related status needs may be reordered; the oldest child in the home may suddenly become the middle or youngest child, the "baby" no longer the baby. Late-arriving stepsiblings change the dynamics of the family. If the father or stepmother is less welcoming of the late-arriving child, professional help or mediation should be sought to avoid the sense of family disruption.

Coping with Privacy Issues

Privacy, or what some like to refer to as "personal space," is essential for most people. In a new family, everyone may have the strange and uncomfortable sensation that they have "no home." Home is now filled with unfamiliar individuals, furnishings, and ways of being and acting. Because everything seems strange, the need for breathing space and personal identity may be paramount. The need for privacy may be the most apparent symptom of this larger need.

Stepmothers and stepchildren may expect these privacy needs to escalate to almost obsessive proportions, especially during the moving-in period, when everyone feels more or less off-balance and insecure. Such uncomfortable feelings may cause possessiveness toward what is known and stable. A stepmother who is unsure of her role in the new family may cling to old habits as a lifeline. Stepchildren who are feeling displaced or uneasy about their futures may cling to worn-out teddy bears and outgrown clothing with a desperate passion.

The slightest intrusion on personal space may be perceived as intolerable and unforgivable. To assure that everyone gets the breathing room they need, give each person a chance to express what he and she regards as sacred. Then respect their wishes—from the stepmother's need for undisturbed baths, to the small child's desire to watch "Sesame Street" curled up with a favorite blanket.

Living Together: It Can and Does Work

Stepmothers were surprised time and time again by the adjustment of children to one another after an initial period of vying for a position. Once children find their place, they usually begin to relate to each other on a personal level. Stepsiblings can and do form close and enduring relationships based on fair treatment, shared interests, and shared history.

General Tips

• Make sure children have time *alone* with their biological parent.

• Make sure children have time *alone* with their stepparent.

• Institute acceptable ways of disagreeing and consequences for unacceptable behavior.

• *Keep out of kids' arguments*; most will stop if you stay out.

Establishing an Atmosphere for Communication

Communication: that great catchall term of modern-day life! "Talk to your family," say the counselors, the books. Your heart says it, too, but to a stepmother who faces the chilling shrieks of a preschooler or the indifferent shrug of an adolescent, such advice may seem unworkable.

Good communication is not a pie-in-the sky dream. Communication is the transmission of one's feelings, attitudes, opinions, or information to another person. There are many different ways of establishing an atmosphere where communication can take place.

Steps to Good Communication

One-sided Conversations

Communication may be one-sided, especially at the beginning of a relationship. One-sided communication may at first seem a misnomer. Only one side speaking? That isn't communication. Everyone knows that communication occurs in a fragrant kitchen, sitting around the table holding mugs of something hot and talking earnestly, or perhaps chatting over icy drinks on the front porch. These pretty illusions materialize occasionally, but they are not the rule. It might help the stepmother to keep in mind the model of the biological mother, who begins talking to her baby long before the infant is capable of speech. She doesn't sit around waiting for the baby to start a conversation or to answer her. Similarly, stepmothers should begin talking to their stepchildren. Do not wait for them to speak first. Stepmothers, as parents, can and indeed should establish the relationship, and one-sided conversing is a good way to begin.

Building Trust

In order for a stepmother to have any type of secure relationship with her stepchildren, she must first establish herself as a person who can be trusted. That means stating her feelings honestly, not snooping, and not disclosing personal secrets without permission. Good communication only occurs between people who feel safe with one another. Good communication necessitates an environment where individuals feel protected and self-assured enough to voice opinions and feelings, hopes, dreams, and confidences.

Children living with stepmothers will have already suffered the loss of their original families. It is very important that stepmothers remember that the past cannot be changed and be patient enough to wait out and override the hurt, resentment, and negative expectations about family relationships that stepchildren may have.

Be Yourself

Stepmothers must try very hard not to pretend. The stepmother who tries her heart out soon may cry her eyes out, summarily rejected by her stepchildren who perceive her as a phony. Children of all ages are particularly sensitive to phoniness; to a child phoniness is one of the most serious adult offenses. By virtue of their physical, financial, and emotional dependence, children must trust the adults in their lives; phoniness threatens this trust. It is better for a stepmother to be deemed cranky, picky, or downright mean than to be dismissed as a phony!

Express Yourself

Stepmothers must risk expressing their own wishes, hopes, dreams, expectations, and needs. Stepchildren cannot possibly meet any stepmother's expectations if they do not know what they are. Stepchildren need to learn about their new stepmothers. They need to know those things that simply drive her up the wall and those things that make her smile. To withhold such information from children is cruel. Again, this may seem one-sided—but it's a beginning.

Listen

Stepmothers need to be active listeners. Some new stepmothers may find a child's life, and the long stories the child tells, a little boring. The finger painting may look just like all the others the child has brought home, but to the child it is especially interesting and unique. Listen to children, and not just to the words: What the child actually did or saw is not as important as how the child perceived the experience—how the child describes that finger painting, or tells that long story.

Listen to the silences as well as the shouts. Try to hear the feelings behind the words, the words behind the sighs or tears or strained smiles. A good stepmother is a bit of a psychic, a bit of a detective. She needs to listen and then to provide a quiet place where a child can feel free to talk.

Be aware of nonverbal communication. Looks, touches, smiles and frowns, body language, and nervous habits all indicate how people really feel about one another. The wise stepmother realizes that hugs, touches, small smiles, and chicken soup for a sniffle convey feelings as well, if not better, than the words she says. The wise stepmother both gives and receives these nonverbal signals.

Set Limits

Once the child begins to talk freely, a whole new set of problems may emerge. Some children and stepmothers are filled with such hurt, anger, resentment, anxiety, or other negative feelings that their negativity explodes. Fair talking limits must be set up in order to avoid hurts that could derail the possibility of communication for long periods of time. Words can hurt more than any slap; verbal abuse, inappropriate language, sarcasm, or insults guised as honesty have no place between family members.

Time-outs

If and when communication gets out of hand—when one or both parties feel that they are not getting anything but hurt out of an exchange—it is time for a "time-out." A time-out means stopping a discussion. If the child insists on continuing, the time-out is enforced by the stepmother; she ceases to respond to the child. Ask the child to leave the room for a little while. If the child refuses, you leave. If necessary, reschedule the discussion for a specific later time.

No Talking Behind Backs

Communication can only occur between parties who are present. Third-party conversations are out! "My mother always says that you..." or "Grandma doesn't see why you can't..." Although it is tantalizing to grab for the bait and begin a grand argument, stepmothers must acknowledge that it takes two to argue and it is impossible to argue with a "ghost." Taking the bait of such statements leaves the stepmother with the option of playing out an adult argument with her stepchild. Not fair, not profitable, and easily avoidable! You can deal with such baitings quite simply. You might calmly respond by not responding. A simple "that's interesting," or something equally noncommittal, lets the stepchild off the hook. He or she has conveyed the information and you've defused it. You might use this opportunity to learn more about your stepchild by turning the question back to the child. The child who says, "My mother says..." might then be responded to like this: "That's interesting, What do you think about it?" Avoiding third-party conversations is very important if you are to feel a sense of control and if the child is to be spared discomfort. Children should not have to be engaged as judges in popularity contests.

Raise Issues

Sometimes it is easier for stepchildren to agree or disagree with their stepmothers than to raise issues themselves. There is no need to wait for a child to get around to formulating and expressing a problem. If a stepmother notices that a child seems gloomy she might say, "I can see that you're upset. If I were you, I'd probably feel gloomy, too." By validating negative feelings, the stepmother will often find that the stepchild is able to begin talking comfortably.

Paula had been "rejected" by her stepson Bobby for weeks. She cooked his favorite dinners; he picked. She drove him to baseball practice, asked him about his games; she got shrugs and silences in response. She bought him tickets to a hockey game and found them torn and wet in the bathroom sink. Paula began to assume that Bobby resented her marriage to his father and her presence in his life. One day she decided it was time to clear the air. On the way home from practice, Paula stopped at a local park and asked Bobby to walk with her. It was an autumn day and he walked beside her, a chubby twelve-year-old, his eyes riveted on the leaves he crunched underfoot. They walked in silence for many minutes before Paula said, "If I were you I'd probably hate me, I'd probably want to just wipe me off the face of the earth, for complicating my life." Bobby stopped and stared at his new stepmother in undisguised astonishment. His eyes softened and locked on hers. "I don't hate... I could never hate you . . . I'm just scared."

Paula and Bobby could have gone on for years, trapped in a relationship that would never have had a chance. If Paula hadn't decided to clear the air by stating her interpretation of Bobby's behavior they would never have had an opportunity to develop a relationship; Paula would have continued to misinterpret Bobby's behavior as hatred, and Bobby might have interpreted Paula's silence as yet another rejection. Paula opened the doors to communication by simply stating what she thought was wrong.

The Pen Is Mightier

Sometimes writing is easier than talking. Little notes can show affection and long letters are a vehicle for discussing complicated issues. Writing provides a way of assuring yourself no interruptions: A written statement can be read, reread, thought about, and saved. Many relationships that were initially awkward are smoothed over by writing. Stick a little note in a lunch box, slide a little letter under a bedroom door. When talking seems tough, writing often seems easy!

Open up the doors for communication. Express your feelings. Set your goals and create an environment where ideas can be exchanged respectfully. It doesn't matter if you begin by talking to the air—sooner or later you will get an answer. Be ready to listen!

Delineating Responsibilities

Most stepmothers feel that their responsibilities mirror those of typical custodial mothers.

Janice is a stepmother to two young children. She defined her responsibilities as "to clothe, shelter, and feed them. To provide personal and medical attention, to help with homework. All the same responsibilities I would have if they were my own flesh and blood."

Andrea buys the food, cooks dinner, does laundry, visits dentists, doctors, and teachers, coordinates visits to maintain family relationships, drives to and from social activities, plays mediator to erupting arguments, dishes out chores, and decides on the consequences of unacceptable behavior.

Denise felt that she had had a lot of responsibility "dumped" on her. Like many stepmothers in her situation, she felt resentful that her husband shrugged off all responsibility for his three young children. She had discovered (after her marriage) that her husband felt that children were "women's work." She cared deeply for her stepchildren but she did not want to be their only caregiver.

Accepting by Default

Too often, deciding who will do what evolves into a lopsided childcare arrangement. When stepmother and father "discussed" child-rearing, the husbands frequently claimed discipline and limit-setting as their contribution and left "the rest" for stepmothers to pick up. Most stepmothers were dissatisfied with such "discussions."

Many stepmothers assume total responsibility for child-care because it seems no one else will. Some, such as Hillary, claimed to feel more competent at handling parenting responsibilities than their husbands. Hillary "took on all the responsibilities of mothering because their father isn't very good at it. Many times the weight and frustration of what my heart told me to do and what was acceptable to the little girls really blew my mind. I never felt sure about how my caring and reprimands would affect the girls and it took almost two years until I began to feel comfortable."

Bonnie similarly did not feel that there was any choice in caring or not caring for her three young stepchildren. She spoke for many stepmothers when she confided that "it was mostly a choice between swimming or drowning. Things had to be done in the family, the children needed to be cared for, spoken to, raised. Someone had to do it and I was the one!"

The Reluctant Go-between

Many stepmothers married to divorced fathers found themselves saddled with an additional responsibility: Their husbands felt that divorce had severed all need to communicate with their children's biological mothers and left this task to their new wives. In almost all cases, this interaction was distasteful and anxiety-producing.

Some stepmothers found themselves accepting responsibilities that made them physically ill. Katherine's husband refused to drive the children to visit their mother, who lived in another town. The mother also refused to come to their town to visit with them. Feeling that the children were suffering from this stalemate, Katherine drove the children to their visits. This task, and the unpleasant reception that awaited her on both ends of her trip, made her anxious. For days before the scheduled visits, Katherine would be nervous, jumpy, and easily startled. On the drives to the next town, her heart would pound and her palms grow sweaty on the steering wheel. When she would arrive the children would race from the car, the mother would rush them into her car, and Katherine would drive home alone. Often she would feel so nauseated and dizzy that she would have to pull the car off the road to compose herself. When she arrived home, her husband, Tom, would greet her frostily, announcing that he thought it was "stupid" that the children's mother couldn't find her way to town.

Although she is still not comfortable about it, Katherine continues to make her periodic drives. Occasionally she tells Tom that she needs a break, but that is rare. Like many stepmothers, Katherine overrides her personal discomfort and continues to drive the children. Why? As Katherine puts it, "I feel like I'm not being supportive if I don't do it."

Eleanor is a stepmother of three teenagers, one boy and two girls. During the eight years of her marriage to Ted, Eleanor has found herself assuming more and more responsibility. At the present time, she feels that she does "everything" that needs doing for her stepchildren. The extent of her involvement has made her feel close to her stepchildren, but she good-naturedly warns other stepmothers to "be careful what you do. Once you do something one time, it will become 'your job.'"

Stepmother's Choice

Stepmothers who actively chose to assume the lion's share of child-related responsibilities seemed to feel more in control of their family than those who did it by default. Obviously this sense of control and satisfaction was related to the husband and stepchildren's acceptance of the stepmother as a primary parent in the family. Beware of accepting responsibility blindly or by default without making a choice. That way leads to resentment.

The New Daddy

Many stepmothers thought they were marrying a "new breed of man"—men who had opted for custody; widowers who had been able to rear their children alone; men who had cared for their children for years before they married again. These women expected that such fathers would be more involved with active parenting than the stereotypical daddy. Certainly, fathers who had been functioning as the sole residential parent had assumed responsibilities that far exceeded the typical tossing of a ball or glancing at a homework assignment. After all, these were "modern men" who would understand what it meant to be child-centered, actively involved, interested in minutiae, sensitive, insightful, even motherly. After all, hadn't women been told for the last decade or so that it was opportunity and interaction rather than gender that made a nurturing parent? These men were certainly nurturers. Right? Wrong.

The "Traditional" Daddy

The report was that most fathers were not nurturing. They functioned in a very conservative, traditional capacity. Even if they had attempted to go through the rituals of nurturing behavior while they were single, they were clearly happy to stop when the stepmother came on the scene. The responsibilities and duties of fathers fell with startling frequency into very traditional quarters: Fathers were responsible for discipline, financial providing, overseeing leisure activities for boys and sports activities for both boys and girls. Less frequently, fathers were described as overseeing chores and homework.

Susan's husband, Freddy, is typical of many fathers. Freddy's involvement with his children centers on discipline because the kids will listen to him but sometimes not to Susan. Susan and Freddy don't always agree about Freddy's brand of discipline (and that, too, is common): Susan often feels that Freddy lets too many things slide, and she knows that he even does the children's chores rather than asking the children to do them. Susan resents Freddy's lack of involvement. After all, she says, "They're his children and he needs to enter into the 'hard training' part as much as I do."

Some fathers were even less involved with their children. There seem to be three oft-cited reasons for this lack of involvement:

- Long working hours.
- Feeling that raising children is "women's work."
- Feeling that children do not require such active involvement.

"Weekend Daddies" All Week Long

Many fathers were noncustodial before they married. They have never been responsible for primary parenting. As new custodial fathers, they often had different ideas about parenting than their wives.

Many stepmothers, such as Allison, stated that their husbands didn't spend enough time with the children. They noted that when they did, they seemed more like buddies than fathers.

For men who are accustomed to being weekend daddies, it will take time to adjust to having children around on a full-time basis. Weekend daddies are notoriously poor at limits setting; many are accustomed to providing gratification in terms of material goods or entertainment. When the relationship between parent and child is limited to short vacations or visits, the tendency is for discipline and/or limit-setting to go out the window. Unfortunately, too many new full-time fathers continue their weekend pattern into the new family situation.

The Daddy Who Always Had "Help"

Many fathers who lived with their children enlisted the assistance of women to help them raise their children. Some custodial fathers moved back to their parents' home so their children could be raised by "Grandma." Wendy's husband lived with his parents before their marriage. His mother cared for the children from the time he left for work until he returned; she became the children's surrogate mother. Both grandmother and grandfather were a great help. When Wendy's husband came home from work, he fed the children dinner and made sure their homework was done.

Now that Wendy and her husband and stepchildren live together, Wendy wishes that her husband would get more involved with the children. She, like many stepmothers, would enjoy building a more solid family. She often feels that she knows her husband's children better than he does—a feeling echoed by stepmother after stepmother.

Deedee resents the fact that her husband, Pat, doesn't seem interested in raising his daughters. The girls, now ten and twelve, never spent much time with their biological mother, even during the years that they lived together. When she and Deedee's husband divorced, the girls were only three and five. After that Pat and the girls lived in his mother's home, and Grandma virtually raised the girls single-handedly. When Deedee married Pat, she felt as though she had just "picked up where his mother left off." She was very angry about this, but she kept it to herself until very recently. It took years for her to gather the courage to talk to Pat about her resentment. Pat's response was surprise; his feeling was that the "job always seemed to just get done."

Other fathers had hired housekeepers who either lived in or came to the home on a daily basis. Many stepmothers resented the fact that such domestic help was dismissed immediately following their marriage—without their consultation and without regard for whether or not the stepmother worked outside the home.

Dream Daddy

A discussion of family responsibility would not be complete without a "success story." Ann and Richard prove that dreams can become reality. Ann's love and admiration for her husband, Richard, shine through her words.

"He's an above-average father. He does more than any man I've ever known. He's very into housework; he even loves doing the laundry! Yard work is a joy to him. I tell him he does too much and, unfortunately, because of his nature, his children have never become very well-versed in their duties. However, he's always very supportive of me and how could I not be satisfied? He'd do everything if I let him."

Amazing? Even more so, when Ann adds that her husband, Richard, is a paraplegic and walks with the aid of crutches and braces. His handicap does not keep him from doing anything he sets his mind to. Ann and Richard are united in their goals for the family and in their commitment to each other.

Common Problems for the New Stepmother

Stepfamilies are different from biological families. A stepmother's family must integrate a number of different and sometimes conflicting lifestyles under one roof. Some things will be subject to compromise, others will not. The challenge lies in deciding which is which, making compromises wherever possible, and realizing which lifestyle components will not bend.

For example, a family might compromise on the subject of dining together—or not. Margaret had always envisioned family dinners like those in the "Father Knows Best" television shows of her childhood. However, when she married Bill, a widower with three teenagers, she was shocked to discover that "Dad and the boys" had always eaten together in front of the evening news. Since this pattern had happily gone on for the past ten years, Margaret realized that she had little chance of winning her campaign for sedate dinners with quiet conversation. More to the point, Margaret realized that her husband and stepsons actually enjoyed their evening meal. Rather than engage in a power struggle, Margaret compromised; dinners were moved from the playroom to the dining room and so was the television set!

Sheila found that she faced a situation that defied compromise. Shortly after her marriage, her twin stepdaughters came down with a terrible head cold. The six-year-old girls were so stuffy and miserable that they looked as though they were constantly crying. When their colds did not disappear after a week at home and in bed, consuming gallons of chicken soup and hot lemonade, Sheila took the girls to their pediatrician. "Where's the cat?" immediately asked the doctor. The twins had a severe allergy to cats; Sheila's seven-year-old-Persian, Commander, had to go.

Table Manners

It is incredible how often the issue of food surfaces. When asked about their stepchildren's most irritating feature, many women mentioned table manners. There is something primal about the sharing of food. It may not be an exaggeration to suggest that the table is the primary arena by which stepmothers gauge the success of the family in general and their individual relationships with their stepchildren. It would seem that in today's world women would have better measures for their success or failures than the dinner table, but the stepmother's responsibility for the table seemed to be hers whether or not she worked outside the home! Indeed, a stepmother's outside job just made her a breadwinner as well as a breadserver.

Privacy Issues

Lack of privacy, the most frequent personal complaint among stepmothers, has two components: real and psychological. Let's deal with the real: children and teenagers DO tend to make noise, litter, knock on doors at inconvenient moments, break things accidentally (or worse, intentionally). Children and adolescents do fall ill or otherwise require attention at inopportune moments. They often make it difficult for their father and his new wife to enjoy those warm feelings that usually characterize a new couple's relationship. Sometimes stepmothers find it difficult even to feel sexy when sharing the same space with breathing, moving, talking, testaments to the existence of her predecessor.

Romance and sex often suffer from a stepmother's sense of insecurity and vulnerability in her new family. Many women, feeling resentful and powerless, seek to address these issues in the bedroom. Often this is not a conscious effort; however, it is difficult for many stepmothers who feel insecure, unappreciated, resentful, picked on, shut out, and constantly reminded of a past they weren't part of to turn on the charm in bed.

Déjà Vu? Back to the Grind?

Some stepmothers described an unpleasant sensation of "returning to the past." Many who were previously married described their current marriages in terms of returning to the daily demands of marriage, to full-time parenting, to housewifely responsibilities. They spoke of going back to the "hectic life of wife and mother" as though they were returning to work after a nice long vacation.

The sensation was not pleasant.

Loss of Personal Time

Diedre seems headed for trouble; her life has simply "changed too much." Before Diedre married and became a stepmother to two girls ages seven and eight, she was very athletic; she had a sport for every season. Now, after only a few years of marriage and stepmotherhood, Diedre finds that she doesn't do any of her former activities—neither sports nor the crafts and hobbies she used to enjoy.

Diedre has given up too much for her new family—in a very real sense she has given up herself. This surrender has taken its personal toll: "I have always enjoyed doing things for the family but I realize now that I am suffering by not allowing time for me," Diedre puts it.

"I feel so old," she says. Diedre is twenty-seven.

Feeling Old

Like many stepmothers, Diedre is neglecting her own needs in the service of her family. Many women immerse themselves in their new families because they are not sure exactly what they are supposed to do. Stepmothers who are overburdened often feel older than their age, as Diedre does. Many feel older because of a sense of time pressure, a feeling of trying to cram more experiences into the present so that the past may be overtaken and eventually erased. There is also a practical explanation for "feeling old": A stepmother often cares for children who are older than her biological children (or the children she "might" have had). This creates a time-warp feeling; stepmothers often feel as though they are operating outside their own biological clocks.

Rules of the House

Discipline, as defined by the stepmothers surveyed, refers to the ability to set limits on behavior in a way that works for the smooth functioning of the family. In no way should discipline include physical, verbal, or emotional abuse. The line between discipline and abuse must be made clear quickly and simply.

Discipline ends in order; abuse ends in hurt. Similarly,

although stepmothers as all parents will develop and use their own styles to enforce such limits, discipline is never related to corporal punishment. Corporal punishment is always inappropriate except perhaps in a life-threatening situation.

Stepmothers almost unanimously described situations where they had consciously chosen to create and/or enforce certain basic rules of living—with varying degrees of luck. Let's try to learn from their experience.

Children Need Limits

Children need structure in order to feel secure; adults need structure in order to plan and manage a household. If any group of individuals is to live together, there must be some general agreement about the way they are going to live.

Some experts advise stepmothers to leave the discipline up to the biological parent, but the experience of stepmothers flies in the face of such advice. Someone who does not discipline is seen as powerless, an outsider and yes, even unloving. Many stepmothers mentioned trigger events, arguments that were provoked by their stepchildren and that forced them into blowing up and/or disciplining, forced them to stop "walking on eggs." Many stated that after such incidents their relationships improved markedly.

Early discipline should involve nothing more than setting down some basic ground rules for living—not a bombardment.

Building Respect

The children must perceive their new stepmother as clear about her own goals and values. In order for stepchildren to perceive you as a credible individual, worthy of respect, you first must see yourself that way. This means no "wimping out"—no running off to your husband at the slightest problem. Authority is assumed as often as granted. No one can be "made" the boss who does not assume the role. Children do not like to see weakness in adults who are in charge. Just look at the horrible time children will give to a red-faced student teacher or an ineffectual camp counselor. Children are not by nature perverse; they simply need to feel safe. They do not feel safe around wishy-washy people.

Put this into adult terms for a moment. What kind of faith would we have in a president who got on the air and announced, "I really don't know what my job is all about or whether or not you're going to trust me. I really love all of you and I hope you'll help me." Such a President would make us all, regardless of political affiliation, very uncomfortable. As adults we want our leaders to be competent and in control; children are no different.

Pat, a forty-year-old stepmother of three school-aged girls, spoke from the heart when she expressed her views on discipline: "Truthfully," she said, "I didn't really feel as if I was being authoritative, just making sure that the girls knew that whenever they were confused there would be one basically constant, basically honest, and absolutely loving person they could rely on to set some boundaries as a safety net."

Stumbling Blocks To Succcessful Discipline

Husbands Who Resist

Mary is the stepmother of two girls, ages eleven and nine, who came to live with the family a year and a half ago. Although she is a teacher, trained in early-childhood education, and the mother of two boys, ages ten and seven, she is having a difficult time adjusting to her stepdaughters. She describes her stepfamily as "struggling," and describes her inability to discipline her stepdaughters. "When I discipline them," she says, "my husband intercedes and they get away without punishment."

Children Who Resist

"You're not my mother": This is the most common refrain from stepchildren resisting discipline. It is thought to be a powerful statement. The way a stepmother responds to this statement will set the tone for all future power struggles. "You're not my mother" might very well be responded to with a simultaneous affirmation and dismissal of that fact: "That's right. Now go ahead and clear the table." It is important to clarify your own position and authority. "I'm not your mother, I'm your stepmother, and now please clear the table as I've asked you to." Stepmothers need to clarify their position and authority. "That's right. I'm your stepmother" is a clear, straightforward way of expressing that.

Outside Interference

Susan is a corrections officer. With her experience on the job, it is ironic that she has trouble with discipline. However, Susan, like many other stepmothers, often feels that her husband does not support her efforts. In addition, those outside the family unit question her authority. Her husband thinks she is too hard on her stepdaughter, who complains to her biological mother whenever Susan attempts to enforce the family rules she has established. Susan feels, and rightly so, that her authority is being undermined.

Legal Resistance

Many stepmothers find their authority and their inclinations about the best interests of their stepchildren overridden by dictates of the court. In fact, the court may be seen as another parent in situations where stepchildren have to comply with legal orders. Time and time again, stepmothers described court decisions that seemed to fly in the face of all logic and reason. They told of situations where stepchildren were required to visit with biological mothers in clearly inappropriate and at times dangerous circumstances. It is important that stepmothers acquaint themselves with court decisions made before their marriage. Because it is extremely difficult to get custody decisions changed, she will most likely have to live with them.

Stephanie was thirty-three when she married her husband and added his two preteen children to her new family along with her own eight-year-old son. Stephanie had been divorced for seven years and was accustomed to an easy relationship of visitation between her son and his noncustodial father, who picked him up at her home every other Friday and returned him before dinner on Sunday night. Stephanie assumed that her stepchildren would visit their mother on the same weekends. She looked forward to alternate weekends alone with her new husband.

Stephanie was not prepared for her husband's "agreement" with her stepchildren's mother or the woman's rigidity. The agreement, which placed uncomfortable restrictions on their weekends, began to dominate Stephanie's thoughts and affect her weekends in a very real way. The agreement specified that the children had to be driven to and picked up from their mother's apartment—a two-hour drive each way, each weekend! Stephanie was further stunned to learn that her husband was also responsible for taking the children to any of their weekend activities, back in their own neighborhood. If the children were to continue playing team sports, there would have to be three or even four round-trips between home and their mother's apartment each time they visited. This hectic schedule destroyed Stephanie's dreams of quiet, romantic, solitary, weekends with her new husband.

"Difficult" Situations

If a potential stepmother and father cannot agree before marriage on child-rearing issues, they should seek professional assistance. If one or both parties is not willing to do so, the marriage should be postponed.

Jeanette and Norman met ten years ago when they were both in their late forties. Both had been widowed at relatively early ages and each had three children in their early teens. Jeanette and Norman discussed the various problems of combining their families and the feasibility of raising six very different teenage personalities under one roof. They came quickly to a mutual decision: They postponed their plans for marriage until the children were "on their own." Because they enjoyed each other's company, they decided to continue seeing each other on an exclusive basis and now, with the wedding of Jeanette's youngest daughter, they are planning their own wedding.

Regina is an outstandingly attractive woman in her early fifties who fell in love with a man who was fifteen years her junior. They enjoyed a fiery love affair and married within several months of their meeting. At the time of their marriage, Regina had three girls living at home; an older daughter was already married. Regina's young husband came to the marriage with five children—whom Regina had never met. Although the flames of her passion continued to burn, she was neither prepared nor equipped to deal with the demands of eight children ranging in age from three to sixteen. Regina quickly came to resent the intrusion of her husband's children. Because she feared seeming incompetent in his eyes, and because she strove to maintain the high romance of their courtship, Regina isolated herself with the problems of her new large family. In less than a year's time, the marriage ended.

Regina's need for control manifested itself in arbitrary and heavy-handed ways. She admits making such "welcoming statements" to her stepchildren as "I'm the one who's in charge now and you'd better accept this fast." The more she attempted to force control over her stepchildren, the more they acted out. Through poor preparation for stepmothering, her lack of familiarity with her stepchildren, her inability to communicate with her husband about child-rearing issues, and her own frustrated expectations, Regina paved the way for the dissolution of her marriage. Biting the bullet is not a good solution.

Hope for Stepmothers

Stepmothers do not have to feel overwhelmed, nor to fear the loss of their marriages along with their sense of self. It is possible to set effective guidelines that will enable a new group of individuals to begin functioning as a family. Running a stepfamily is a matter of figuring out what is important to you and deciding how much you're willing to give to attain your goal. Setting up a stepfamily is a little like the childhood game of Tropical Island. Perhaps you recall that the premise of this game was that a group of individuals was stranded on a tropical island and needed to create a new society from scratch. One of the first necessities for this new "civilization" was a set of rules and consequences. It is the same for stepfamilies. In order for a group to function there must be a common set of rules and consequences. Take a deep breath and follow along...

Guidleines for Establishing Discipline

Clarify Personal Needs

Many stepmothers run into trouble with their husbands, stepchildren, and ultimately themselves because they simply are not clear about what they really want and believe in. Feelings of discomfort and anxiety quickly turn to resentment as they wait—and wait and wait—for their stepchildren to begin to "do what they're supposed to" and for their husbands to "back them up." Stepchildren cannot "do" what they do not know and husbands cannot "back up" what is left unsaid. Stepmothers need to clarify what they need to live comfortably.

Start by writing a list of nonnegotiables and negotiables. The list will have two columns and must be limited to concrete actions rather than feelings. Do not worry if the things on this list seem silly. Everyone is entitled to personal quirks. Once you've made this list, look it over carefully. If there is anything on it that you can learn to live with, or overlook, add it to the column marked "Needs that are negotiable." (Perhaps you really could learn to close the door on your stepchild's messy room.) When you have finished, put your list away. During the next day or two, add or delete any needs that come up in your day-to-day living.

Discuss Needs with Your Husband

When you feel comfortable with your list, find some time with your husband to discuss it. Ideally, he will be willing and able to add some of his own needs to this list. Discuss this combined list, then make time to discuss it with the children. It is very important that the list be presented and discussed as a joint effort: The children can add their negotiable and nonnegotiable needs to the list, too.

Limit Discussion to Specifics

All family members should try to keep their needs concrete and unemotional. Needs must refer to definite actions rather than feelings. Such statements as "I just want everyone to be happy and get along" or "I want everyone to leave me alone" don't belong on the list.

Listen to Each Other With Respect

Respect each other's nonnegotiables. In order for a stepmother to have her own needs respected, she must be willing to listen and attempt to comply with the reasonable needs of her husband and her stepchildren.

Develop Family Rules and Consequences

Based upon the needs of all parties, the father and stepmother should now be able to set up family rules and consequences for misbehavior. These family rules need to be agreed upon by stepmother and father. If there are severe stumbling blocks in values and conflicting approaches for consequences that cannot be resolved privately, father and stepmother should seek professional help.

Inform the Children

Once the stepmother and father are in firm agreement on basic rules and consequences, it's time to tell the children about them. At this point there should be no discussion. It is important that the children see that their parents have discussed and decided the issues.

Keep the rules and the consequences to a minimum so that the family is not overwhelmed. Impress upon the children that these are nonnegotiable household rules. Explain the rules and the consequences clearly; do not get into rationalizing or defending your decisions. Deal with negative remarks calmly: "I know this is new for you" or "Thanks for your opinion, but these are the rules."

Stick to Your Guns

Get ready to enforce your rules. Be prepared to have them tested. But if at any point in the formation of family rules and consequences you realize that you have made a mistake or have changed your position on something— *change it.* It is better to give in or give up on a particular rule or point if you are not going to be able to enforce it wholeheartedly.

Paula, a bright thirty-five-year-old stepmother of a teenage girl, found that she had grown increasingly uncomfortable with her stepdaughter's spending habits. Paula had imposed what she thought was a generous limit of fifty dollars per shopping spree. However, Paula came to realize that she herself had made her stepdaughter a "Frankenstein Shopping Monster." When she and her husband married, her stepdaughter had been a ten-year-old tomboy with a wardrobe of faded T-shirts and worn jeans. Paula taught her everything she knew about fashion—a considerable body of knowledge. She took her to the finest stores and instructed her in the benefits of natural fibers and custom styling. Now, at fifteen, Paula's stepdaughter will wear only designer clothes! Paula's rule about fifty dollars was impractical in consideration of these tastes. She had to reevaluate her stepdaughter's clothing allowance in view of the fact that she had given the girl very conflicting messages by steering her to designer labels and shops. This was difficult, because her husband, who had recently become quite successful in private business, enjoyed spending his newly accumulated wealth by "spoiling" his daughter. Now Paula and her husband had a new problem to solve: how to steer their daughter so that she didn't become too materialistic.

The best rule to follow is: Be firm but flexible. You'll have to revise your list of negotiable and nonnegotiable needs as the children grow older and their needs change. Be careful that your list does not become outmoded!

You're finally all moved in, you've begun establishing a basic sense of order and taken some important steps toward becoming a functioning family.

Not all stepmothers live with their stepchildren; these noncustodial stepmothers face a host of challenges all their own. The following chapter is dedicated to those noncustodial stepmothers who confront the challenges of a full-time relationship on what seems to be a part-time basis.

Chapter 9

NONCUSTODIAL STEPMOTHERS

Noncustodial stepmothers share many of the same concerns as other stepmothers, however, their relationship with their stepchildren is subject to a host of additional concerns. Noncustodial stepmothers must regularly deal with their husband's feelings concerning his relationship with his children. Too often such feelings are negative—including *anger* that may remain from his past relationship with the children's mother, anger which may continue to be fueled during his new marriage. Stepmothers may find that a husband's anger begins a cycle of negativity ranging from guilt to disappointment and sadness. The way in which such emotions are expressed and dealt with directly impacts on a stepmother's life.

Noncustodial stepmothers also deal with an array of issues that are specific to their special situation. As these stepmoms well know, visiting stepchildren bring more baggage with them than the kind that carries their pajamas! Stepchildren may be unsure of their "place" in their father and stepmother's home and express their uncertainty in a variety of ways, many of which can make for less than pleasant times together. And, though the role of stepmother is a pretty fuzzy one, the role of noncustodial stepmother is even fuzzier! A stepmother's insecurity about her own identity often runs headlong into a stepchild's uncertainty. When this collision occurs in the environment of the father's negativity, the very air may seem to crackle with tension.

Who Is a Noncustodial Stepmother?
Obviously, the title implies the situation—a noncustodial stepmother is married to a father who does not have either

legal or physical custody of his children, who more than likely live with their biological or adoptive mother. This role is often burdened with feelings of anger, guilt, disappointment, and sadness—usually originating from the husband's relationship with his children. These feelings not only spill over onto the stepmother's relationship with her stepchildren, but may actively shape that relationship. Let's take a look at the way this can happen.

Father's Negative Feelings

Anger. Anger is perhaps the most common starting place for many noncustodial fathers. Anger may be left over from the breakup with the children's mother or may spring from a husband's perception about the way he is being treated by the children's mother or even the children themselves. Husbands may begin to sound like Paul, the father of Sam, aged twelve, who says, "Honestly, as far as I'm concerned, I feel like I'm nothing more than a dollar sign to my son's mother. It's been this way since we separated, and, frankly, I think a lot of this has rubbed off on my son. After years without even a Father's Day card, what am I supposed to think. I know my new family suffers because of the money I have to give Sam's mother and sometimes—I don't know— it just makes me mad."

How may husbands act when they are angry? Many simply withdraw, others may argue openly with children and their mothers. Many husbands like Paul, who are hurt and angry, may fluctuate between anger and guilt.

Guilt. Husbands may feel guilt that springs, as we have seen, from their own anger towards their children. Guilt is often seen as a more acceptable emotion than anger, especially towards one's children. Husbands may also feel guilt over "leaving" or not living with their children. This guilt may escalate when the father feels happy in his new relationship—especially if the stepmother has children from a previous marriage living with them or if the stepmother and father have children of their own. The guilty father has become all too familiar today. Such "Disneyland Daddies" may try to assuage their guilt by "doing and buying." Husbands may also step up time alone with their children, isolating the stepmother and any other children in the household.

Disappointment. A husband may have secretly or openly fantasized that his new marriage would have improved his relationship with his children and perhaps even smoothed out any remaining rough spots with the children's mother. When difficult relationships remain difficult, or more than likely become even more difficult, the husband may feel angry or guilty. When husbands begin to feel either angry, guilty, disappointed, or any combination of these over time, they may grow sad.

Sadness. Husbands may begin to feel depressed with the sense that nothing can be done to change poor relationships with children or that the new marriage is threatening his relationship with his children.

Obviously, an angry, guilty, disappointed, and/or sad husband is going to have an impact on a marriage. When these feelings seem to start from somewhere outside the marriage, and yet threaten the future happiness of that marriage, stepmothers are bound to have some strong feelings of their own. If the couple is recently married, such negative feelings come into direct conflict with the expectations of the newlywed stepmother.

Many fathers continue to act out their cyclic feelings of anger, guilt, disappointment, and sadness in the same ways they did in their prior marriages. They may overspend, attempting to deluge their children in "happiness." They may continue to visit with their children as though the stepmother did not exist. They may imbue their children with a power that may be inappropriate. A stepmother of two, now married for eleven years, expresses the conflict a newlywed woman may feel when confronted with her husband's negativity:

"All I remember of those early years was having to console Jim. Here I was twenty-four years old and deliriously happy. Jim was older and we'd had a romantic courtship for two years. We often met after work for candlelight dinners in wonderful restaurants. Flowers for no reason at all, sweet good-night phone calls—the list of good things just went on and on. It wasn't hard to accept that Jim spent the weekends with his children; in fact, I respected him for it. There were even times when his eyes would mist up when he talked about them, and his strong feelings about his kids made me love him even more. And then we were married.

The children didn't come to the ceremony, but I didn't think too much about it at the time—after all, they were only ten and eight at the time. It wasn't until that first week after our honeymoon that I began to see how tormented Jim was about not living with his children. The children came to stay with us every weekend, and Jim, it seemed, spent the time in between lamenting how much he missed them when they weren't with us. He was so guilty about "breaking up their home" that he seemed to be almost afraid of them. It may be hard to believe, but we actually had to wait to have our own children until *his* children were ready!

"I was so happy before we were married, and then, well it just didn't seem right to continue to be so happy when he was so obviously unhappy. The thing that bothered me most was that I couldn't *do* anything about any of it. It was just "the situation" as Jim would say. After awhile, I guess, it was harder to continue feeling sorry for Jim. I guess I began to feel a little sorry for myself and what had happened to us. There didn't seem to be an "us" anymore.

Carrie is not atypical of many noncustodial stepmothers. All stepmothers become stepmothers because they are married to men who have children. Yet, few realize the extent to which their husband's relationship with these children may impact on their life. Many stepmothers experience a range of emotions that place them in a cycle that starts with anger—at the husband, then at the stepchildren and their mother—then progresses to guilt—for being a "bad" wife and an incompetent stepmother (i.e. when a visit doesn't seem happy and fun)—then to sadness about the whole situation, which in turn triggers anger all over again.

Jealousy. Stepmothers have a hard time with jealousy directed towards stepchildren and their mother. If this emotion is understood as springing from a sense of being threatened, it is easy to understand how and why a stepmother can feel jealous. However, when a stepmother begins to accept the stepchild as part of her own household, these feelings of insecurity and "threat" begin to ease.

Sometimes, this acceptance may actually help ease tension that may have developed over time between husbands and their children's mother. However, a word of caution is due here; the children's mother may feel her own sense of "threat" and insecurity. It is wise to remember that a threatened mother may be a very unpleasant person to have in one's life on an ongoing basis. The complicated dynamics of a relationship between stepmothers and mothers could probably fill a volume on its own. There is no doubt that trying to minimize the "threat" a mother perceives from a stepmother is certainly worth a try, but realistically this may or may not be feasible. On a more positive note, stepmothers who do not seek to *replace* mothers, but who form genuine feelings for their stepchildren, will often win a place in even the most skeptical mother's heart. Finally, if difficult relations with the children's mother persist—remember that old saw about "actions speaking louder than words?" Your *actual* relationship with your stepchildren, and not their mother's perception of that relationship, will, in time, come to be the way your stepchildren know you.

What's a Stepmother to Do?

Must all stepmothers be angry, guilty, disappointed, sad, or jealous? Absolutely not. In order to move away from such negative feelings, stepmothers need to change their lenses. As we have seen, such feelings often begin with the husband. Instead of viewing the situation from the husband's point of view, stepmothers can use their distance from the situation to see things in a new light. This new perspective can present opportunities for relating to one another. Stepmothers start with a clean slate with their stepchildren and can and do form relationships that are unique to their situation. But wait just a minute! It's not that easy, you may be saying. Stepchildren have their own feelings, too! And very often those feelings don't seem to include welcoming a new stepmother into their lives! What can a stepmother do, to not only get through visits, but to make them as pleasant as possible for all concerned?

The Visiting Stepchild

The very first thing a stepmom can do is realize that stepchildren are not visitors or guests at the home their father and his wife share. They are members of the family. It may be easier for new stepmothers to begin thinking of their stepchildren in this way if they first think of them as in-laws.

Now, that is not to say that just being a "family member" guarantees that everyone will love one another. What it does imply is that family membership is *nonrevocable*. Imagine for a moment that a husband has a particularly unpleasant Aunt Tillie. During her last visit, Aunt Tillie refused to clean up after herself no matter how many polite reminders she was given—leaving trails of wet towels everywhere, spilling crumbs on the living room couch, and hanging wet stockings in the family bathroom. The list could go on and we could imagine all sorts of unpleasant and grievous behavior, but no matter what Aunt Tillie *did*, at the end of her visit, Aunt Tillie would still be... well, Aunt Tillie. Too often, there seems to be a sense that a stepchild can be ex-communicated from family membership. Of course, this feeling may not even be in the forefront of anyone's mind, but it may feel that way to the stepchild who is being treated like a visitor.

Family Member Vs. Visitor

This notion of family member vs. visitor is at the root of much of the difficulty experienced during stepchildren's visits. Think hard. Do you really think of your stepchild as a member of the family? Perhaps privately (meaning truthfully) you see them as visitors or guests or even (if things have gotten bad enough) as intruders. This perception will greatly affect the way you treat your stepchildren and vice versa. Guests, for example, are usually not expected to do daily chores. In fact, if they do anything, they are soundly thanked for their help. On the other hand, guests seem to expect that they will be entertained in some way or have the focus of attention directed toward them.

Family members, on the other hand, are expected to be involved in a more two-way relationship, to be aware of the little idiosyncracies of other members of the family, and to have his/her own expectations of having their own needs understood as well. There is a basis of "comfort" between family members, a sort of unspoken agreement that "we know each other for who we are... and accept each other anyway!"

Often a curious thing happens when stepchildren visit—

they are treated like guests on the one hand and expected to fit in like family members on the other! There is a certain barrier erected by household family members between themselves and those who visit. This invisible shield separates those who *belong* from those who don't. The way in which we let people know that they're on the other side of this barrier may take a variety of forms: politeness, exclusion from "inside information," outright hostility. However, whatever the form, the result is that the stepchild is on one side of the barrier and the family on the other. The real rub is that the stepchild's *father* is on the other side. Sometimes this distancing of stepchildren is, frankly, conscious. However, more often a stepmother will want to get close but just not seem to be able to find a way. Such stepmothers may go out of their way to treat their stepchildren nicer and nicer during their visits only to find things go from bad to worse.

Take Marie and her eleven-year-old stepson Jake who visits every Friday afternoon through Sunday evening. Marie is a pediatric R.N. at a large teaching hospital who works on a rotating day and evening shift Monday through Friday. In order to have weekends free to spend with her two daughters April (eleven) and Mandy (nine) from a previous marriage and the baby, three-year-old Todd, Jake's half-brother, Marie works two or three double shifts during the week. But weekends are not only for fun, but also for laundry, vacuuming, dusting, and so on. Marie expects April and Mandy to do their part, even little Todd has his own chores, but what is Jake expected to do? "Why nothing really," says Marie. "It just doesn't seem fair. I mean he hasn't been here all week making a mess." So what does Jake do while the rest of the house is doing chores? "Oh, he usually watches TV or plays a computer game or something. Frankly, it's not fair, but it does make me a little annoyed to see him just sitting around like that—just lifting his feet while the girls vacuum around him—and I know it makes the other kids mad—but it's really not his fault."

Marie, like many stepmothers, is trying very hard to be fair, but treating Jake and stepchildren like him differently sets them up as outsiders. When children feel that their family status is unacknowledged, they may begin to try very hard to show that they do indeed have a "family" relationship. For example, Marie also relates that "Jake can be so angry sometimes; I don't really understand it. I'm afraid to ask him to do anything. Well, like last weekend, I picked him up after school and he came in and dropped his books and his jacket right inside the front door. When I asked him to pick them up, he said right out of nowhere, 'This is my father's house.'"

A stepmother in Marie's position is often afraid to confront her husband—especially if he is feeling any of the negative emotions discussed earlier. Many stepmothers swallow their own feelings and try to redouble efforts at being "nice," treating stepchildren even more like guests. This may help the stepmother for a short time—some even find themselves counting down until the visit is over. However, if this feeling like a nonfamily member is causing unpleasant or unruly behavior, maybe the simplest thing a stepmother can do is—STOP—stop treating stepchildren like guests. One of a stepchild's worst fears is that he or she will be abandoned, and treating a stepchild like a nonfamily member aggravates this fear to the point where the child feels something has to be done to stop the hurt! Some of the signs that a stepchild may feel threatened with respect to being treated as a nonfamily member are statements such as:

"*He's* my father," or

"I've known him longer than you," or

"I know what *he* likes."

Although remarks like these and the charming attitude that usually comes along with them may seem aggressive, they are more likely in response to the stepchild's feeling of being threatened or excluded. The stepmother that sees her stepchildren as vulnerable is a stepmother who will begin to have easier, more pleasant visits.

What's a Stepmother to Do?
Starting With a Clean Slate—Visits

Change Your Frame of Mind

Simply beginning to think of stepchildren as household family members rather than intruding guests will shift the atmosphere. But, what then? Certainly, we are not

Pollyannas, and we understand that relationships cannot be "wished into being" with the flick of a mental mind-set. Furthermore, many stepmothers *have* been trying to include stepchildren in the family only to feel their efforts rejected.

Honesty Really Is the Best Policy

Stepchildren seem to have built-in radar for detecting false feelings. Stepmothers who are unsure about their feelings for their stepchildren are far better off *not* pretending to feel a love they just don't feel yet. On the other hand, stepmothers who feel loving toward their stepchildren need to understand and respect that their feelings may be very different from their stepchild's. The point is, it is far better for all concerned to share fears and hopes directly so that real issues can be worked through.

Understand the Stepchild's "Two-Headed" Dilemma— Loyalty Conflict

Stepchildren are often faced with a perceived dilemma that may seem unresolvable to them. On the one hand, the child wants to have a relationship with his or her father. This relationship now includes a wife and perhaps other children. However, the child may feel that giving in and enjoying that relationship is disloyal to mother. These loyalty conflicts may be supported directly by the child's mother, may arise from the child's holding on to the relationship between mother and father as part of his or her identity, or may be a combination of both.

Here is where the stepmother's attitude is critical. Treating and accepting the stepchild as a member of the family may help soothe the conflict for the stepchild—the stepchild *is* already a member of the family, so there is no choice necessary on the child's part. Taking away the stepchild's concern about choosing between families may go a long way toward reducing the tension that underlies difficult visits.

Jealousy

Imagine feeling a combination of anxiety, protectiveness toward your mother, fear, and uncertainty about your welcome. Imagine feeling some or all of these feelings and then visiting people who seem to enjoy being "at home" with, of all people, your very own father. Given such a situation, it might be difficult to be warm, loving, and receptive to the new people in your father's life.

Stepchildren often feel just this way. In order to reduce feelings of jealousy, it is absolutely crucial that the stepchild understands that he or she is a member of the family household—a membership that is guaranteed and irrevocable simply through his or her father. When that relationship is accepted and honored, there may still be feelings of jealousy, but the intolerable feeling that stepchildren often have of being replaced will be soothed.

House Rules—Different Households/Different Rules

This may seem to be a larger problem than it actually is. Children can and do understand the difference in different rules in different places. Certainly children understand (and if they don't, they need to learn) that one behaves differently in a library than on a playground, in the principal's office than in an amusement park, and so forth. Children may become confused (or try to test) the rules of family. Parents in each house must agree that children will conform to the rules of the other household when under its care.

There is a proviso here: For example, Casey is the new stepmother of a fifteen-year-old stepson. It seems that Joey's mother permits him to smoke marijuana in the house. On several weekends, Joey has arrived obviously "under the influence." In addition, Joey's grades have dropped and the school has contacted the father. In extreme cases such as these, where there is danger to the child, the other parent must be contacted. If it is impossible to gain cooperation from the custodial parent, and if the danger is considered severe, professional help should be sought for guidance. Most of the time, however, differences in household rules center around chores, bedtimes, and so forth. It is important that such differences be stated just as that—differences— without preference or judgment.

House Rituals

One of the ways we human beings begin to develop a secure identity is by knowing what to expect. Fear of the unknown is one of the greatest fears. And to address this fear, people often try to do things the same way over and over again so that the world becomes a bit more "knowable" and just downright less threatening. There are almost as many rituals as there are people. Every family has its own way of doing things and doesn't even give them much thought. They say things like "in our family we always _____." For a stepchild, acknowledgment of his or her place in the household will be underlined by rituals.

Rituals don't have to be large—one doesn't need to get out a marching band and fireworks every time the stepchild arrives—no, rituals are more likely to be small ways of doing things that define the family and the stepchild's place in it. Perhaps it's something as simple as stopping off for groceries on the way back from being picked up for a visit, a place to hang one's coat and put away one's things, or throwing the laundry in the basket before one leaves. Rituals also include the way time is spent among family members—working in "family times," perhaps one or two meals that the family shares together, and/or time set aside for just stepmother and stepchild or stepchild and father. There are no set list of rituals. They will be as unique as your family.

When you become centered on yourself, understand that you have a family that includes your stepchild, understand that unpleasant behavior is usually a mask for vulnerability, understand that you, as a stepmother, do not have to give in to unacceptable behavior, and when you no longer treat your stepchildren like intruders, you will feel that tense need to "protect" the family ebb away. When a stepchild is accepted into the family, the father may feel a reduction in any guilt, anger, disappointment, and sadness he may have been feeling. As a result, fathers may have less need to make up for losses they imagine they have caused their children. Fathers may begin to actually develop better, more "real" relationships with their children as they are permitted to interact with them in a *family* situation, rather than as one on one Disneyland daddies. As tensions ebb away, visits usually become less difficult, and everyone may actually be able to relax and even begin to enjoy their time together.

Vacations

Legal custody arrangements or geographic realities often have stepchildren spending long vacation periods together.

Sometimes, these are the only times stepchildren get to spend with the family. In cases where children have regular visits, they will obviously become secure in their place in the family. Vacation periods are little more than extended visits with all the same rules and privileges of family membership. When children's visits are more or less limited to vacation periods, an initial adjustment period may be felt by all. The initial adjustment period may be considerably eased by helping children to feel at home before their arrival.

Sending photographs of "home," father, stepmother, and the rest of the household, will help make everything seem a little more familiar to the children before they get there. Daily phone calls before they leave will help shape their expectations and verify rituals that have been established during past visits (or if this is a first visit, to establish some rituals to make the child feel more at home). Such rituals can be as simple as "getting your special blanket down for you" or "looking forward to our special breakfast together." Anything that helps the child feel that his or her visit is an important part of the household will help ease any feelings of strangeness and smooth that initial adjustment period. It is especially helpful if children have a ritual to look forward to as soon as they arrive. For example, Bob and Betty have always greeted Bob's two girls at the airport with a bottle of ginger ale to drink in the car to settle their stomachs after their long plane ride. Remember, the way of decreasing tension and the chance of an unpleasant visit is by increasing security and familiarity before the visit even begins!

Vacations—Away

Vacations are simply visits that take place away from the father and stepmother's house (and cost a lot more money than staying home). Many folks believe in the magic of vacations. This belief holds that if you take a difficult situation and move it far away where everyone will more than likely be closer together, things will improve! Obviously this doesn't work—and often makes matters worse! Before planning a get-away family vacation, be sure that the stepchild feels like a member of the family. If not, tensions are sure to rise, often in direct proportion to how much every member feels they are sacrificing in terms of time and money. Many fathers and new stepmothers expect that a glamorous vacation to an exciting spot will miraculously begin a wonderful relationship with a stepchild or change a difficult one. Again, it cannot be emphasized enough that difficult relationships with stepchildren spring from a variety of insecurities related to a sense of family membership. A quiet time at home building security and acceptance, getting to know the rules of the household and the quirks of each other, and finding a place for oneself within the family is the stuff great vacations are made from.

If the relationship with stepchildren is more or less in place and a vacation is planned—remember the togetherness rule. "Too much is suffocating and too little is isolating." That goes for everyone. A good family vacation should include time for the entire family to be together, time for the children to be alone together (with supervision if necessary, of course), and time for the individual parents and children as well.

A Final Note: All Is *Not* "Step" Related

There is a natural tendency sometimes to think that all stepchildren's behavior is related to the "step" relationship. Although much of a child's behavior may be, it is very important to remember that stepchildren, hard as it may be for a very beleaguered stepmother to imagine, actually have lives and concerns that have nothing to do with the stepfamily. It is also essential to remember that stepchildren *are* children, and their thinking and behavior will reflect their age and the level of their emotional and intellectual development. Conflicts sometimes arise not so much from the "step" relationship, as from misunderstanding about just where children are in their development.

Very young children, for example, may have trouble separating fantasy from reality and be truly frightened by fairy tale stepmothers. School-age children may be concerned about doing things with their friends—team sports, clubs and so on—where adolescents will be normally involved in moving physically and emotionally away from any and all kinds of family. (For a more complete discussion of children's development see Chapter 5.)

So, who is the noncustodial stepmother? A stepmother who facilitates the bond between father and child, who understands the uncertainty, the jealousy, and the insecurity spawned from living apart from a parent. A noncustodial stepmother comes to understand that her life has been forever changed by her stepchildren. A noncustodial stepmother understands that she is a stepmother *every* day.

Now it's time to face the fact that your new family embraces a much larger cast of characters than those living under the same roof. Stepfamilies have complicated extended families that may include several sets of grandparents, aunts, uncles, and multitudes of cousins. These numbers both increase and threaten the possibility for future support and happiness.

Chapter 10

THE EXTENDED FAMILY

We tend to idealize extended families, seeing them as groups of people beaming at one another around perennially gleaming holiday tables. Each face reflects their obvious genetic connections; each exchanged glance is imbued with a glow that forgives little indiscretions.

It's usually not quite like that; the idealized extended family is usually an illusion. Family differences, competition for love and affection, and values that conflict with the established "family" doctrine are common.

Stepmothers often discover, to their dismay, that they must integrate their own complex extended family with their husband and stepchildren's families, creating, perhaps, an overextended family. The possibilities for joy and togetherness can be diminished as well as enlarged through the newly complicated family structure.

Begin with the Children's Grandparents

It is important that the stepmother be aware of her stepchildren's relationship with their grandparents, particularly the maternal ones. If they have a close and loving relationship and have been accustomed to having their grandparents in their lives, the stepmother must get to know the grandparents, assure them of her support, and hope for their support in return. Remember the obvious: The maternal grandparents are the parents of your stepchildren's mother, and they're going to remain loyal to her. Even when they are pleased that their grandchildren have a loving stepmother, their allegiance to their daughter—or to her memory—may prevent them from welcoming you wholeheartedly.

Most grandparents fear that a stepmother will affect

their relationship with their grandchildren. Maternal grandparents seem to feel this fear more keenly than paternal grandparents. The fear is real. It may be difficult to establish and maintain a relationship in the face of conflicts in loyalties in the case of divorced biological mothers or unfinished grieving if their daughter has died.

It is imperative that you do everything in your power to see that this relationship is in no way damaged by your arrival. The children have already suffered too many losses by the time you enter their lives. They have weathered the storms of divorce or dealt with the trauma of death. They do not need any more losses, dissension, or confusion.

If the stepchildren have *not* had a good or active relationship with grandparents, and if the grandparents seem to want one, you might try to foster a new closeness. Sometimes a stepmother can mend a fragmented relationship or help build a new one.

When Lorrianne became stepmother to Alana and Chad, ages four and eight, Lorraine felt that the children should get to know their grandparents. Alana and Chad had not seen their biological mother—a drug abuser—for three years when Lorrianne became their stepmother. Lorrianne fondly remembered her own grandparents; she felt that it was her duty to contact her stepchildren's grandparents and reestablish contact. Lorrianne's story had a happy ending. It seemed that the grandparents had been staying away because they were ashamed of their daughter's addiction and because their daughter had told them that the children had a "new life" that totally excluded them. Mr. and Mrs. B. were thrilled by the prospect of getting to know their grandchildren. Photographs were exchanged, regular weekly phone calls were made, and last Christmas Mr. and Mrs. B traveled to Lorrianne's home for the holidays.

What to Expect

Most stepmothers reported that their stepchildren had limited or no contact with their maternal relatives, either before or after the stepmother's entrance into their lives. Although a few reported improved relationships with grandparents, aunts, uncles, and cousins due to their efforts, most reported that even the limited contact their stepchildren had with these relatives ended with the new marriage.

Typically, if the stepchildren had been living with their father before the marriage they had limited or no contact with relatives on their mother's side. If the children had lived with their mother, the stepmother usually found that the children had maintained a relationship with their maternal relatives and that a change in custody, not easily accepted, tended to end the contact.

Julie felt threatened from the very beginning of her marriage. Her little stepson's maternal grandparents did everything in their power to prevent her from assuming responsibility for the boy. They went to great lengths, both in the courts and through personal harassment. She decided not to give in to the unpleasantness. Instead, she took charge and turned this potentially catastrophic situation into a success story.

When Julie married her husband, Joey was little more than a toddler. Joey's maternal grandmother actually tried to kidnap him! Says Julie, "She hated me for taking her daughter's place and was afraid that because of me, she'd lose Joey." Julie continued to call Joey's grandmother each week. When the woman refused to speak to her or to the child, she sent weekly letters and photographs. When the grandmother realized that Julie was encouraging a relationship between Joey and herself, she began to warm up. Finally, she agreed to drop her custody suit and began to speak with Julie about her grandson. Finally, the two women discovered that they need not compete for Joey's affection. Now, they spend time together as a family and everyone is much happier— especially Julie's husband.

Susan decided to facilitate the good relationship that her stepchildren formerly enjoyed with their maternal grandparents. "From the beginning, the grandparents sent cards and letters. Then they didn't write to us for a while. We never heard from Grandpa—just Grandma. After a year or so I called and said that the children really missed them. Grandma said she was so glad I'd called: Her daughter had told her I wouldn't allow the children to see their grandparents. I told them it wasn't true and that they could see their grandchildren any time they wanted to! They sent two airplane tickets and the boys stayed with them for two weeks last summer. Contact has been reestablished! They plan to come out this spring to visit the children—and us."

Take It Easy

On the other hand, if grandparents or older children resist meeting or forming any sort of relationship, it's best to back off and let things be. Too often, a well-meaning stepmother may push a relationship that is in no one's best interest. Stepchildren do not need any more complications. Children who are genuinely adamant about not visiting grandparents are best left alone.

In-laws

Most stepmothers reported very good, close relationships with their in-laws. Many paternal grandparents had played a very involved role in their grandchildren's lives prior to their son's new marriage. In a number of cases, they had assumed a majority of responsibility for the care of their grandchildren. Once these grandparents felt confident that their relationship was not threatened by the new stepmother, things usually went very smoothly. In fact, in more than a few cases, the relationship between stepchildren and their paternal relatives markedly improved as a direct result of the stepmother's intervention.

Of course, there are always cases where only the strength of the human spirit permits a person to carry on. Katherine headed that strength. She married a man who had been the subject of the town's most notorious scandal— a man whose wife "ran off" with another man, the teenage father of the baby she was carrying. When he and Katherine married, the girls were still in diapers. In addition to suffering the challenges all stepmothers face, Katherine became a veritable pariah to her family and friends. Her marriage to a divorced Catholic brought severe criticism from family members. Both families felt that Katherine's husband should not have married. Katherine thought that time would soften the harshness of their feelings, but it didn't. She raised both girls in the town where she had been born and raised herself, shunned by church and friends. Katherine maintained at least a "holiday contact" with both families for the sake of her stepdaughters and the son who was born in the fifth year of her marriage. The situation never did improve in the extended family, but Katherine managed to build loving and close relationships within her own family. Last year Katherine's elder stepdaughter married, and Katherine has just received the news that she will soon become a stepgrandmother. She continued to take from her family and in-laws the best of what they could offer, and to give what she could in return. After nineteen years of marriage, she is a testament to the powers of perspective, managing to retain the "family" feeling that was so important to her.

Your In-laws and Your Biological Children

Some stepmothers mentioned feeling a little hurt and resentful about their in-laws' cool treatment of their own children. They were disappointed that their in-laws didn't try to accept the stepmothers' biological children with the same effort that they, as stepmothers, had made for the in-laws' grandchildren. Other stepmothers groaned about being subjected to seemingly endless recitations of "past history." For some, it became increasingly difficult to sit through stories and photo-sharing sessions that predated their existence. Other in-laws seemed to have little difficulty accepting the stepmother's children into their lives. Careful handling can make a real difference.

Your Side of the Family

Almost all stepmothers were satisfied with the relationship between their own relatives and their stepchildren. For the most part, they found that after a short period of awkwardness their relatives welcomed their stepchildren into the family. Time and time again, stepmothers stressed their satisfaction when their families proved able to treat their stepchildren as "real" members of the family.

Surprisingly, stepmothers also reported that their own relatives seemed to be able to treat biological children and stepchildren equally. Only a tiny percentage mentioned that their relatives treated their stepchildren and biological children differently. When they did, their behavior drew prompt comment from the stepmothers, who made the unacceptability of such favoritism known in no uncertain terms. More than one stepmother mentioned that she had decided to forgo family get-togethers when she felt that her stepchildren were ignored or hurt by her family's markedly unequal treatment of her stepchildren and her own children from a previous marriage.

Your Stepchildren and Your Family

Stepchildren were generally eager to become part of their stepmother's family, quickly coming to accept them as their own family members. Any coolness between stepchildren and stepgrandparents was more likely to result from the adults' reluctance to foster a close relationship than from the stepchild's ambivalence.

What Do You Need?

Stepmothers need support from their relatives on both sides, their own and their husbands'. Support means sensitivity—in all the little ways.

Like gift-giving. One stepmother said, "Relatives should not show partiality. It's cruel, and children pick up on it. My in-laws will either completely disregard my son when it comes to gift-giving occasions or give him a token gift that's worse than none at all. While my stepsons got Reeboks for Christmas, my son got socks. For sixth-grade graduation my stepson got a computer, my son got a card and a ten-dollar bill. I've gotten to the point where I don't even want their gifts at all."

SENSITIVITY

Stepchildren who have been abandoned by death or divorce by their biological mothers need special sensitivity; such children should not have to tolerate any additional "rejections." Sensitivity may mean not removing photos of the stepchildren's biological mother, but rather adding some current photos to the display. Sensitivity may mean trying to talk more about "recent" history at family get-togethers.

Some Tips for Getting Along

Don't Let Yourself Feel Left Out

Stepmothers can help everyone by setting the tone for the new family. Instead of sitting around feeling helpless and resentful while the family talks about the past, try to add something from the present to the conversation, or something from your own past.

Give It Time

If you truly want your own parents to be involved with your stepchildren, try discussing your feelings, then step back to give a relationship time to evolve. This relationship, like all others, takes time to grow. It helps if your relatives are given an opportunity to get to know their stepchildren gradually, and preferably one at a time!

Familiarize Family Members With One Another

Introduce new family members to each other before they meet. Write letters, exchange snapshots, talk on the phone.

Don't Push New Relationships

If you would like your stepchildren to call your relatives Grandma and Gramps you might suggest it, but do not push! It is better to discuss preference with various family members. Stepmothers may be needlessly hurt by family members who are perceived as cold when they are really only hesitant about their new roles. Talk it over!

Be Upbeat

Many times, stepmothers unwittingly damage chances for a successful extended family relationship by prematurely sharing complaints with family and in-laws. It is difficult for your family to accept stepchildren, whom they may perceive as problems for you, and it is likewise difficult for your in-laws to accept you or your children if you are griping about their grandchildren or their son! Be pleasant and calm when initiating new family relationships.

Give It Time

Make sure that stepchildren have a chance to get to know your relatives and that your new in-laws have an opportunity to get to know any children you may have from a previous marriage. You cannot force these relationships but you can provide the opportunity for sharing. Again, the first steps may fall to you and your husband: Open your home as well as your heart if you desire a close family. Like any other relationship, these relationships will mature over time. One cannot wave a magic wand and wish a relationship into existence, as many stepmothers try to do and fail. Relationships are not legislated by wedding vows, desire, or demands—they develop over time.

The member of the extended family who often causes the most difficulty is the stepchildren's biological mother. Whether living or dead, involved or absent, her impact on the family will be keenly felt. A stepmother must confront a host of both practical and emotional issues that revolve around her stepchildren's mother. The following chapter tackles those issues.

Chapter 11

THE BIOLOGICAL MOTHER

*I have come to the realization that evil really does exist.
I've met her.*
                    —A frustrated stepmother

Ask a stepmother about her stepchildren's biological mother and prepare to be deluged by rage, resentment, and frustration. Greedy, self-centered, vain, materialistic, spiteful, vengeful, egotistic, hedonistic, perverted, insane, ghoulish, and "controlling my life from the grave" are some of their descriptors.

The bad feeling that exists between stepmothers and biological mothers springs from both practical and emotional issues, all of which can be handled by a change in perspective.

The stepmothers I spoke with were unprepared for the impact their stepchildren's mothers would have on their lives. Somehow, they seem to have expected those women—now dead or divorced—to stay in the past. But the biological mother kept reappearing, even though she sometimes did so as a ghost.

Biological mothers linger in the background of new stepmothers' lives. Their presence, either actual or in memory, poses a threat to the new marriages—a threat that surprised most of the women I spoke with. They simply had not anticipated how difficult it would be to incorporate another woman, living or dead, into their marriage and family life. Nor had they anticipated their new husbands' reluctance to discuss the difficulty of coping with the problem.

The Noncustodial Mother

Many stepmothers married to divorced fathers sought to keep their lives in the present, disassociating themselves from their stepchildren's absentee mother. Such stepmothers seemed to be pretending to naiveté, accepting the most casual explanations for why stepchildren lived with their fathers rather than their mothers. Courts are still very conservative, and custody still overwhelmingly favors biological mothers. Hence fathers with custody more often than not signal a biological mother with "problems" or a "problem" child. The complexities of these situations make it almost impossible for stepmothers to have any sort of meaningful dialogue with their stepchildren's biological mothers.

Many stepmothers reported feeling like nothing more than glorified baby-sitters. "Motherhood" is theoretically a privilege and a responsibility, yet many stepmothers felt that this role had been split, with the biological mother claiming all the privileges and leaving all the responsibility.

Stepmothers can realistically expect to feel aggravated, frustrated, jealous, and angry with their stepchildren's biological mothers at some time during their marriages. However, having said this, let's also assert that stepmothers *can cope* with these confusing emotions. Once the emotionalism has been explored and removed, stepmothers supported by their husbands can deal effectively with the issues presented by their stepchildren's biological mothers.

What to Expect

Changing Circumstances

"Oh, my stepchildren haven't seen their 'mother' for *years!*" This common quote is rued by scores of stepmothers who discover later that circumstances can and do change. Even biological mothers who have left "forever" sometimes return.

Your Stepchildren's Relationship With Their Mother

Most stepmothers misgauged the level of closeness between their stepchildren and their biological mothers.

Some stepmothers anticipated a high degree of involvement by the biological mother, which would leave large chunks of free time for the stepmother, her "own" children and her husband; often they found that this did not happen.

Other stepmothers anticipated a low level of involvement, which would permit the stepmother to have uninfringed authority and "significance" in her stepchildren's lives. This, too, was often not the case.

Mothers without custody generally maintain little *direct* contact; therefore, the stepmother is usually responsible for unrelieved childcare. Many stepmothers found that they were responsible for the care of their stepchildren *all the time,* while their own children frequently visited their fathers—periods which had previously freed them from childcare.

Even when there is little direct contact, stepmothers quickly discover that a child's biological mother is a vivid presence in a child's life, even if that mother left home right after the child's birth and has not reappeared since! The *concept* of "mother" lives within each child and the desire to know and resolve this relationship is a driving need for many children. Stepchildren who have not seen their biological mothers in many years demonstrate some of the same behavior patterns as adopted children, yearning to "find" their biological mothers and resolve their personal histories.

You Can't Escape

It's uncomfortable to have someone in your life whom you may never have seen and may not like when you finally meet. As a stepmother you must learn to incorporate the existence of your stepchildren's biological mother into your life. It won't do simply to ignore her existence. Denial never works, and it can only serve to inflate the intrusive quality of the biological mother when she does appear. Stepmothers often resent being forced by their husbands or stepchildren, either directly or indirectly, into contact with women they would not otherwise choose to have in their lives. But in order to keep your sanity, you will have to adjust.

Facing Difficult Issues

Stepmothers and stepfamilies want to be normal more than anything else. The very fact that children are living with their fathers suggests something abnormal to many people. It is still widely expected that in the event of divorce children will remain with their mothers. Biological mothers generally seek, and are awarded, custody of children except in extraordinary circumstances. Although many fathers are becoming nurturing, primary parents, most mothers who live apart from their children do so because of unusual circumstances including physical or mental illness, substance abuse, or abandonment.

A stepmother may find that she is forced to learn about, to confront, to cope with, and to explain uncomfortable life issues: alcoholism, abandonment, drug abuse, neglect, or some other form of aberrant behavior on the part of her stepchildren's mother. Noncustodial mothers are generally painted with an unflattering brush by full-time stepmothers. Their objectivity on the topic of their stepchildren's mothers is questionable, but noncustodial mothers themselves confirm many of these perceptions.

A study undertaken by Patricia Pasckowicz reported the feelings of one hundred women who are noncustodial mothers.* The issues of nurturing ability and desire for full-time mothering were raised by both absentee mothers and stepmothers, surprisingly with many of the same conclusions. Absentee mothers often demonstrated a lack of nurturing ability or desire to play a mothering role. Ms. Pasckowicz reported that the majority of noncustodial mothers in her study had some history of mental illness. Boredom, inadequate finances, a need for self-actualization, and rage were some of the reasons mothers gave to explain their absence from their children's lives. Some mothers were sensitive to their own inability to manage the stress of child-care; these women feared that they might pose a danger to their children if they had to be full-time mothers. In such cases mothers felt that leaving their children was a responsible act of love.

Absentee Mothers (New York: Universe Books, 1982).

Poor Support Systems—or None

Rhonda is an office manager in her early fifties. Ten years ago, she married a widower with three children. Rhonda had four daughters. Shortly after her marriage, She was shocked to discover that her husband expected her to assume all responsibilities for all the children. Like many men of his generation, he genuinely believed that raising children was women's work. This belief system also explained his unwillingness to take any responsibility for his children's poor behavior. Rhonda wilted under the demands of seven children, two different religions, and tremendous interfamily conflict. Her grievances were summarily dismissed by her husband, Frank, who expressed disappointment that she "wasn't the woman he thought she was when they married." Rhonda's frustration is evident. This is how she speaks of her stepchildren's mother: "I wish that she had never died and that I had never met her husband!"

Stepmothers often operate under great stress, without support. Friends and family may be either too uncomfortable or unfamiliar with the stepmother's particular problems to be genuinely helpful. Stepmothers typically do not know any other full-time stepmothers; the necessary network simply isn't there.

Prejudice in Favor of "Mothers"

Stepmothers are often expected (or required by the courts) to relinquish part-time care of their stepchildren to a mother who may be unbalanced, incompetent, or even abusive—a person with whom, if not for the "accident" of birth, they would not permit their stepchildren to have any contact. Stepmothers must balance their distrust of an actual unreliable mother against their own built-in reverence for the sanctity of motherhood as an abstraction. A stepmother may find that even her closest friends or relatives are unsupportive of any criticism she may level at her stepchildren's mother.

Compounding her frustration and jealousy about the general respect the world accords to biological mothers may be her own prejudice in favor of motherhood. Stepmothers' psyches were shaped by the same cultural biases we all share. Many stepmothers spoke of finding themselves in the strange position of feeling uncomfortable about breaking the taboo and speaking out against a biological mother. Sometimes they found themselves actually protecting undesirable, neglectful, even abusive mothers.

Children who have been mistreated by their mothers need their stepmother's help in coming to terms with their ambivalent feelings about their mother. A stepmother can provide a stable home and a listening ear, but for serious issues of abuse (either past or present), she should seek out a qualified objective professional.

A Rock and a Hard Place

It's hard to be in a no-win situation—expected by husbands, family, and friends to act as a "real" mother, yet chastised by these same people criticizing the biological mother. Stepmothers are expected to identify and care for their stepchildren as nothing less than their own, yet at the same time to yield all claims to *real* control to the biological mother. Dealing with this situation will require a heroic measure of tact, forbearance, courage, and—most difficult of all—patience.

The Green Monster

Very few women are brought up knowing how to integrate their husbands' prior mates into their marriages. Stepmothers are often called upon to do exactly that. It is an accepted psychological precept that jealousy blossoms in an environment of insecurity; stepmothers are often notoriously insecure in their relationship with their stepchildren and husbands and therefore especially susceptible to jealousy of the prior intimate connection the stepchildren represent.

Biological mothers also succumb to jealousy of stepmothers. This jealousy seems to spring from a feeling that the stepmother has usurped her place; it often has no connection to the biological mother's past or present feelings for mothering, marriage, or the children's father. Such jealousy often results in an apparent campaign to remove the stepmother from the picture. Jealous mothers may seek to damage the stepmother's marriage, her relationship with her stepchildren, and her self-esteem. Some of her weapons are sharp indeed.

Provocative Behavior

Biological mothers often act in seductive and manipulative ways. Stepmothers report frequent phone calls to speak with their husbands about personal matters, asking for favors, loans, or advice. Frequent reminders of shared personal history—anniversaries and other special events—make stepmothers very uncomfortable. Some women are a bit more blatant, dressing inappropriately in negligees or otherwise seductive outfits when husbands drop off or pick up children.

Bad-Mouthing of Husband

Where some mothers are jealous or critical of the stepmother, others seek to befriend her. Their motives are not always immediately clear. One young stepmother was pleasantly surprised when her teenage stepchildren's mother approached her with an offer of friendship. It took this young woman about six months to realize that her new friend's confidences about her former husband's countless affairs and inadequate sexual performance were anything but friendly.

"Pumping" or Bad-Mouthing to Children

Some biological mothers use their time with their children to "pump" for information about the stepmother's life, her spending habits, her personal idiosyncrasies. This can result in an insecure stepmother's spending lots of unnecessary time making up rules and testing her stepchildren's loyalty. The good news is that the pumping cannot last forever: Even the youngest child will quickly grow bored with snooping. Stepmothers need to learn to act graciously—no matter what. A little imagination helps when you feel as though you're being attacked. If you can imagine that you are a grand "Lady of the Manor" in whose mouth butter wouldn't melt, you will be less likely to be drawn into combat. As a child you were probably advised not to "sink to the level" of taunters, and this advice still serves. Adopting a gracious and cool role will make you feel better about yourself and will set a better example for your stepchildren.

No Brownie Points from "Her"

Most mothers without custody either surrendered it willingly, did not contest their children's desire to change living arrangements, or had their children removed from their care. Despite the circumstances, most stepmothers felt that those mothers never considered them as anything more than temporary caretakers of "their children." This feeling also is probably responsible for much of the rage stepmothers feel. And it's not just their imagination. One of these mothers actually verbalized what the stepmother had assumed she felt all along: "She can raise them, if that makes her happy. They'll come to me when they're grown."

Coping With Inconsistency

Despite the lack of actual participation in her children's lives, the biological mother is often an active "presence," orchestrating her relationship with her children from the wings. The biological mother's level of involvement is also generally sporadic. Only a few of the surveyed stepmothers reported that their stepchildren visited with their mothers on a regular basis. No contact whatsoever was more common. The most typical involvement is a random pattern of telephoning.

Mothers who had been totally absent from their children's lives often reappeared shortly after the stepmother's wedding. Often this increased involvement was short-lived; the pattern that predated the stepmother's appearance tended to resume within time.

When Debbie married and became a stepmother to Theresa, the eight-year-old had not seen or heard from her biological mother in seven years. Her only contact had been the birthday card she received each year. However, within five months of Debbie's marriage, Terry's mother resurfaced, moved back to town, and began exercising her legal prerogative for every-other-weekend visitation. After six months of rather strained visits, one day she failed to show up. She did not reappear for the next six years.

Most cases are not as extreme as Debbie's. Michelle's case is more typical. When Michelle married, Brian and Steven, her two stepsons, had no weekly meetings with their mother, though she lived nearby. Their contact with her was limited to occasional holiday visits and two weeks in the summer. However, when Michelle became a stepmother, the boys' mother sought to replicate the visitation schedule that Michelle's daughters had with their father: If Michelle's daughters saw their father for dinner each week, she wanted to see Brian and Steven for dinner; if Michelle's daughters spent a weekend with their father, she wanted Brian and Steve. After several weeks, dinners began to be canceled. Months would go by when she would see the boys only at an occasional school sporting event. Visitation has now returned to the pattern that predated Michelle's marriage.

Stepmothers struggling to build a relationship are upset by such inconsistency. Changes in patterns of visitation make planning difficult and threaten a stepmother's sense of control within her new family. Women who are struggling to adjust to major changes in lifestyle may find that they have little patience with biological mothers who rearrange visitation for personal convenience, jealousy, or whim.

It's Hard on the Kids

Except in the cases of very young children, stepchildren were often ambivalent, apathetic, or apologetic about their relationship with their mothers. These attitudes can make it difficult for stepmothers and fathers to help them. In addition, stepchildren may sense or imagine that positive feelings for their mothers are unacceptable to the new family. Faced with the choice between rocking the boat in pleasant waters or braving the hostile territory of a rejecting mother, many children retreat. Stepmothers reported that children were frequently apathetic or reluctant to talk about their mothers. Many times children chose to move away from any relationship at all with their mothers, refusing visits and needing to be coaxed to the telephone to receive her calls. Often they threw away or quickly hid letters or cards from their mothers. Trying to avoid trouble or painful emotions is understandable in a child; for the stepmother, it is a danger signal she must recognize—and respond to.

Stepmothers were eloquent in their descriptions of the "push-me-pull-you" tactics of their stepchildren's mothers—and the children themselves.

The Telephone—a Handy Weapon

The telephone was the most-often-reported vehicle of harassment. Many stepmothers spoke of telephone calls—sometimes twenty or thirty a day—that were either unpleasant or were immediate hang-ups. Telephone calls at inconvenient and intrusive hours, in the middle of the night, in early morning hours, and at other times when the intent of the call was obviously to harass rather than communicate were frequently reported. Such harassment cannot be handled in the ways available to the general public. Stepmothers cannot hang up when they hear *her* voice or change to an unlisted phone number; biological mothers are usually entitled by law to have telephone access to their children. Similarly bothersome to stepmothers is the scenario where the mother ignores her existence, hanging up when she hears the stepmother's voice or asking for the children or the husband without even giving her a cursory "Hello."

Susie's stepchildren are both of preschool age. Susie finds herself growing increasingly uncomfortable and resentful as she reads bedtime stories to the children while her husband spends his evenings listening to her stepchildren's mother complain about her poor sex life over the telephone.

In one extreme case reported, the biological mother is actually in prison! She uses her allotted phone calls to harass her children's new stepmother, Linda, speaking directly to Linda about "the children and what they need and what their father doesn't provide for them." It is not difficult to understand why Linda would like to tell this woman to "butt out."

Betty, a teacher in her thirties, is frustrated by attempts to undermine her authority. When she married almost two years ago her husband's two girls, aged nine and seven, joined her two boys, then eight and five. Betty states that initially her relationship with her stepdaughter's mother was "great." The mother had left the family to "find herself" (a la *Kramer vs. Kramer*). Then, suddenly, she seemed to become threatened and began to cause trouble by undermining Betty's authority with the girls through constant phone calls. Although this mother has stated repeatedly that she isn't the mothering type and that the girls *are* better off with Betty, she continues to intrude in Betty's relationship with the girls. Betty speaks for many stepmothers when she says, "Be a mother or let me do it."

AVOIDING THE TRAPS

Sensing their lack of power and control, stepmothers may risk becoming obsessive about their stepchildren's biological mothers if they are not careful. Beware of tactics that don't work:

Denial of Her Existence

Some stepmothers try to cope by ignoring the biological mother's very existence. This only serves to exacerbate the tension when the mother does resurface; denying her existence is untrue and erodes the stepmother's control and credibility. On the practical level it means that each new reappearance necessitates a new readjustment—and that is very wearing.

Bottling Up Feelings

Hiding feelings doesn't work either; the tension is still there even when the reasons for the "vibrations" are hidden. Husbands react negatively to this tension, and stepchildren are especially attuned to the stress that their stepmother feels. Resentment, disapproval, anger, and other negative emotions are hard to disguise and rarely hidden. Meredith thought she was doing a good job putting on a good face until her two teenage stepchildren confided to a family member that their stepmother would have "cleaning fits" whenever their mother telephoned.

Pretending

Many stepmothers feel that they must be civil or even pleasant to a woman for whom they harbor no pleasant feelings. Many feel that they must tolerate or even encourage relationships that are nearly impossible for them to maintain in the face of their strong negative feelings. Such stepmothers often feel isolated, angry, resentful, frustrated, and overwhelmed, and run the risk of suffering extreme stress. It's better to admit that you don't like your stepchildren's mother and limit your efforts to bare-bones politeness.

Nora is a thirty-eight-year-old stepmother. She and her husband have been married for nine-and-a-half years and have raised Nora's son from a previous marriage. During the course of their marriage, arranging visitation with Bill's sons was always a problem. The boys lived in another state, and the logistics of timing and short notice accommodations were always a problem. The visits were problematic, too: Bill's boys were destructive and had a different set of values concerning property and lifestyle than Nora's.

Six months ago one of Bill's sons, who was the same age as Nora's son, decided to live with them. Actual problems have been minimal, but Nora feels tremendous stress because she's been trying to hide her negative feelings toward the woman who brought up her stepson so badly. Her anger is barely contained. "I think she's the poorest example of motherhood, of womanhood, of humanity that I've ever come across. Her existence has caused more chaos, grief, and upset in my marriage than anything else. She has affected my life emotionally, financially, and psychologically. She has created trauma for the children and for my husband.... But I *can't,"* continues Nora, *"ever* speak badly about her in front of the children, although I choke on having to be polite to such a woman."

Nora won't find relief from stress as long as she forbids herself to express her negative feelings. Like Nora, many stepmothers suffer from extreme stress when they try to act in ways that run counter to their deepest convictions and perceptions. Stepmothers almost unilaterally agree that they should try to avoid saying negative things about their stepchildren's mothers. In some cases these attempts border on the ludicrous, such as when Ellen states, "She is a horrible excuse for a human being," then adds quickly, "but I would never express these feelings to my stepchildren." Some stepmothers confronting the challenge of coexisting with the mentally ill or socially deviant mothers of their stepchildren try to avoid discussing unpleasant circumstances—such attempts typify the same type of impossible irony as asking Mrs. Lincoln, "But aside from the assassination, how was the play?"

The Urge to Overprotect

Sheila, an attractive woman in her early forties, has decided to help her two stepdaughters have a happy childhood. She makes up stories and "covers" for her stepdaughters' mother, an alcoholic who is consistent only in her inconsistency. Sheila describes how she tells scores of white lies to protect the girls from disappointment, even pretending to receive phone calls from the girls' mother explaining her inability to arrive for visitations. For the past six years, Sheila's stepdaughters have never had a birthday that their mother remembered, *but they don't know that:* Sheila has sent cards and presents in their mother's name. Sheila's dark eyes flash as she states that "her stepdaughters are going to have the best mother possible. Even if I have to invent her." This scenario scarcely needs comment; such covering up only prevents the girls from developing the skills they will need to cope with their mother as she really is.

No one would suggest that stepmothers give license to their personal resentment or insecurities and lash out at their stepchildren's mothers. On the other hand, it is vital that stepmothers be advocates for their stepchildren. To stand idly by, not saying anything when a mother behaves badly, just because she is the mother, gives unwarranted power to a title and further confuses the child by validating the mother's inappropriate behavior. Somewhere, somehow, a stepmother must strike a balance.

What to Do?

Sometimes, Nothing!

What can you do about inappropriate, provocative, frustrating, or otherwise maddening behavior? Nothing. You cannot change someone else's behavior. You *can* gain a tremendous amount of relief by letting go of the things you can't change and taking charge of what you can: Your own behavior! Don't use your problems with your stepchildren's mother as a convenient "hanger" for anything else that's going wrong in your life or your marriage; being obsessed with someone else's behavior diminishes your individuality and sidesteps important issues, including the issue of how your stepchildren and their mother will build their *own* relationship.

Given the anger and hostility many stepmothers expressed, you'd almost think they wished there were *no*

relationship between their stepchildren and their biological
mothers. Although a few stepmothers did fantasize about a
complete severance of contact, most had very different hopes
in mind: They wanted noncustodial mothers to learn to be
more consistent in their affection; they wished their
stepchildren could receive consistent love and support; they
strongly desired visitation that was constant and dependable.
Stepmothers also hoped those mothers would eventually be
open to receiving regular communication and be competent
enough to answer the tough questions children posed about
their behavior. In a word, stepmothers wanted the mothers
to act responsibly.

Stepmothers wanted the children to have a solid, sane
relationship with their mothers, even when this conflicted
with their own personal emotions and interests. Stepmothers
seek happiness for their stepchildren; and if this happiness
involves contact with their biological mothers, so be it.

Stepmothers have learned, through their commitment to
their stepchildren, that it is possible to love different people
in different ways. There is plenty of love to go around: More
love for the child's mother does *not* mean less love for the
stepmother.

Long ago, Judge Solomon decided that the true mother
was the woman who had the best interests of the baby at
heart—but you are not a judge. You may have the best of
intentions when you decide to foster the mother's
relationship with her children, but you cannot assume
control for someone else's actions. You cannot *give* your
stepchildren a good relationship with their mother. You
can be responsible only for your own relationship with
the children. The success or failure of the mother's
relationship with her child is *her* responsibility.

The bottom line is this: *Do* take charge of your own
behavior, but *don't* try to play God—or judge—toward others.

Take Charge of Your Own Life

Karen, a thirty-five-year-old former bartender, is an
extraordinary example of the damage that passivity can cause.
Karen became a stepmother to *two* sets of stepchildren. She
didn't know that the second set was coming to live with her
new family until two months after her marriage, when her
husband said he "must have forgotten" to tell her. Karen's

four stepchildren, a girl and three boys, range in age from five to thirteen. When she married, the two oldest children were in their father's custody because their mother is mentally ill. The two younger boys arrived unexpectedly because *their* mother "just couldn't handle them" and had a boyfriend who didn't feel like having children around. Karen often feels like a warden to her stepchildren—or a servant. Her stepchildren call her by her first name or refer to her as "the stepmother." There is an almost eerie sense of detachment and resignation running through Karen's responses. She refers to her stepchildren's mothers as "Wife Number 1" and "Wife Number 2," or "The Mothers."

Although Karen has responsibility for all childcare, she is told what she may and may not do by Wife Number 2 and receives no help from her husband who is, in her words, "usually not home." Karen talks to the mentally ill mother every morning on the telephone. Although these calls are time-consuming and often unpleasant, and are of no benefit to the children, Karen seems unwilling to take charge and make changes in the routine.

To make matters worse, Karen's husband has told her that she may not have a baby as "she has enough children already." He recently gave away her dog because one of the children didn't like it. He gave away her parakeet because he didn't like its chirping. Karen was sad, but she said nothing.

Karen is an example of the extremes that passivity can lead to. If a stepmother is to be happy and successful in her role, she must take charge of her own life.

Don't "Take Over" for Your Husband

Stepmothers need not agree to perform their husband's unpleasant tasks. Many stepmothers reported that, despite their own personal feelings, the task of communicating with the children's mother often fell to them, either because they were simply more available or because the mother and father did not want to communicate. Whatever the reason, acting as a liaison with the biological mother is usually uncomfortable and stressful for a stepmother.

One woman stated, "My husband doesn't feel it is necessary or appropriate to talk to her." This husband probably speaks for many men who assume they are demonstrating their commitment to their new marriages by totally alienating their children's mothers. This may be a well-intentioned gesture. However, we all know what road is paved with good intentions. The stepmother who is forced to serve as a go-between for her stepchildren and their mother can also expect to build a tremendous amount of resentment.

Another stepmother spoke of being required to drive her children to meet their mother in a town two hundred miles from her home because her husband refused to even "look at the woman" and the mother didn't "feel like seeing anybody in the old neighborhood." The children would look forward to their "sleepovers" and Toni could not stand to see them disappointed by their battling parents. Toni felt that she really was in a no-win situation. If she didn't "volunteer" to drive the children to their visit, she would have to tell them they couldn't go; yet the stress involved in these trips was eventually too much to handle.

Toni was given explicit instructions by the children's mother, who didn't want to have to "look at her face"; she was told exactly where to park and precisely what time to arrive at the meeting place which was changed each weekend. Instructions were delivered early in the week and revised and repeated during subsequent telephone conversations until the weekend arrived. Toni spent weekend after weekend hovering in parking lots, waiting with her two young stepchildren for the sight of the mother's silver sports car. When they spotted the car, the children would leap out and run to meet their mother before she would have to look at their stepmother; the children, at ages five and seven, thought this was all great fun. Toni drove the two hundred miles home alone, only to return the next evening to repeat the process in reverse, welcoming two invariably red-eyed and silent children. One day, on the lonely return trip, Toni broke her grueling routine and did not go straight home. Instead she spent the day walking along the shore—and thinking. By the end of the day she had made a critical decision: she would not assume total responsibility for those trips. She and her husband entered counseling and began to deal with the visitation in a way that did not threaten their marriage and Toni's self-esteem.

Stop Competing for the "Mother" Title

Some stepmothers are engaged in a never-ending battle; they resent the unconditional love granted the biological mother regardless of her actions or attitudes. Let it go! You're the one who's on the job each day. Take charge of your relationship with your stepchildren—concentrate on that.

Accept Unequal Financial Responsibility

Sometimes stepmothers must tighten their belts because of the large alimony payments their husbands make. Often they resent the fact that a husband is required to pay child support for children who live with the biological mother, whereas the mother has no financial responsibility for her children who live with their father and stepmother.

The inequality of financial responsibility goes hand-in-hand with the imbalance of responsibility for childcare. Stepmothers are often frustrated by the courts' failure to review the noncustodial mother's ability to pay for her children. Although the law provides for both parents to assume financial responsibility for children, it is rare for a noncustodial mother to make any sort of financial contribution.

Unless the stepmother wants to "fight the system," she must accept the unpleasant fact that such issues are outside her control, step away from the problem, and concentrate on enhancing her own role within the family.

Focus on the Present

What is happening *now?* Certainly no one is suggesting that you try to wipe out the past, but dealing with the present is more productive, though sometimes more difficult. You may be tempted to succumb to the soap opera of your husband's past life, but it's far healthier to continue asking yourself, "What does this have to do with life *now?*" Remember: You are more likely to be able to keep the past in perspective than he is. One of the reasons men marry again is for a new start. Unless past behavior directly affects what you're doing now, help your husband to "retire" his past and to live more happily in his new present—with you.

Callie was thirty when she became a stepmother to three preteen children. A school psychologist by profession, she was certain that she could successfully integrate her three stepchildren into her life and that she, her husband, and the new baby who arrived a year later could form a new family. Callie was unprepared to learn that her stepchildren had been sexually abused by their mother throughout their childhoods. Callie was protective and supportive of her stepchildren's disclosures to her; she welcomed their trust and set about getting therapy for them. Callie found that her condemnation of the mother's behavior raised uncomfortable questions about her husband's role. Why, she wondered, had her husband failed to recognize the signs? Why didn't her stepchildren tell their father at the time?

Callie began to live in her husband's past. As she became more familiar with the specifics of the children's abuse and their fears, she questioned her husband's lack of intervention. Although he owned up to his responsibility and apologized to the children privately and in family therapy, Callie's respect for him was seriously threatened. Her obsession with his past began to erode her marriage and spill over into her relationship with her stepchildren. Callie grew increasingly unable to deal with present situations and to accept that her husband had changed from his former role of absentee father. Although he was now eager and able to be a much better parent, her obsession with his behavior almost destroyed a perfectly functional marriage and stepfamily. Callie, and all other stepmothers, must learn to "let go of the past."

Set Your Own Limits

Stepmothers *can* control the way they will be treated by others, biological mothers included. There is no excuse for wimpiness. To be respected by others, you must be self-respecting. One needs only to remember Toni and Karen, and other stepmothers like them who subjected themselves to humiliating dictates by unreasonable women who were probably only testing the waters. Take charge of your own behavior and set limits on the kinds of behavior you will—and will not—accept from others.

So You've Married a Widower

Stepmothers whose husbands are widowers must deal with a completely different set of concerns. First they feel a confused mixture of emotions in reference to their departed predecessor, secretly perceiving her as an unassailable competitor. Often, stepmothers are plagued by guilt and discomfort or shamed by their inexplicable feelings of resentment and jealousy for a woman who is no longer alive. Because of social or religious taboos, stepmothers often feel uncomfortable about voicing their negative feelings.

The death of a mother does not end her relationship with her children. The stepmother must confront the "presence" of the biological mother every day as she deals with the children. She must, in addition, deal with her own feelings about mortality and ritual as they relate to her new marriage, and she must confront the challenge of helping her stepchildren—and perhaps her husband— through any unfinished grieving or unresolved issues.

Any stepmother can feel a bit shaky. Stepmothers who have married widowers live in a climate ripe for insecurity. When a woman marries a divorced man she can calm her insecurity with the very real knowledge that her husband chose her, no matter who initiated his former separation. Marrying a widower is different; stepmothers are often plagued by the nagging and unanswerable question, "Would he have ever married me?" The practical answer to this question is probably no. A stepmother usually follows a marriage that was viable. If her husband's marriage was a happy one, she may need to accept his reminiscing without feeling threatened. The stepmother must not plague herself with questions about what would have happened if "she" had not died and try to live in the present and look forward to the future.

What to Expect

A certain natural idealization takes place when a loved one dies. Stepchildren, husband and many of the people who now inhabit the stepmother's world may idealize the biological mother.

Living With a Saint

Many stepmothers in this situation believed that they would have had an easier time if their stepchildren's mother were still living. Stepmothers described time and time again how difficult it was to live with the notion of a departed "saint."

Miriam, a twenty-nine-year-old federal security guard, has been a stepmother for almost three years. Her stepson and stepdaughter are now fifteen and nineteen; their mother died six years ago. Living in the shadow of a "deceased mother" is a discomfort for Miriam, a deeply religious woman. The stepdaughter is away at college but her behavior during vacations causes Miriam to dread her visits. The moment the girl arrives home she inspects the house for any "changes." If something has been moved, she flies into a rage, reminding Miriam that her mother "worked hard to buy a house and nice things for her kids." Miriam understands that her stepdaughter misses her mother and is having a hard time adjusting to her father's marriage, but she resents the tension her stepdaughter brings home with her. Miriam's husband is a mild-mannered man who tells her just to go ahead and do what she wants with the house. But when the shouting starts, he disappears.

Miriam illustrates the plight of many stepmothers who try to respect their stepchildren's fond memories without going underground themselves. Despite her best intentions, she is still hurt and frustrated by her stepdaughter's unrelenting disapproval. She lives like a shadow in the house of her predecessor, working to contribute to the mortgage payments, fearful of changing so much as the faded bathroom wallpaper. Her resentment grows.

What Miriam hasn't realized yet is that this is her problem. Her stepdaughter is getting on with her life; she is doing well in college and plans to move to her own apartment when she graduates. Miriam's guilt and discomfort get in her way.

Houses are a big issue for this group of stepmothers. Houses are repositories of memories and commitments and physical reminders of the departed mother. Stepmothers are sensitive to the nostalgia of their stepchildren and their very real pain. However, there is a middle ground between enshrining and trashing.

Stepmothers can help their stepchildren focus on keepsake items that are portable and movable.

Stepchildren need to believe that their mother's memory is not being erased. Children who have lost their mothers are typically very resistant to change. You can help your stepchildren and yourself come to terms with the past by striking a balance between retaining the memories and moving forward.

Look for the Signs—and Read Them

Your appearance as a mother figure can trigger all sorts of discomfort and unfinished business in your stepchildren. Children may have been too young at the time of death to understand the full implications. Those who were ten or older at the time of their mother's death may have failed to grieve as well. Older children frequently are not given an opportunity to grieve when their mothers die. They typically assume a "responsible" role for their father and other family members. Many lose their "childhoods" with the death of their mother, as they assume adult responsibilities. It is not uncommon for children, especially girls, to undertake the care of the home and younger children. Such a child may resent the appearance of a stepmother and the loss of her own adult role in the family. The wise stepmother can give the child one of life's greatest gifts: his or her stolen childhood.

What to Do?

Build a Present History

When a stepmother can share her own history, she becomes more comfortable about accepting her husband's and stepchildren's history. The deceased mother does not have to be made either a villain or a saint.

When a stepmother can make the deceased mother part of her own history by learning about her, by listening when others speak of her, she will feel more in control and more secure in her relationship with her new family.

When You Can't Confront "Her"...

The biggest problem facing the stepmother is the societal taboo against speaking negatively of the dead. Stepmothers will probably find a friendlier ear and an easier conscience if they speak about their own feelings and reactions. A stepmother who has just been told by her mother-in-law that "Lois always baked the loveliest cookies for Thanksgiving" might confide that being compared to Lois hurts her. Such a stepmother might find, to her surprise, that the mother-in-law had not intended to make a comparison. Because stepmothers are afraid to speak out, they often find themselves living in someone else's past instead of their own present.

Help Your Stepchildren Deal With Their Grief

You cannot erase the past, but you *can* modify it. You can be of enormous help to stepchildren who have had to deal with death at an early age. These children have suffered an unparalleled trauma. The person with whom they shared the closest of human bonds, and in whom they probably placed the bulk of their trust, suddenly and irrevocably vanished from their lives.

Many children harbor unresolved feelings of grief for their mothers. Older children may have been too "busy" and responsible to grieve; younger ones may never have been given the opportunity to talk about their mother and to grieve for her. Relatives and well-meaning friends are often uncomfortable with children's pain and try to shield them from sadness. Sometimes they mistakenly assume— or hope—that the children are "too young to be affected." Your younger stepchildren may have been told a bunch of euphemisms: Their mother "went to sleep" or "went to live with God" or "went away on a long trip." Most young children are not taken to funerals or urged to partake in any of the traditional rituals that attend death in our culture—rituals that were designed, in part, to help us cope with the death of a loved one. You will inherit the results of this lack of grieving. Simply put, your presence confirms the fact that "Mother is *never* coming home."

Assume Responsibility Gradually

Some stepmothers seem to have an easy time of it—at least at first. They must be careful to not find themselves imprisoned in the good intentions of their stepchildren. Charlotte was such a stepmother. At age fifty-two she married a man with teenage daughters. After months of visiting the girls and her fiancé at his home, she was certain that their relationship would be smooth and problem-free. However, Charlotte soon discovered that she was treated as a visitor after her marriage as well as before. Her stepdaughters did not permit her to assume any responsibility in the home. They did not want her to cook or arrange furniture, and they even whisked away and arranged the flowers her husband occasionally brought to her. Any suggestions Charlotte made about redecorating, meal-planning, or vacation were greeted by polite silence. It quickly became clear to her that she had moved into a shrine her stepdaughters created and maintained. If she had not taken matters firmly into her hands, she might still be living in her "gilded cage."

Encourage Conversation

A stepmother can help make her husband and children of all ages comfortable by including conversation about the deceased mother as part of everyday talk. Encourage your stepchildren to share their memories and their history. You can help them overcome the feeling that their mother's life is being "erased" by encouraging them to cherish personal keepsakes. Furniture that the stepchild outgrows can be stored away, but only when the child is ready to part with it. Sometimes a stepmother can help by weaning an attachment for large household items to smaller personal items— for example, from a dining room set to "Mother's candlesticks."

Share the Memories

Stepmothers can take their children to the grave site, suggest they write a story about their mother, take them to church to light a candle or to synagogue to say a memorial prayer, or help them to go through any other rituals that allow them to experience the grieving process they may have skipped.

Doreen has a close and loving relationship with her four stepchildren. She has been a stepmother for the past eight years and appreciates the gratifying results of her stepchildren's loving childhood. Doreen would love to meet the woman who gave birth to these wonderful children. As the years go on, she often wishes that she could have known her stepchildren's mother. Doreen has found a way to integrate the memory of this woman into her own life as a sort of "guardian angel."

Living with the memory of the children's mother is much more practical than spending time and energy pretending she didn't ever exist.

Do Not Compete

Obviously it is impossible to compete with someone who is no longer living, but many stepmothers try to do just that. Try to avoid any attempt to replace or replicate a departed mother. There is no sense in competing. Children can, and do, come to love their stepmothers deeply and with real and deserved affection. Spoiling this genuine feeling by competing with an idealized mother can only bring disappointment and frustration for everyone.

Attempting to build a new family is a challenging endeavor. The following chapter addresses the ways that a new baby changes the stepfamily: ways that may be surprising!

Chapter 12

THE NEW BABY

What does a stressed-out, overworked, and in many cases overwhelmed woman need? A baby!

Many stepmothers described a powerful desire to add a baby to their family. Why? Some had never had a child before; of course they wanted one now! Some couples desired a "nuclear" family experience: "his-mine-and-ours." Others felt that a baby would cement or legitimize the new family, as if the marriage would not be taken seriously until the new couple had produced a child of their own.

The Need to Be Called "Mommy"

Some stepmothers simply felt the pull of biology, despite their previous negative feelings about childbearing. It's hard to comprehend the part that day-to-day childcare plays in such a decision. Stepmothers who have borne children often approach motherhood in a sort of backwards fashion: Expected to assume responsibility for nurturing and rearing their stepchildren, they begin to operate competently but with a marked feeling of "Is this all there is?" Those who enthusiastically jumped into child-rearing find that they handled the responsibility well but now yearn for the reciprocal love and affection that is missing from their relationships with their stepchildren. Stepmothers who feel satisfied and fulfilled in their relationship with their stepchildren may be eager to undertake child-rearing from the beginning, with an infant. And many childless stepmothers simply want a baby because they've never had one. They had decided to marry with the strong intention of having a baby, they see their stepchildren as "incidental," and they are at great risk for feeling put-upon and resentful by the reality of *living* with children.

Husbands—Sometimes Not So Sure

Some husbands seem absolutely delighted to begin the fathering experience again. Many are more financially secure than when their older children were born and have more time to spend with their babies. Others are less enthusiastic having looked forward to a romantic marriage that would grow in intimacy as their older children left home. Still others are reluctant to experience the stresses of fathering again or fear creating stress for their existing children.

The simple, commonsense approach for any woman contemplating marriage is to discuss the possibility of children before marriage. If having babies is important to her, she should say so before she walks down the aisle. She should not assume that a man with children will want to have more. On the other hand, a woman who does not want children should also speak out. She cannot simply assume that a man does not want a child with her. The prospect of adding children to a family is too important to be left unexplored.

A Child Of "Our Own"

For a stepmother who has been married previously and has borne children, a new and happy marriage may suggest a different brand of parenting. Involved in a committed relationship, she may feel a need to create a child that will belong only to her and her new husband. Couples with children from former marriages must share their children with others—the noncustodial parents. A new baby offers another chance—a chance to nurture a child within the confines of the couple relationship only, without the complexities of visitation and extended family relationships that have been severed by divorce. A husband is nearly as likely to feel this pull toward parenthood as is a wife.

A Baby "Cements" a Family

Some stepmothers spoke of the need for a child as if the new baby would "cement" and unify the family mixture. A baby would create a biological tie between stepchildren, stepparents, and stepsiblings, thereby creating a real connection among the family members. Many stepmothers also spoke of giving the family a feeling of legitimacy.

Virtually all stepmothers who had had a new baby reported that a baby did, indeed, give the family a feeling of togetherness and cohesiveness that had been lacking. More importantly, it fulfilled the stepmother's need to love openly. After a period of perhaps strained or conflicted feelings toward stepchildren, these women welcomed the luxury of being able to love unconditionally.

Stepmothers frequently mentioned the need to have a baby of their own, to be called "Mommy," to be accepted by a tiny, nonjudgmental human being who did not have to be shared with any other mother figure.

At twenty-eight, Judy married for the first time and became a stepmother to her husband's two preteen children. Within two years she and her husband decided to add a baby to their family. Judy seemed to speak for many stepmothers when she said, "I needed so badly to love *freely*. *I* was a wounded and rejected stepmother and I felt the new baby would pull us all together as a real family. I think that has happened to some extent."

Connie had raised her stepdaughter for six years before she had a powerful desire to become a "real" mother. Connie stated that "I think now I wanted to be 'legal.'" She was surprised to discover that her feelings for her infant son did not surpass the intense feeling she had for her eight-year-old stepdaughter. Connie said that she "often felt guilty that I didn't love him more than I loved my stepdaughter." She was surprised that her feelings for her infant son were not immediate; she needed to get to know him first.

Anticipating the Response

From Your Stepchildren

"When the baby came home from the hospital, Timmy wanted to pick her up right away to soothe her. I felt very good about that. Later, he'd get mad when he was asked to feed her when I was busy. I was disappointed."

"John loves having a baby brother, although sometimes he cries too much. I explain that babies need to cry. John's most negative reaction was disappointment that he couldn't do more with the baby. We helped him find more ways he could help."

"Jenny spends time with the baby and loves her very

much. Her teacher told me that Jenny acted as if the baby were hers. Jenny calls him 'my' baby."

From Your Husband

The big news is really no surprise: Fathers who were generally uninvolved with their first set of children continued to be uninvolved with the new baby. This was a source of great disappointment for women who felt that their husbands would be very different with a child from the new marriage—a child of their "own." These stepmothers seemed to have forgotten that their stepchildren *are* their husband's "own" children. Although there were several cases where fathers became much more involved with later additions than with their older children, this was the exception rather than the rule. Very few leopards change their spots.

From Yourself

Stepmothers found that they were more relaxed with their stepchildren after the arrival of the new baby. This probably has less to do with anything mystical or psychological than with the simple fact that there is less time for "harping," as one stepmother put it. "Comfortable, relaxed, less strict, easy, casual." These words were often repeated when stepmothers relayed what had changed in their families after the arrival of the new baby. There seemed to be a general release in tension, perhaps because the birth of a baby signaled the end of the period of trying so hard to prove they were "mothers." Now, they *really* were.

Increased Confidence

Stepmothers also looked forward to and realized a sense of closeness with their babies that had been missing from their relationships with their stepchildren. Miranda, a stepmother with a new baby girl, expressed this sense of confidence. Even though her baby was just an infant, Miranda felt truly comfortable with her. Miranda verbalized a hidden suspicion of many stepmothers: She would feel more comfortable with her own child because, as she put it, "She has no choice but to stay with me."

Increased Sense of Power

Many stepmothers seemed to relax with the feeling that they would be accorded unconditional rights to raise their new babies as they saw fit. So many stepmothers mentioned the word "rights" when referring to their new babies that this need to raise a child without outside intrusion seems to be more than speculative.

Less Controlling

The advent of a baby encouraged the other children in the family to assume a more independent role. As Hillary stated, "When the new baby came I was so busy that I didn't have time to constantly remind my teenage stepson to "take a jacket" or to "take out the garbage." Because the baby demanded so much of her time, the other children were expected to do more for themselves. This expectation seemed actually to lead to increased independence.

Bonding As a Family

Many, many stepmothers decided to have a baby with the idea that the baby would make everybody "feel like a family." And did that happen? The answer is YES! Stepmothers reported feeling "more secure," "more normal," even, as one stepmother stated, "more real."

Julie strongly felt that baby Iris had created a "blood tie" among members of the family that had not existed before her birth. "It's made the kids feel more a part of each other by sharing a blood tie in Iris. They can feel a little bit of each other in her. They are *all* brothers and sisters when Iris is discussed."

Women desired to have their "own" babies in an effort to meet strong emotional, psychological, and biological drives. These new babies at first seemed to carry a heavy load, to function as "glue" bonding together pieces of a family that didn't always fit. At first glance this may seem too tall an order for a baby, but these new family babies seemed to meet this demand. Their arrival often relaxed household tensions and supplied a focus that everyone could share and enjoy.

Chapter 13

SPECIAL OCCASIONS

Holidays, birthdays, anniversaries, and other special occasions are times when people share happiness in a traditional manner. For many people the thought of such special days prompts visions of happy family faces smiling from the pages of photograph albums or flickering on a movie screen or a home videocassette. We are a culture of occasion-celebrators. Brightly wrapped gifts and crinkly paper, flowers and candy on Mother's and Valentine's days. Holidays, birthdays, anniversaries, and personal events permit all of us to give in to our penchant for celebration. The dream of the happy family celebrating together is perhaps one of the most closely guarded "national treasures."

Stepmothers share this dream, too. Stepmothers revel in the Mother's Day bouquet, the lacy Valentine, the happy family around the laden holiday table. But alas, many stepmothers are disappointed and unhappy around holiday times, finding that what should be happy occasions are instead tests of their personal worthiness and collective validity as families. They find that traditions are largely defined by families and that differences in the "way things are done" can cause unnecessary complications. Special days, including stepmothers' birthdays, anniversaries, holidays, and Mother's Day can be joyful events for stepmothers. But it takes some doing.

The handling of birthdays, anniversaries, achievement celebrations, and holidays is simply a matter of limit-setting and taking charge. Stepmothers have to be sure of themselves and their right to happiness; stepchildren need to be made aware of expectations and should be protected from impossible decision-making. Unacceptable behavior must not be tolerated. A hostile, sullen stepchild can ruin a celebration or a vacation. Set the limits, work as a team with your husband, and stick to your guns.

The stepmother who creates traditions will orchestrate the mood of those celebrations. She must always set the "tone" of the day. Stepmothers who define limits, avoid competition, and create their own traditions will avoid senseless wrangling and unnecessary tension and unhappiness.

What is a family if not a group of people with shared traditions? Traditions and celebrations weave together through time to create a unique family pattern. Stepmothers who accept the importance of traditions not only feel more in control of their lives but are happier for this sharing of life's special events.

Getting Started

Plan Ahead

The easiest way to avoid disappointment is by verbalizing your expectations before the event. Stepchildren have no psychic powers. If, for example, a stepmother would enjoy a "day off" on her birthday, she should announce, "Today is my birthday and I'm taking a day off" rather than to grumble through a day of chores. Many stepchildren need reminding of birthdays and other special days. If your husband is not particularly diligent about reminding the children of special days, make a calendar with everyone's birthday or put a note on the refrigerator or bulletin board a few days before the event. It will save everyone a lot of unnecessary grief.

By the Same Rules

In order for the stepmother and her stepchildren to form a "family" relationship, they have to play by the same rules. Stepchildren who know what is expected usually will feel safe and be cooperative. The stepmother must always remember that she is the adult in this relationship, and adults are straightforward about what they want; they don't play games or expect miracles.

Lisa *did* expect miracles. She kept silent about her birthday and let an entire weekend pass without saying a word. Her husband and stepchildren went about their business, oblivious to her pain. As a result, Lisa lost the opportunity to celebrate her first birthday with her new family. Her stepchildren had no way of knowing that this was her day, and her husband simply forgot. How much better for everyone if Lisa had announced, at some earlier point in the week, that she was having a birthday and wanted to celebrate it!

Creating New Traditions

In order to avoid disappointment and to keep holiday occasions happy, make them special. Stepmothers need to create family and personal traditions that are different from those celebrated by their stepchildren in the past. Creating new traditions that do not conflict with old ones serves three important purposes:

- The stepmother assumes control of the occasion;
- The stepchild does not feel that loyalties are being tested;
- The stepfamily gains another shared experience.

Accommodating the Noncustodial Mother

When the children's mother is living nearby and visiting regularly, holidays may be particularly stressful. For her own happiness and the success of her relationship, the stepmother should try to avoid making the children decide between families. Any stepmother who has ever tried to decide between celebrating with the in-laws or with her own family will empathize with this dilemma—a dilemma that is intensified for children. Try to avoid shifting the child around from holiday to holiday. This will only give everyone the feeling of celebrating on alternate years. You and your new family can celebrate each holiday without tearing the child apart. Having a Thanksgiving feast on Friday instead of Thursday does not diminish the importance of the holiday. Some stepmothers suggested specific techniques. If the stepchild has other commitments for Thanksgiving dinner, the stepmother might establish her own Thanksgiving dinner at an earlier or later day— and perhaps serve a goose instead of a turkey.

Celebrating Traditional and Other Holidays

Birthdays

Birthdays seem to be a particularly sensitive issue for stepmothers. For a stepmother who may feel shaky in her relationship with her stepchildren, a forgotten or disappointing birthday may rock self-confidence and be perceived as an outright attack. If you've always enjoyed birthday celebrations, these traditions must be explained to your stepchildren—and to your new husband. You should also think about starting *new* traditions with your stepchildren. Special dinners, treats, trips, presents, or rituals are fun for children of all ages. Any new way of celebrating can be introduced as just that: something new. Children may feel uncomfortable at first about a new way of celebrating, so take care that no one feels that the old way is being devalued.

The Anniversary

The stepmother and father's anniversary is another area that may be particularly sensitive. She may perceive her stepchildren's response to the wedding anniversary as a statement of their feelings about the marriage and the family. The wedding anniversary in stepfamilies does indeed assume a different connotation than it does in biological families. The anniversary commonly marks the family beginning rather than honoring the couple's own relationship. Again, in order to avoid disappointment, set up expectations early— and keep plans simple. The anniversary is an opportunity for a couple to reaffirm their feelings for each other and to do something alone. For stepparents who have fallen into the pattern of doing everything as a family, this is one day that they may guiltlessly celebrate as a couple.

Mother's Day

Mother's Day is a real bugaboo for most stepmothers. It is perceived as the day on which they receive—or do *not* receive—recognition for "mothering" their stepchildren. Even the most levelheaded stepmother may find herself swept away when a grade-schooler hands her a handmade Mother's Day card. A bouquet of flowers from a teenage stepson will melt the coolest stepmother's heart. Consciously or not, many stepmothers set up Mother's Day as the day they receive a "grade" for this job.

When stepchildren have a living mother, the holiday is more complicated: Mother's Day highlights the duality of a stepmother's role. Many stepmothers resent that they act as a mother all year, perhaps even being called "Mother" or "Mom," then must relinquish their stepchildren for the day. The more distanced the relationship between stepchildren and biological mothers, the greater the stepmothers' resentment.

A stepmother of two little girls, Sandra positively glows when she describes the "cards, kisses, hugs, and handmade gifts" she receives from her stepdaughters. However, her face quickly falls when she adds, "But when they have to— as part of the visitation agreement—go off with their mom, it hurts so much."

Of course it hurts. For a woman who has played "Mother" for 364 days of the year, it simply doesn't seem fair to release children on the day set aside to celebrate such dedication. And yet in some bizarre form of "fair play," the stepmothers themselves are often most reluctant to challenge the Mother's Day rights of the biological mother. They bend over backwards, almost literally stepping into the background so that the stepchildren can have their day with Mother. One solution is to celebrate either before or after the actual holiday, establish your own tradition.

Stepmothers must also find the strength to overrule unreasonable dictates of the biological mother that affect her relationship with her stepchildren. Mary's nine-year-old stepdaughter is afraid to commemorate Mother's Day with her stepmother because she claims "her mother would kill her." The mother in this case abandoned her child at eighteen months. The girl's mother stayed out of contact until the child was seven, then began phoning infrequently and had visited with the child two or three times.

This mother is clearly placing her child in an unfair position—yet despite the inherent unfairness the child is still painfully torn. What can a stepmother do to help the child deal with the situation? You can remove yourself from the role of co-conspirator by refusing to honor demands that result in discomfort for both you and your stepchild and by helping your stepchild understand that the responsibility for facilitating a relationship lies with the people *involved* in the relationship. A smart stepmother will respond to fears that "my mother will kill me if..." by suggesting that the mother communicate directly with the child's father. Children need to be taken out of the middle of such unpleasant demands. Mary could tell her stepdaughter, "I'm sorry your mother is upset that you will celebrate Mother's Day with us. Maybe she'll call me some time and talk to me about this." After a response such as this, the planning and enjoyment of the holiday can continue.

Preserving the Holiday Spirit

Whereas birthdays and Mother's Day highlight the individual stepmother, and anniversaries are special to the couple, other holidays incorporate the extended families and can cause tremendous discomfort. In a more perfect world, everyone would compromise. In our inperfect world, people must make choices.

Disappointment, hurt, anguish, anger—these are just some of the feelings stepmothers experience on days that are supposed to be happy occasions. Let's not kid ourselves: Stepchildren harbor a great deal of anger, and special occasions are ideal times to ventilate their negative feelings in front of an audience. Many stepchildren and their parents feel pulled in all directions around holidays and special occasions—occasions when their feelings of divided loyalty are most severely tested. If the children's biological mother is living, "where" the holiday is celebrated may be an issue, as well as "how." If she is deceased, memories of past holidays may cloud present attempts at celebration. Past traditions tend to assume a sacred quality, and the stepmother's efforts to add her own style may be rejected out of hand. Discussing your stepchildren's fears may relax them enough to accept a different way of celebrating. Assuring children that new traditions do not erase past memories may be a big help.

Many stepmothers spoke of the heartache of Christmas. Several stated that they had simply instituted different gift-giving traditions. For example, if stepchildren will be visiting their mother on Christmas Day, then the big stepfamily gift-giving ceremony could take place on Christmas Eve. For stepmothers who are fed up with bickering, tears, and resentment around Christmas, gift-giving occasions may be borrowed from other countries.

Stepmothers who chose to delay their gift-exchanging until Three Kings Day, the Feast of Epiphany, were pleased with their solution. Because Three Kings Day falls nearly a week after New Year's, the stepmother and her family will be able to enjoy an "exclusive" celebration.

Other stepmothers celebrate Chanukah by selecting one day as their special day for gift-exchanging and a festive dinner and candlelighting in the evening. Because this Feast of Lights spans an eight-day period, stepmothers can usually reserve one day for their family's special celebration.

The Feast of the Passover typically involves two large holiday dinners at the beginning and end of an eight-day period. Although the first seder (dinner) is accorded primacy over the second, it is again more beneficial for the stepmother and her family to modify a tradition than to haggle over winning the children for the first seder.

In addition to the "big-name" holidays, additional ones of religious, national, and personal significance can be elevated in the stepfamily—Valentine's Day, Memorial Day, Halloween, "Moving-in Day," even Labor Day.

Graduations—Confirmations—Weddings—Special Days

Most stepmothers can come up with a list of very rational reasons why their stepchildren's mothers or maternal relatives don't "deserve" to attend special events in their stepchildren's lives. However, such reasons are irrelevant. The stepmother need ask herself only one question when confronted with such occasions: Who is the *center* of the event? If the answer is herself or her husband, then obviously the children's mother can be excluded. If the answer is the stepchild, then the best interests of the child must be primary. Who is graduating? Who is getting married, or receiving the honor, or rushing to the finish line, or making the speech? The stepchild is the focus of his own special event. The committed stepmother is sensitive to her stepchild's wishes and puts aside petty jealousies. She is able to see how this event fits into the larger picture of her stepchild's life. She does not fall into the trap of perceiving such events as public validations of her role.

Stepmothers should not be excluded from events, but they should be gracious and loving enough to think about expanding traditional roles to include *all* desired participants. Two sets of parents may walk down the aisle before and after the bride; two women may respond to the "mother's" prayer at a Bar Mitzvah. Stepmothers should shine the limelight where it belongs—on the celebrating child.

Vacations

Vacation periods are often difficult to negotiate because they are not always under the control of stepmothers and fathers. Vacation plans usually revolve around adults' work schedules and childrens' school and extracurricular schedules. In addition to the real problems posed by schedules that overlap or conflict, some adults may choose vacations as the time to "power trip," making planning seem almost impossible. Stepmothers and fathers may find, to their unpleasant surprise, that their vacation plans are continually undermined by the children's mother. This does not have to happen. Planning a vacation involving three or more adults and children is not simple, but it is possible. The safest rule is to *plan well in advance.* Because of the number of individuals involved and unforeseen problems that may crop up—such as illness or injury—*make contingency plans* as well. Imagine your worst-case scenario and plan how to have a happy vacation despite it!

Many stepmothers spoke of having their *own* vacation plans sabotaged by mothers who changed plans at the last moment, leaving the children stranded. Don't let a vacation be totally dependent on your stepchildren's mother. Make an alternate plan in case she backs out: Willing grandparents, camp, or live-in baby-sitters can be arranged long in advance.

Other stepmothers found enthusiasm for family vacations dampened when their stepchildren were pressured by their mothers to change their plans and vacation with her. Help stepchildren avoid feeling guilty by taking adult responsibility for vacation plans. Communicate directly or by mail with the noncustodial mother confirming travel plans—and go!

Chapter 14

LEGAL & FINANCIAL CONSIDERATIONS

Although a full-time stepmother functions as the primary parent in her stepchildren's lives, she has in effect no legal relationship with them. As far as the law is concerned, stepmothers are nonpersons with neither rights nor responsibilities for their stepchildren.

Stepmothers also may discover that they are involved in protracted court battles that began before or after their marriages. The extreme discomfort many stepmothers suffer as a direct result of these long and often ugly court battles is an important contributing factor to the failure of many of their marriages. The very definition of a custodial stepmother implies that stepchildren are living with their father full-time; however, the legal custody of children is always subject to review and modification by either the father or the mother. Because custody and visitation are subject to change, stepmothers often must swim against an undercurrent of ongoing litigation.

Custody

Most statistics put the recorded number of children living with fathers at about 10 to 11 percent. (This figure may be much higher, since many children live with their fathers without benefit of legal custody.) Fathers seeking custody are frequently told that unless the biological mother is psychiatrically or physically incapacitated—confined to an institution or hospital—they would do better to save their time and money. In fact, one stepmother reported that her husband was given this advice despite the fact that the children's biological mother did *not* want custody!

But Things Are Changing

Now that women in the work force is the norm rather than the exception, and divorce is so common, parental rules in society and in the courts are being redefined. In cases where fathers dispute the mother's right to custody, they now win 63 percent of the time. These changing custody decisions imply more custodial stepmothers on the horizon.

Stepmother's Role in Custody Battles

Many stepmothers describe custody battles as excruciating. They feel they are participating in their husbands' seemingly never-ending divorce action. The emotional devastation of divorce is commonly acknowledged; such devastation often escalates into a full-scale conflagration when a stepmother appears.

Stepmothers suffer from these courtroom battles on many levels. Their marriages suffer as the language and strategies of the courtroom seem to dominate their lives. Often they feel that their own lives are being put on hold until custody decisions are finally resolved. They may resent the lack of attention given to the children they bear with their husbands and may be increasingly upset by the constant tension, feeling that their actions and relationships are monitored by the adversary attorneys. Indeed, stepmothers involved with their husbands' custody battles may feel excluded, frustrated, even shamed.

Stepmothers are often excluded from the courtroom proper—prevented even from witnessing events that will directly affect their lives. Although they are often expected to make themselves available for interviews and examinations, they may not be permitted to witness the presentation of these reports in court. The biological mother may request their exclusion, since custody is usually tied to the original divorce action. If custody *is* awarded, it will be awarded to the father only—not to the stepmother and father, together.

The very language of the courtroom may be hurtful to the stepmother: the language of divorce. Despite the passage of time and changing circumstances of the parties, the stepmother's husband is returned, for the purposes of the court, to the children's biological mother, who has now resumed the title of "wife."

The stepmother exists on the edge of a sharply honed two-edged blade. If she attempts to support her husband and is committed to her stepchildren, she will necessarily find herself living in her husband and stepchildren's past in a way that is often humiliating.

What to Expect: Common Custody Procedures

Despite the statistics, stepmothers speak again and again about the pain and anxiety of custody battles—battles that usually end with *everyone losing!* The courts use the expression "best interests of the child" in considering and announcing custody decisions. But who determines what is best? The father? The biological mother? The new father/stepmother couple? The children? The court? At present, the court often relies on "expert" opinion. A custody battle may involve individual interviews with a court-approved psychiatrist, usually at a state-regulated agency. In addition, the homes of both parties will usually be visited by a worker from the city or county social service agency; the children will be interviewed and re-interviewed; even teachers, friends, extended family members, friends of the children and of *all* the parents, and religious and community leaders may be questioned. The attorneys representing the biological mother and the father submit these reports to a judge. Sometimes the children are represented by a court-appointed attorney of their own.

Unfortunately, many fathers, stepmothers, and biological mothers become embroiled in a battle that is in *everyone's* worst interest. The custody battle assumes a life of its own. Stepmothers speak of months of nonstop conversation about custody, legal maneuvers, and changing attorneys. Often the months turn into years. As one veteran attorney at a New York family court confided, "The family court has two speeds: SLOW and STOP." However, while the reports are garnered, the interviews continue, the court appearances drag on, and the attorneys' fees mount, the children are continuing to grow. And such battles take their toll on the *way* these children grow, becoming almost a way of life. The stepmother and the father may find that they never develop a life of their own. Instead, they sacrifice the present to the past.

For these reasons, it is best to avoid the courts, if at all possible. Too many fathers, stepmothers, and biological mothers enter the courts seeking validation and confirmation of personal worth rather than legal recourse. Unless the father has a clear legal reason to enter litigation, try to keep him away from the court.

Arbitration

Arbitration is much more expedient and satisfying than litigation. The hiring of a professional mediator can resolve emotional issues in a smooth, practical way. Arbitration gets to the core of the issues and is less expensive than litigation in time, money, and emotions.

Although arbitration and mediation may be a less painful way to resolve custody and visitation issues, this choice may not be the stepmothers' to make. So what can she do to protect her marriage, stepchildren, and self-esteem in a custody or visitation battle?

Hard Choices

Many stepmothers try to act as their husband's advocate. They read legal journals, confer with attorneys, keep court papers, drive to court appearances. The more control they seek to assert, the more they suffer when they are excluded from the court procedure. A short personal letter to the presiding judge defining your relationship to the stepchildren and your interest in the proceedings may prompt the judge's permission for you to attend as more than an "interested party." Then again, it may not.

Support Your Husband, but Remember It Is His Fight

Stepmothers need to step back and away from issues where they have no real control. Jill almost destroyed the happy life she shared with her husband, Joel, and her two stepdaughters. Now she must live with the can of worms she opened by exerting pressure on her husband to bring action against the children's biological mother, who had left the country five years before. Jill prodded her husband to clear the way for her to adopt her adolescent stepdaughters. Litigation began and Jill immersed herself in the procedure of the court. However, what she assumed would be a simple issue became incredibly entangled when the girls' mother returned to the country and decided to counter-sue for full custody. Jill was excluded from all courtroom procedures. That left her husband, who was not as well-versed nor as *vested* in the sole-custody issue, fighting a battle he had not begun!

Don't Look for Bargains—Hire the Most Competent Attorney

Custody battles are nothing more than business as usual for the courts. Although there is frequent reference to "best interests," the legalese of the court applies to custody decisions as well as to corporate takeovers. "Old boy" networks operate in all courts, and a well-meaning but unknown attorney who gives satisfaction outside the courtroom may be disastrously ineffective inside it. Seek out the best-known and most influential custody attorney. Although such expertise is expensive, it is well worth the cost because of what is at stake.

Once you've hired a stellar attorney, turn the case over to him or her and step back! Do not become embroiled with the issues of the court. Failing to understand that family law is a sort of "game," some stepmothers persist in viewing all the "players" from an emotional perspective. They may also ignore the advice they are paying for and extend and complicate the proceedings. If you don't know how to play the game, leave it to the professionals.

Continue With Your Life

Discussions revolving around court actions must be confined to a particular time and place. If possible, all such discussions should occur outside the home, preferably at an attorney's office. Stepmothers often realize, before anyone else does, that "custody" exists only on paper and in the imagination of those who desire it. Although a legal "win" is satisfying, custody decisions are ultimately secured in the home rather than the courtroom. Indeed, the very term "custody" is at best a misnomer, suggesting either ownership or coercive confinement. Apart from the children of divorced parents, who do the terms "custody" and "visitation" apply to but criminals and social deviants? Children are not subject to ownership. A stepmother's relationship to her stepchildren is defined not by legality or biology but by interaction, shared experience, and commitment.

Case Closed at Eighteen

There is an end to custody cases. At the very least, stepmothers can look forward to the future by remembering that there is finiteness to debates over custody. Sometimes, in the heat of battle, everyone loses sight of the fact that even the best attorney cannot prevent a child from growing up. When children reach eighteen, their cases are closed. But the childrens' lives are not, and with that in mind a stepmother will continue to attempt to live in the present as she raises her stepchildren.

One eighteen-year-old wrote to his stepmother after a protracted and ultimately unsettled suit, "Thank you for being the only one who remembered that I was having a *life* while they were having a *battle.*"

Other Legal Matters: Estates, Adoption, Guardianship, Stepmother-custody, Financial Responsibility

Although stepmothers do not have a legal relationship with their stepchildren, many seek to protect the interests of the children they raise by including them as primary recipients of their estate. Stepchildren will *not* automatically be entitled to any inheritance from their stepmother's estate unless they are specifically named in her will.

Most stepmothers who had a will or carried life insurance stated that their stepchildren were beneficiaries, to share in equal amounts with any biological children.

Adoption

Only a tiny percentage of the stepmothers surveyed reported that they had adopted their stepchildren. In the cases where the mother was not living, they didn't feel it was necessary: Their stepchildren *were* "their children." In cases where the biological mother was living, they usually didn't feel that she would permit this. This is interesting in view of the fact that many stepfathers (whose stepchildren have living fathers) *do* adopt. It is also interesting in view of the fact that the overwhelming number of stepmothers viewed themselves as the primary maternal figure in their stepchildren's lives. One can only speculate on the stress caused by living under such contradictory circumstances.

Legal Custody for the Widowed Stepmother

Although stepmothers time and time again protested that they functioned as mothers in every way, their statements about what would happen if their husbands died belied their protestations. A majority of stepmothers felt that their stepchildren would return to their biological mothers, despite the poor quality of the mother's relationship with the children or the unsuitability of the mother's living situation and/or personal circumstances. A small percentage of stepmothers were adamant about their stepchildren in the event of their husband's death. Some of them described financial arrangements they had made—trust accounts and financial guardians—to keep the biological mother from having a custody motive.

Mary was the exception to the rule—a widowed stepmother who secured legal custody. Mary's husband died after they'd been married for only a short time, leaving Mary with two young stepsons and an infant daughter. Mary fought for, and won, custody of her young stepsons, and has raised them to adulthood as a single parent.

Many stepmothers voiced passivity, not preference, when they said that their stepchildren would return to their mothers in the event of their husbands' death. When asked to describe the type of legal relationship they felt a stepmother *should* have with her stepchildren, they presented a very different picture.

Anne married Joe when she was in her mid-twenties. It was her first marriage and his second. Anne had no children; the mother of Joe's two sons had left when the boys were little more than infants. At the time of Anne's marriage, her stepsons were eighteen months and three years old. Anne and Joe had been married for nine years when Anne became pregnant and gave birth to another son. However, before the new baby was a year old, Joe filed for divorce. Anne's stepsons, who were ten and twelve, were sent cross-country to live with their paternal grandparents. Neither mother nor father assumed or wanted custody of the boys. Because there are no legal provisions for divorced stepmothers, Anne was awarded no visitation. Although she tried repeatedly to locate the boys, she was not able to. She still hopes that at some time, when they reach eighteen, they will seek out their stepmother and half-brother.

Financial Responsibility

Many stepmothers did not realize, at the time of their marriages, that they might be financially responsible for their stepchildren. Although there is no standard legal obligation for a stepmother to support her stepchildren, many women discovered that they were expected to contribute, and did so willingly. Most stepmothers were surprised to learn that these mothers had no financial responsibility for the support of their children in most states.

Stepmothers also found that their personal financial background weighed heavily when their stepchildren reached college age. Many colleges in the nation determine financial eligibility based on computations that include the stepmother's financial status. The stepmother's salary and other assets become a factor in determining eligibility for financing and loans.

Legal Guardianship

Most stepmothers were unaware that they could be appointed guardians of their stepchildren. Check with an attorney for procedures; they differ from state to state.

Hope for Change

As more children begin to live in stepmother-headed households, more changes will occur. It may be that *all* parents—step and biological—could come together to renegotiate a legal agreement that delineates responsibilities when the father and stepmother marry and/or assume full-time responsibility for the children. A new agreement, thus negotiated and arbitrated, would give all the adults in a child's life a sense of power and control over the new situation and perhaps diminish the jealousy, insecurity, and low self-esteem that underlie many court actions. Such an agreement could modify previous custody and visitation agreements and take into consideration the new circumstances of the newly created family. Both step- and biological mothers would feel that they had some say in what was going to happen with their children in their new family situation.

Legal responsibilities and privileges accorded to stepmothers will certainly make them feel more definite about their role as primary caretakers and less like mothers in name only. Such negotiations and arbitrations would serve to bring the new family into the present.

Life experiences are not subject to legislation. Life has a way of intruding on the best-laid plans of stepmothers, who may find their day-to-day lives played out against a background of complicated crises.

C h a p t e r   1 5

WHAT DO I DO NOW

Life goes on—even for a stepmother. Her stepchildren's mother dies or moves away or out of their lives. Custody is changed; stepchildren move in or out or away from home. Husbands die or divorce. Stepchildren grow up and move away.

Coping with Change

The Death of the Children's Biological Mother

In situations where unresolved conflicts have remained for stepchildren, their grief may be particularly intense and burdened by guilt. Stepchildren often feel unduly responsible for the unhappiness or death of their mothers despite their disappointing relationship during her life. The death of a mother represents the death of a dream—a dream of reconciliation between mother and child or between mother and father. For a variety of reasons, the death of a mother is almost invariably painful.

Stepchildren, in their pain, often lash out at their stepmother, implying either directly or through their attitudes or actions that they hold her responsible. What to do? As with any inappropriate behavior, a calm response, supporting the child's pain, and limiting the inappropriate acting out will be most productive.

Loss of Contact With the Biological Mother

A mother who just fades away can send even the most well-adjusted child into an emotional tailspin. The stepmother's role here is cautious support. Typically, children will question their own role and that of their stepmother and father in their mother's disappearance. Rejection or perceived rejection by a parent is always painful. Children need to be helped to deal with the reality of the loss and to avoid both unrealistic guilt over their part in "driving off" the parent and the sense that they "should" experience guilt but do not. A stepmother can reassure the children that she has no intention of changing her own relationship with them.

Custody Changes

Stepchildren often face changes in custody, due to the court decisions, parents' decisions, or their own preference. However the change of custody comes about, it will affect the child's life and the stepmother's. If the child moves from the stepmother's home to the biological mother's, the stepmother will have to deal with the deep emotional effects of loss of control and status as a full-time parent as well as with the real sadness at losing day-to-day contact with the child.

If the stepmother welcomes the change, there may be a relaxation of stress; the stepmother and stepchild may get along better when they don't live together. If the change was against the wishes of the stepmother, her husband, and perhaps the child, the stepmother will have to deal with everyone's feelings of loss. Although the stepmother may grieve or continue to "fight," the time she spends with her stepchild should be as free as possible of feelings of grief and powerlessness. An out-of-control and vulnerable stepmother is *not helpful*. A stepmother can help by maintaining her own calm, efficient, and loving household as a safe haven for the stepchild.

Some children bounce from parent to parent, depending on whim or on who is offering the best situation at the best time. Bouncing is not good either for parents or for children. Changes in custody should be serious decisions, not subject to the whims of children or their parents. Any change in custody should, ideally, be on a trial basis, with the child "visiting" the new home for a while before the change is formalized.

Death or Divorce of Father

If the stepmother should become widowed or divorced while her stepchildren are still legally minors, she will be faced with painful custody decisions. In the case of divorce, the stepmother will often lose all rights to her stepchildren, including visitation; some stepmothers are beginning to test this lack of visitation rights in the courts, but at present most lose all contact unless their stepchildren elect and are permitted to maintain the contact.

In the case of the husband's death, the stepmother will face similar difficulties, despite any provisions in her husband's will or the choice of the children she has raised. Some stepmothers have successfully challenged custodial decisions in the courts, but the chances of her retaining custody of her minor children is still quite remote.

If stepchildren are no longer minors when death or divorce occurs, stepmothers will confront the realities of their personal relationship with their stepchildren. If the stepmother has developed a real connection with her adult stepchildren, that relationship will in all likelihood continue.

Family Crises

Many stepfamilies are formed as an indirect result of a crisis. A mother dies or becomes mentally or physically ill; a stepchild gets into trouble at school or becomes an addict; sometimes a child and a mother, and perhaps a new stepfather, simply can't get along. Other crises spring from complications inherent in the nature of the stepfamily—a family without biological ties or accepted cultural taboos. Possible crises abound.

What to Expect

Many stepchildren harbor secrets they have been unable to share with anyone. The move into a stable and secure environment may prompt a stepchild to entrust these secrets to a stepmother, who is perceived as caring and committed. Often the secrets involve neglect, abuse of one kind or another, or family behavior that is unacceptable by anyone's standards.

The abuse may be physical, sexual, or emotional. Dealing with a child who confides in you about such problems requires a cool, clear head. You must decide when—and how—to get involved and to deal with your husband, who may respond by "shooting the messenger."

Past Abuse

Sometimes stepchildren remember incidents of abuse that occurred long before the stepmother appeared on the scene.

Andrea, a twenty-eight-year-old physical therapist, was married for five years before her stepdaughter came to live with her. Caroline had been abused by her mother's husband for a period of two years. When Caroline began to trust her stepmother, she felt secure enough to share her long-hidden secret. Such delayed "telling" is common between stepmother and stepchild. It may take years for a child who has been abused to trust and to share such secrets. Stepmothers who are so entrusted must view the confidence as an indication of the stability and security that the stepchild perceives in the new relationship and must not overreact or rush to share the news with the child's father. It is usually best to get professional help and advice for the child, even though the abuse occurred in the past.

Current Abuse

When stepchildren confide abuse that is going on in the present—during current visitation periods, for example—direct action is essential. Again, great delicacy will be required in sharing the bad news with the child's father—and dealing with the consequences of his reaction.

What to Do

The typical stepmother is not a psychologist and most stepmothers don't have experts in residence. When a child shares a confidence, a stepmother must react promptly, wisely, and calmly. It helps to take the process step by step:

Listen

Let the child talk. Ask questions. Try to get the facts as clear as possible without getting too many details. If you are unsure about anything, don't be afraid to ask.

React

Don't be afraid to react to your stepchild's confidences. Stepchildren need honest reactions to their trust. They are confiding in the hope that you will do something!

Commit to Action

It is not enough just to listen or to respond sympathetically. A stepmother, like the fairy in *Sleeping Beauty*, cannot undo the past, but she can and should try to lessen the impact and improve the prospects for the future. She may not know what can or should be done, but she should assure the child that she will help—or will *get* help.

Discuss With Your Husband

Stepmothers will need to discuss their stepchildren's confidences with their husbands. Fathers may be shocked, appalled, unbelieving, or plagued with guilt. If the abuse occurred in the past and was unknown to the father, he may suffer guilt. If the problem is current, the father may be enraged. The stepmother is caught in the middle.

Find a Solution

The decision to prosecute or not is a very personal one. The possibility of gaining a conviction will depend on a variety of factors including the child's willingness to testify and the presence of physical or other evidence of abuse. Family court systems are notoriously slow, and investigations involve long, complicated procedures.

Many families seek to change or modify legal custody or visitation based on their commitment to their child's veracity. Family court is not the province for retributive justice. Many stepmothers find that family court is prejudiced in favor of keeping family relationships *together* and restructuring fractured family relationships. Because of this predisposition, stepchildren are often subjected to long, complicated processes that end with no change in custody or with *renewed* visitation. The most important thing to remember before deciding upon court action is that once the issue is before the courts, you lose a great deal of control over your family's life. If a child is in real danger or distress, the issue belongs in *criminal court*.

Many stepmothers spoke discouragingly of the court system in relation to situations involving the abuse or distress of their stepchildren. The court is generally sympathetic to the claims of biological mothers and is still loath to accept the realities of incest and maternal abuse. When abuse or neglect occurs between mother and child, the court seems to have difficulty accepting this distortion of the "sanctity of the mother-child relationship."

A Cautionary Tale

Aimee's stepson began having academic, social, and personal problems during his junior year in high school. Rather timid, Kevin suddenly began to be plagued by skin rashes and insomnia, and his grades plummeted. When Aimee questioned the boy, he confided that he had just recently "remembered" that he had been sexually abused by his mother beginning when he was about seven years old. Because the mother lived in another town and had had no contact either with Kevin or with his thirteen-year-old sister for the past two years, Aimee and her husband arranged for private therapy for the boy and continued with their lives. After several sessions with the therapist, the boy recalled a more recent episode of sexual abuse occurring during his last overnight visit with his mother. Shortly after this new disclosure, Aimee's stepdaughter slid a letter under her stepmother's bedroom door.

Don't want to ruin your day but you always say to write if I have a problem. Here goes. I don't want you to be upset but Kevin is not the only one who was "abused." I was too. I guess I was a different kind of kid but I just told her after the first couple of times to cut it out. Now, you know why I don't care if I don't see her. Now you know why it's kind of hard for me sometimes to talk about personal stuff. I know nothing can be done about this stuff but I just didn't want Kevin to think he was the only one and that I got away free.

Luv, Me

Aimee decided to act. She called a state hot-line for child abuse and reported the mother. Child Protective Services responded quickly. Within twenty-four hours a caseworker had been sent to the house and had spoken with both children. Aimee assured the kids that they would be able to "close" this issue. By the time the report was made, Kevin was seventeen and his sister, Kimberly, was fifteen. Both children were eager to speak about the abuse and seemed relieved that something would be done at long last. The caseworker for the Department of Social Services suggested that the case be remanded to the family court so that visitation (which was still a legal "right" for the mother, although not exercised) could be terminated. The family agreed. Neither Aimee nor her husband sought an attorney, feeling that the case was straightforward. The mother adjourned the case twice and by the time it came up the third time, Kevin was away at college. Aimee and her husband decided to drop his name from the petition, as he would soon be eighteen. When the judge ordered forensic examinations (for all parties), Aimee, her husband, and her stepdaughter attended eagerly, convinced that such an examination would validate Kimberly's allegations as well as determine the mother's mental incompetence. The court-appointed psychiatrist was a warm and concerned professional who related well to all three members of the family: She felt that Kimberly was a well-adjusted child and did not require any additional therapy.

Aimee and her husband returned to court. Aimee asked for, and was granted, permission by the judge to be present in the courtroom. At this procedure, the judge stated that he had *no* reports of abuse and that the children had denied all the charges. Aimee, who held copies of all the investigative reports in her lap, desperately tried to get the judge's attention. The judge took notice of her waving hand and interjections and cautioned her to remain silent. When he continued to chastise her husband for repeating "unfounded" allegations, Aimee ignored the judge's warning and spoke aloud. She didn't get much further than a beginning, "What ..." before she was ejected from the courtroom. This might have been for the best—Aimee's exclusion allowed her to miss the judge's order that visitation between Kimberly and her "natural" mother begin immediately in a private therapist's office, with all such expenses paid for by the petitioner—Aimee's husband. When Kimberly informed her law guardian that she had no intention of seeing her biological mother unless it was in court, she was informed that she had no choice and that if she refused she and her father could be held in contempt of court: jail for Dad and a foster home for Kimberly could be the punishment if she did not abide by the court's decision.

Aimee secured the services of an attorney well-known for her advocacy of women's issues such as rape and battering. The attorney met with Kimberly and suggested that Kimberly did have the right to refuse visitation—which she did. Kimberly's failure to comply with the judge's recommendations caused him to become enraged; when the court convened again, he ordered weekly visitation supervised by a social worker at the Department of Social Services. Aimee's husband was ordered to drive Kimberly to these meetings and threatened with imprisonment and Kimberly's removal to a foster home for failure to do so. Kimberly was forced to comply. She placed a headset on her ears, turned up her music, and read a magazine each time she was forced to visit with her mother.

After years in court and tens of thousands of dollars in legal fees, the judge finally agreed to hear Kimberly. Shortly before her eighteenth birthday, he ruled he could not force visitation.

If a child is in present danger, obviously the abuse will need to be reported, but if the problem occurred in the past and is but a recollection, private therapy is probably the least intrusive and most effective recourse. Remember, if you open up a can of worms you will have to dispose of them.

Sexual Issues Within the New Stepfamily

Stepfamilies are unrelated by biology, so therefore sexual attraction may not seem subject to the same taboos that apply in biological families. However, many stepfamilies function as biological families and would like to see stepsiblings regard each other as *siblings,* rather than as possible mates.

Incest taboos are not biologically programmed, but rather created by society; they are taught in biological families and need to be taught in stepfamilies as well. What is and is not acceptable must be stated simply and with great clarity.

Set Limits

Stepmothers can set clear limits about what is and is not acceptable behavior within the family. The way stepsiblings dress around one another, the way she and her husband dress and behave in front of them, and the way the stepmother demonstrates and receives affection from her stepchildren must be consistently reinforced by both statement and action. Initially, stepmothers may find that a good deal of testing of boundaries goes on, especially when older children and adolescents begin living together and especially in situations where the stepmother and her stepchildren are close in age.

Obviously, it will be difficult for individuals who are initially strangers to develop a family feeling when faced with a parade of sexuality. Bonnie came to her marriage with two teenage daughters; her husband brought one fifteen-year-old son. Bonnie's new stepson had a good deal of trouble beginning to think about his new "sisters" as sisters when they continued to march between their rooms in various stages of undress. The air was charged with sexual tension. Bonnie's adolescent stepson chose to deal with it by acting out, becoming uncharacteristically aggressive. This prompted his mother and stepfather to "get on his case" and encourage him to be "nicer and more loving to his sisters."

Kathy's seventeen-year-old stepson, faced with a similar situation, chose a different route. After two months of living in the next room and sharing a bathroom with his new sister, his father and stepmother were pleasantly surprised at how quickly the "children" learned to get along. Both parents thought it was sweet when Kathy's fifteen-year-old daughter would kiss her "big brother" good night. Both parents thought it was also sweet that the boy blushed when his "sister" complimented him on his good looks or asked him to apply suntan lotion to her back. And when the girl began to walk around the house in her bikini underwear they thought it was a sign that the kids really considered themselves brother and sister, a notion that was quickly dispelled by a scream one summer night. After a day in the sun and an evening snuggling in the TV room with a sister dressed only in sheer shorty pajamas, the boy entered his "sister's" bedroom and made sexual advances to her. The family was shocked and the boy was sent to finish out his senior year with his grandparents in another town.

Basic Rules for Teenage Stepsiblings

Limits on behavior can prevent or at least curb inappropriate stepsibling behavior.

• Opposite-sex stepsiblings should have their own sleeping quarters. Bathroom doors should be closed during use.
• Robes and cover-ups are proper attire for all members of the household. Discussion of individual sexual behavior is inappropriate.
• Parents' sexuality remains a private issue.

Sexual Issues for Stepmothers and Stepsons

Sometimes women become stepmothers to adolescent and older "boys" who are unable to think about their fathers' wives in a "maternal" or nurturing sense. Stepmothers can do much by their action and behavior to set the tone for the kind of behavior they find acceptable. The stepmother who lounges about in a sheer negligee, having intimate talks with her teenage son while waiting for "Daddy" to come home, is sending mixed messages and asking for trouble. When stepmothers are much younger than their husbands, they may find themselves confronting stepsons who are their own age. The fact that these "boys" are younger versions of their husbands may prompt unsettled feelings in a young stepmother. Watch out!

Becoming Aware

Stepmothers needn't be scared off by images of sex-crazed adolescents invading their homes—or by their "own" children suddenly changing into monsters. Most of the problems reported by stepmothers resulted from a denial of adolescent sexuality—a sexuality that needs to be redefined within the context of the new family.

Children who have grown up in single-sex, single-parent homes often have difficulty knowing just what is and is not, appropriate "family" behavior. A balance must be struck somewhere between overemphasizing sexuality (by hovering and unfounded suspicion) and oblivion—such as thinking it's cute when teenagers flaunt their sexuality.

Girls who grow up in all-female homes will tend to be freer about their manner of dress. They may need help understanding the changing mores of the new home that now includes male family members—including your husband, who may be as uncomfortable with inappropriate dress or flirtatious behavior as his sons are.

Women who have raised sons may be accustomed to expressing physical affection in a manner that is misinterpreted with stepsons who have no history with the stepmother as a caretaker.

Boys who have been raised in all-male homes will, like their stepsisters, need to be re-educated about their manner of dress or undress in the house. Boys who have been raised in an all-male household may have a locker-room mentality and at first resent or misunderstand the need for covering up.

Girls who have been raised by their fathers may resent even the implication that their casual behavior with their fathers was provocative.

Time Helps

With time, living-together taboos seem to emerge, just as they do in college dormitories where young men and women share facilities. As many adult couples have found, living together is sometimes the best remedy for inappropriate romances. Sharing living quarters and personal items from toothpaste to telephones, coupled with day-to-day proximity, adds an insider's view of another person's private life. Curlers, pimple cream, sulks, screaming matches with parents, tears, and giggles may help to extinguish inappropriate flames of sexual attraction. If familiarity does *not* dull the edge, the family must confront the problem and either deal with it themselves or seek professional help.

Children With Special Problems and Needs

As mentioned before, many children come to live with their fathers because of problems their mothers are unable or unwilling to handle. Such children may have difficulties with substance abuse—or a history of antisocial behavior involving truancy, running away, aggressive or sexually promiscuous behavior. Other stepchildren are plagued by emotional problems—eating disorders, depression, even suicidal tendencies. Still others have physical disabilities or conditions that make their care difficult. Stepmothers in such circumstances need strong personal and family support and qualified professional assistance.

You will need to become as knowledgeable as possible about your stepchild's particular problem in order to deal with it. You will need to learn, and face, all the facts about the child's difficulty and how it will affect family members' daily lives. A child with special needs must be treated as normally as possible, whether the handicap is a physical disease, a learning disability, a disfiguring birthmark, or just simply a difficult or problematic disposition.

As Dr. Spock tells us, a handicapped child's happiness and effectiveness depends on that child's attitude and the attitude of other family members toward the difficulty. The important factors that make a person (with or without defects) grow up happy and outgoing are parents who thoroughly enjoy and approve and who do little worrying, urging, fussing, or criticizing. The handicapped child who grows up learning to give and take with other children from an early age is the child who grows up happily. It is those parents who are unhappy or ashamed about their child's appearance who will tend to produce an unhappy child.

In growing dissatisfied with himself or herself, Dr. Spock feels that the child becomes exactly what the parents feared: a burden. "If they take his disfiguring birthmark, or the deformed ear, as of no great importance; act as it they consider him a normal child; let him go places like anyone else; don't worry about stares and whispered remarks—then the child gets the idea he is a regular guy and thinks little of his peculiarity. As for the stares and whispers, the child with a noticeable defect has to get used to them, and the younger the easier." Dr. Spock feels strongly that children are much better off without pity. "Pity is like a drug."

Stepmothers can be more helpful to a disabled child than the actual parent, who may be burdened by guilt for their genetic contribution to the disease or deformity. Because of their lack of a biological relationship and their more objective demeanor, stepmothers can help their stepchildren reach their full potential. "Naturally a child with a defect needs understanding, and he often needs special handling," cautions Dr. Spock. "The slow child should not be expected to do a job that is proven to be beyond his mental development, and one with stiff hands shouldn't be criticized for poor penmanship. On the other hand, don't sell your child short by assuming that he can't do something, or be taught to do something. It is the confidence of parents and teachers that keeps a child moving forward. But the child with a defect can be reasonably polite, take turns, do his share of the chores. Everyone is happier and more pleasant when he knows he's expected to be considerate. The child with a handicap wants to be treated the same, held to the same rules as other children."

Dr. Spock and other childcare experts agree that in order to grow happily and to contribute to families and the larger community, children need to be loved and accepted for who they are. A child's disability may be profound or may be only a matter of the adults' perception. Treating a child with overconcern and refusing to accept the child can lower his or her self-esteem. Dr. Spock tells of a ten-year-old boy who is short for his age. Although the parents have been assured that he has no disease, they view his small stature as a deformity and continue to show their concern by urging the boy to eat larger portions so that he will grow faster. Being compared favorably for other qualities—telling a child that his looks don't matter because he is so smart, or so witty—only emphasizes the idea of competition and rivalry. There are times when a short child, or a homely one, or a nearsighted one, wants to be told how unimportant the handicap is. Confident reassurance is then a great help. But if the parents are uneasy, always bringing up the subject, the child becomes convinced that he is an inferior person.

—Spock, Benjamin, *Baby and Child Care*, pp. 666-667.

Set the Tone for Acceptance

Brothers and sisters take their attitude from the parents: If the parents accept the handicapped child wholeheartedly and matter-of-factly, the other children in the family are likely to do so, too. They become indifferent to the remarks of other children.

Stepmothers may find that they are inundated by friends and family with unsolicited advice about experts and treatment programs concerning their stepchild's disability. In order to feel comfortable with the particular handicap, stepmothers will need to confer with the child's physician and any specialists with whom the child is interacting. Sometimes stepmothers find it helpful to attend or organize a support group for children with similar special needs.

Don't Hesitate to Seek Help

Caring for a child with a handicap or a "difficult" child usually means extra effort. To make the best plans for that child requires real wisdom, which is hard to come by, especially when you have little experience. All this adds up to the fact that, as the parent of a troubled or handicapped child, you need guidance. Find an opportunity to discuss whether or not it is feasible to manage the care of the child at home and, if so, what practical strategies are involved in this care. Educate yourself to cope with the impact of the child's disability on other family members, the advantages and disadvantages of various educational local and residential programs, and a host of other issues. Clarifying such matters may take months, even years of research and discussion with qualified professionals and other parents. There are usually social workers in state bureaus for the blind, deaf, crippled, and retarded and on the staffs of the schools and clinics that care for such children. In rural districts there might be a county welfare worker, and in cities there are social workers in family and children's social agencies.

If you are not sure where to get help, write to the Department of Welfare in your state capital. If you live in a city, call the United Way or United Good Neighbors for an agency referral. Parents of children with various handicaps and conditions have organized themselves into local chapters and national associations that share their special problems and solutions. They hear talks by professionals in the field and exert their influence to get better facilities for their children. They raise funds for research and treatment. You can get information about special schooling from your state Department of Education and about professional resources from your state Department of

Health.

Once the stepmother feels that she has a good working knowledge of the child's disability, current limitations, and prognosis, she can usually treat the child as a person rather than as a disability. Some well-meaning parents and friends become so involved with the disability that they lose sight of the child. A stepmother, unshackled from debilitating guilt, can provide the love and confidence her stepchild needs.

Crises affect families deeply. Stepmothers have to be careful not to become overcontrolling and obsessive about redressing wrongs or to grow resentful about the problems. Husbands may either turn away from problems that began in what one husband called "another lifetime" or turn inward with guilt. Other husbands are unable or unwilling to take responsibility for their children's current symptoms. Although crises can and often do bring families together, a crisis that originated outside the present family can also divide it.

Don't hesitate to seek professional advice. If you are unsure about how to find a therapist, ask a doctor you trust for a referral, contact a local hospital or mental health association, or ask a rabbi, minister, priest, or any other person you trust and respect for assistance. Try to get several names and shop around until you find a person with whom you feel comfortable.

When You Can't Get Help

Obviously, the best solution is to find a family counselor and haul the whole bunch into family therapy. Realistically, this doesn't always work. Often, husbands and/or stepchildren are unwilling to enter therapy or feel that they can't afford it. If you are in a situation where counseling is not an option, *read, read,* and *read some more!* Become knowledgeable about your stepchild's particular problem. Share what you have learned with the family. Present age-appropriate options for the child to consider and help him make choices in working through, and ultimately moving away from, his problems. Encourage your stepchildren to talk through their concerns.

Living with problem situations is extraordinarily stressful

for a stepmother. In order to avoid feeling overloaded, resentful, and overwhelmed, find a place where you can unload your feelings safely. When you are stressed out or angry, you need an outlet. Whether or not the family is in counseling, you may benefit from individual therapy or a stepmother group.

Stepmothers who are bewildered or frustrated about their roles often lack self-confidence. You need to learn to manage your stress and become calmer and happier—and you can, by turning to the next chapter.

Chapter 16

Stress Management

Stepmothers suffer from an incredible amount of stress. Juggling a career, a new marriage, and a new family, often in a climate of nonsupport or outright hostility, is decidedly stressful.

Many stepmothers feel that they have no homes—no place where they can unwind and recharge. Indeed, when there are conflicts with stepchildren and/or husbands, home often feels like dangerous territory rather than a calm, safe haven. A tension-home filled can actually be perceived as a *cause* of stress.

What to Expect: Five Common Areas of Stress

Lack of Recognition

Mental health experts have long recognized that a one-sided relationship is both stressful and doomed to failure. When a person perceives that she is doing "all the giving," she is bound to feel resentful. Many stepmothers willingly assume the bulk of childcare responsibilities only to discover that their efforts are unappreciated, even unrecognized by their husbands. Compounding the buildup of stress is the stepmother's feeling that she cannot express her feelings, that speaking out is either inappropriate or impractical.

Jackie is one such stepmother. At twenty-nine she feels that "most disappointing is when, after all the consideration, after all the doing and caring as if they were your own, there is not an ounce of gratitude, thanks, or appreciation." Most disappointing is an attitude from your husband that "you're expected to do it all, that you have no right to feel tired, hurt, or angry about any part of the situation."

Other stepmothers feel cheated: They feel that they have

been assigned all the responsibility for their stepchildren, without any of the fun times, celebrations, and recognition. Jane, a thirty-three-year-old stepmother of three, often feels as though she's "paying the penalty for other people's irresponsibility." Jane states that "I feel I'm always expected to clean up, or correct other people's messes or mistakes. It makes me angry when my own family or my own son must pay consequences for actions and deeds they didn't have any part of. I'm angry at the injustice of the situation, the blindness and injustice of people, and the pomposity of a court system and appointed representatives that treat me like I don't exist."

This question of "invisibility" crops up again and again; as mentioned earlier, stepmothers feel that they are "just not there." In some cases, this perception is accurate, as stepchildren seek to reconcile loyalty conflicts by ignoring their stepmothers. Sally can't stand it when the kids "act as if I'm a stranger" when she picks them up from a weekend with their mother. Sally feels betrayed and incredibly angry, even though she knows they're coping with a difficult situation that involves loyalty conflicts.

Rebecca reports that her very existence is ignored by her stepchildren. After two years, her stepdaughter still has problems adjusting to "having a stepmother"—she just "forgets to tell people" that she has one. Rebecca is hurt and upset when she meets teachers, camp counselors, parents of the child's friends, and others who don't even know that she exists. Rebecca claims that she feels eerily "dead."

Other stepmothers have their existence recognized, but fail to receive any approval for their role in child-rearing. Harriet is still dismayed over the lack of support from her in-laws. Even though she has raised her sixteen-year-old stepson for the past nine years, her in-laws persist in ignoring Harriet, crediting only their son, or grandson, luck, or even themselves for any achievements or accomplishments. Harriet realizes that she shouldn't care so much about approval or recognition from others, but like many stepmothers, she continues to seek such validation long after it has become obvious that this recognition will not be forthcoming.

"Sometimes it's just little things that get to me, like

the time I helped our boy with a big school project on dogs. We worked for days, gathering the materials, going to the library, and making the actual project. When it was all finished I took him out for pizza and bowling. Weeks later, I found a report that he had written where he praised his grandmother for taking him to a dog show. I never told him I saw that report but it still hurts to think about it!"

Lack of Affection

While some stepmothers are upset about their lack of recognition, others feel more stress over the lack of affection between themselves and their stepchildren.

Dorothy, a stepmother with grown children, remembers this lack of affection as a prominent cause of the stress that gradually eroded her relationship with her stepchildren. Dorothy did not feel any warmth or affection from them. A biological mother of four and stepmother to three, Dorothy had expected that her hugs and kisses would eventually be returned. However, after some initial tries, she was hurt and backed off when her stepchildren struggled from her embraces. From time to time, she would reach out again, only to be rebuffed. The years passed and Dorothy grew used to living without any demonstrations of affection by her stepchildren. Now that they're adults, she no longer even tries to be affectionate. The past eleven years have muted her feelings for her stepchildren.

Irene invited all her nine-year-old stepdaughter's classmates and friends for a huge surprise birthday party. Irene even went so far as to dress up in a clown costume and bake the birthday cake. Much to her disappointment, her stepdaughter refused to be in any pictures with her. When Irene tried to sneak into one picture, the girl ran from the room and screamed in front of all her friends that she hated her. Irene was crushed.

Lack of Acceptance

Many stepmothers are rattled by the lack of stability, acceptance, and respect for their role in their stepchildren's lives. Stepmothers may, with all good intentions, create important roles for themselves in their new families. They may continue executing these roles, only to find themselves occasionally thrown off balance either by the chilling devaluation of their role by insensitive remarks or by "surprise" appearances by the children's mother. Remarks from those outside the stepfamily can be especially stressful. A teacher's "But where is her *real* mother?" may ring in the ears of a stepmother who has raised this child for six of her ten years of life.

Tanya, stepmother to two boys aged nine and seven, says, "It's the inconsistency that really gets to you; not knowing what I'm expected to do. Like taking my stepsons to their Little League dinner after attending every game all season and finding 'her' in my seat, or going to the school open house and finding 'her' sitting in the boys' seats. There's no rhyme or reason to it. She disappears from their lives for months at a time and then resurfaces at these public times, just as if she'd never been gone. Of course, to the world she looks like a great mother, and I look like the wicked jerk if I say anything at all." Such inconsistency builds stress; being unable to prepare for the future and feeling unbalanced, attacked, and incapable of receiving support is stressful.

Lack of Control

The most stressful issue for stepmothers is their perceived lack of control. They usually function as primary parents for their stepchildren and as such begin to feel responsible for their stepchildren's day-to-day lives and instrumental in affecting their future. When these parental efforts are frustrated or blocked, many stepmothers feel a tremendous amount of stress.

Diane is faced with unrelenting stress every other weekend when she is forced by court order to send her eight-year-old stepson, against his wishes, to his mother's home. Diane "can't stand being unable to protect my stepson from the negative, abusive aspects of his life." The boy's mother is an alcoholic and frequently abusive, both physically and emotionally. Although Diane and her husband have repeatedly sought termination of such visits in the court, they have been unsuccessful, and they just don't have the money to continue fighting. Diane has sought to balance the instability of her stepson's life by providing a positive example and a "dry" household. She well knows the effects of alcohol; her own father was an alcoholic. Diane has been prevented by the child's mother from taking the boy to Al-Anon meetings; the biological mother retains joint custody, which gives her the legal power to consent or decline consent for any and all extracurricular activities. "Sometimes I feel so frustrated I could cry and I do. It kills me to have him go on these visits—if this wasn't his mother, I wouldn't even let him spend one minute there."

Other stepmothers find that they are not permitted to assume parental roles for their stepchildren either by their husbands or because the children resist. Such stepmothers are often confused about what to do. Ultimately, their sense of identity may begin to suffer.

Marie finds that not being a central figure in her household really bothers her. Like all too many stepmothers, Marie lives with a dichotomy between her professional and personal life: Professionally, she is a middle manager who functions in a leadership position. At home, she has no control—"I go from respected executive to nonperson as soon as I walk through my front door."

Other stepmothers are frustrated by trying to influence their stepchildren's lives in ways that just don't seem to work. Renee discovered, after five years of marriage, that her stepchildren would not "turn out like her" after all. It was very difficult for her to accept the fact that patterns of behavior and personality traits are often so firmly entrenched.

Another primary cause of stress for stepmothers is feeling unjustly blamed for events and issues over which they have little control. Too often, they feel that they are the family "dump" into which everyone's garbage is spilled. Last year Merryl, a new stepmother of two teenagers, was blamed for her stepchildren's bad grades. After all, said her husband, Merryl had been "told over and over again to check the girls' homework each evening." Yet her husband is aware of the girls' uncooperativeness. Merryl had tried to check the girls' homework and had been told to "get out of our room and off our case"; her husband told her to back off, stop nagging, and respect the girls' privacy. Although Merryl knows that she is not at fault, she feels puzzled and powerless.

Other stepmothers *really* have no control; their control is totally tied to their husband's physical presence. Carol is one such stepmother. Her husband often travels on business and, when he leaves, her two preteen stepchildren seem to become "totally different children." They refuse to "mind" Carol, telling her to her face that if she tells their father they will just deny everything they've done. At these times Carol feels like a hostage in her own home. The stress builds as Carol struggles between capitulating, telling her husband, or trying to handle this out-of-control situation on her own.

No Time Off

Many stepmothers are "stressed out" when they discover that, contrary to previous expectations, they have no time off from child-rearing. Often stepchildren, even those with living mothers, do not visit with her because of unsatisfactory situations or relationships.

Stepmothers often feel uncomfortable requesting that in-laws, their own relatives (or even their husbands!), act as "baby-sitters," fearing that others will question their commitment to their stepchildren. Because of this unwillingness to ask for help and the very real problem of finding people who will "baby-sit" for one, two, three, four, or more children at one time and in one place, stepmothers often find that they have committed themselves to unrelenting childcare.

Marlene didn't expect that she'd *never* have a vacation. When she and Neal married, she thought her three stepchildren would spend their vacations with their mother, as they always had. That arrangement changed when Marlene came on the scene. Now the kids stay home for vacations, which leaves no vacations or weekends alone for Marlene and her husband.

What to Do

Stepmothers do not have to wait for recognition, appreciation, and control of their lives; they can take charge by themselves. You can minimize your stress by changing your perspective. Thinking about stress as a reaction to pressure places you in charge. When stress is perceived as a reaction, you can begin to feel that you not only induce your own stress, but have the power to reduce it as well.

As a stepmother, you need to be kind to yourself. You do *not* need anyone's approval and validation. You must validate, confirm, and accept the importance of your role in your stepchildren's and husband's lives.

In order to reduce stress immediately and substantially, view yourself as you would wish yourself to be—gracious, calm and able to tolerate whatever stressful forces come your way.

Refuse to Be Stressed

Stress is a killer. In the same way that a stepmother watches her diet, her alcohol intake, and other unhealthy factors, she must manage her own stress. Doing so is not very complicated: Most of it is caused by a feeling that one has lost the ability to manage a situation or to prevent an unpleasant event from occurring.

Try these simple steps:

Ask for What You Need

"I need a hug. I need to be left alone. I need to be told you love me..." Say the words. There is no crime or shame in asking for what you need. More often than you would imagine, husbands, stepchildren, in-laws, your own relatives, and friends will be happy to comply. You don't come with an instruction manual—people won't know what works for you unless you tell them. Waiting around for people to figure out what you need is unfair to them and to you.

Give Yourself What You Want

If it's a hug, take it. If it's to be left alone, remove yourself from the room. If it's a candlelight dinner, orchestrate it! People who are not "needy" are more attractive to others because they're more fun to be around. You may find that once you give to yourself, others are more willing to give to you, too. Or you may find that you just don't *need* as much anymore.

There is no reason for any human being to feel invisible. No one can make us feel unworthy but ourselves. Respect is accorded to those who respect themselves.

Focus on the Practical

Sometimes, in response to the tremendous emotional issues that seem to bombard them, stepmothers get totally mired in the undercurrents of life. Bright, highly educated women lose sight of both the forest *and* the trees. They may pick apart and analyze each statement uttered, look for hidden meanings in the most casual behavior. Such over-analysis produces tremendous stress in *everyone*. Whenever possible, try to focus on the practical and do-able, leaving the heavy analysis and introspection for only the most critical issues.

Let Go of the Things That Are Not in Your Control

Stepmothers said that the biggest stressor was lack of control. The best way to obliterate this type of stress is: LET GO! Stepmothers need to acknowledge that certain aspects of life are outside their control. The stepmother who can separate herself successfully from those things that she truly cannot control will find that she is living a relatively stress-free life.

Accept Responsibility Only for Your Own Actions

A primary stress producer is accepting blame and responsibility for others' actions. Stress builds up when a stepmother seeks to rewrite history, to redress past wrongs, or to live someone else's consequences. Opt out of this game. Don't accept anyone else's responsibility. Help your stepchildren toward this goal by not permitting them to blame you for events of the past. This is the only way you can teach them to be more responsible for their own actions.

Find Support Systems

Stepmothers often feel that they have no one to talk to about their concerns, and they may be right. Friends, family, and even some professionals may be unaware of their concerns. Some stepmothers have spoken to people who were inappropriate sources, only to find their ignorance and lack of sensitivity *added* stress to the situation. Stepmothers *do* need support systems.

Individual therapy provides an arena where women can talk about themselves in a noncritical, nonjudgmental setting. It's a luxury that boosts self-esteem and speeds the ability to handle the challenges of stepmothering.

"People need people." Most full-time stepmothers don't know any *other* full-time stepmothers. This isolation is in great part responsible for the stress they feel. Breaking this isolation isn't always easy, but if there is a stepfamily group in your area, find it. If there is not, you can advertise in the local newspaper for members.

If you can't manage therapy or find or create a stepmother group, or even locate another stepmother to talk to, get out a pen. Isolated stepmothers find that journaling is very helpful. In addition to getting those feelings on paper, it's possible to chronicle your progress through the various stages of stepmothering.

Date Your Husband

Stepmothers often shelve their role as *women*. Good "couple time"—and a vacation from superparenting—are refreshing. Remember what you loved about your husband when you were dating and why you thought you'd be able to handle all this! Recapture that feeling and you will find your stress melting away.

Work Outside the Home if Possible

Many women leave their jobs when they marry and become stepmothers. Sometimes they enjoy being able to give up their work, only to find that they were unprepared for the negative side effects. Stepmothers who had not worked outside the home tended to identify themselves through their families; they expected to work harder at making everyone happy. Such stepmothers, unfortunately, tended also to expect too much too soon; more often than not, everyone was unhappier than might have been expected.

Whether working within, outside the home, or both, stepmothers need to define themselves other than through their families. Since a new family takes years to build, a woman who insists on defining herself through the family tends to magnify each success and failure and to react to family matters much too personally. Stepmothers who have some other means of fulfilling themselves will find that they are less stressed and more successful in their family relationships.

Keep hobbies, activities, and personal interests alive, too. You'll be less stressed and more interesting to your family and to yourself.

How to Defuse a Stressful Situation

Despite careful planning and self-preserving tactics, most stepmothers will occasionally bump into a situation that is especially stress-producing. In order to minimize personal stress and retain a measure of dignity and self-respect:

• Remember how you would "like to be" and act as though you "are."

• Take deep breaths.

• Speak in low tones.

• Speak slowly.

• Avoid responding if you're feeling overly emotional.

Sometimes stepmothers are faced with direct attacks by their stepchildren. Remember that such are little more than window dressing for deeply felt emotions.

There is a certain repetitiveness to the remarks children most frequently level at their stepmothers. Those remarks hit below the belt and snatch the breath away. It is possible to understand these commonly launched barbs and thereby lessen the stress they induce.

Try to respond to the *feelings* underlying harsh statements rather than to the statements themselves. Below are examples of remarks and appropriate responses.

"You're not my mother!"
"Of course not. I'm your stepmother."

"I hate you!"
"I'm sorry you're angry."

"I wish my father never married you!"
"I know, but I'm glad he *did.*"

"You ruin everything!"
"I'm sorry you're disappointed."
My brother [sister, grandmother, mother, teacher] says that…"
That's interesting, but how do you feel?"

"Don't kiss me! [touch me, tickle me, etc.]"
"Okay—for now."

"This is not your house! [boat, car, dog, etc.]"
"You're right. It's not mine, it's ours."

Avoid stress by simply avoiding "the game." Children are not appropriate adversaries. You can use a child's statements, even if they are hurtful, to forge a deeper and more understanding relationship. You need not be saccharine or phony, but you do need to refrain from responding to statements that are really nothing more than bait for arguments with your stepchildren.

Stressful Remarks from Others

Stressful remarks do not come only from children. Often teachers, neighbors, family, and friends inadvertently or intentionally make statements that cause stress levels to soar. Hearing "Are you so-and-so's mother?" gives stepmothers pause because they think it sounds cold to respond, "No, I'm his [or her] stepmother." On the other hand, just saying "Yes" may make the stepmother uncomfortable, especially if the person continues, "I mean so-and-so's *real* mother." Probably the best response is something like "Yes—everything but the giving birth. I'm so-and-so's stepmother." A response like this reduces your stress, identifying exactly who you are and how important you consider your role. Avoid getting emotional and just provide the information you want the person to have or to turn the question back, as you've learned to do with your stepchildren.

Spend Time Alone

Stepmothers need time alone, away from the concerns of family life, whether in a bubble bath or out to dinner with college chums. Whether you do something as rigorous as attending an aerobics class or as introspective as practicing the piano, you need time apart, and alone. Because so much of your energy is directed outward, your individual time is necessary if you are to stay calm and in balance.

Recognize Your Power

Although many stepmothers feel powerless they are often perceived as anything *but* by others. Stepmothers are much more powerful than they imagine. In fact, much of the stress they bump up against is a direct response to their perceived strength. The resistance from stepchildren, the bad-mouthing from biological mothers, the devaluing by in-laws—all are often reactions to the stepmother's perceived *power*.

Stepmothers spend too much time trying to justify their existence; such attempts lead to stress. There is no need for a stepmother either to define or to justify her existence. Stepmothers, like mothers, brothers, sisters, grandmothers, and grandfathers, uncles, and aunts, just *are*. They are as different and as alike as members of any other family group. When stepmothers stop trying to defend themselves and to justify their actions, they will feel a tremendous decrease in their level of stress.

A stepmother's relationship with her stepchildren can be one of life's most challenging; it can also provide deep personal satisfaction. Many people have asked, "Why would anyone want to become a stepmother?" The answer lies in a stepmother's heart. Stepmothering can and does "work," and when it does, a family is forged. That adds immeasurably to a woman's personal fulfillment.

The primacy and critical nature of a stepmother's relationship with her stepchildren is obvious; stepmothers live with and care for their stepchildren on a daily and ongoing basis. That is all—and that is enough.

All relationships are fluid, dynamic, and subject to both subtle and substantial shifts; in this respect stepmothers' relationships with their families are no different. Each stepmother enjoys a unique relationship with her own family; all stepmothers share a collective lore.

Whether a stepmother begins parenting with confidence or trepidation, most quickly discover that it is a new kind of mothering. It often begins and sometimes continues without the freer intimacy that characterizes biological motherhood.

Talking, family conferences, letter-writing between members of the family, personal journals, a strong support system, and personal and/or family counseling can help a stepmother over the rough spots.

Throughout these pages stepmothers have struggled to express the essence of what they have gained from their relationships with their stepchildren. Although their experiences are diverse, there seem to be some striking and important common gains: Stepmothers gain a sense of their own personal limitations—including a realization that they cannot accomplish everything according to their specifications and in their own time. Although many struggle against these limits, such acceptance ultimately has such interesting by-products as a sense of lessened pressure and a lessened concern with getting everything right.

The understanding that one cannot control everything, and a lessening of the desire to do so, prepares stepmothers for self-acceptance. Self-acceptance in turn enables interaction with others in a clearer, freer, more individual way than ever before.

Stepmothers must juggle a jumbled and conflicted spectrum of feelings. But sorting out the feelings allows her to eventually understand and accept the feelings of each family member.

Finally, the most fortunate stepmothers find themselves privy to a deep understanding of the way relationships evolve though time and shared experience. Stepmothers learn that parenting is hard work, not to be taken either lightly or for granted. They understand that relationships grow from a shared commitment, loyalty, respect and a common history—and may, if they are lucky—come to rest under the banner of love.

The author welcomes your response and reactions, personal and/or professional, to this book. To share your responses to the book or your experience with this subject, address correspondence to:

Pearl Ketover Prilik
c/o WRS Publishing
P. O. Box 21207 • Waco, TX 76702

A p p e n d i x

R e s o u r c e s   f o r   S t e p m o t h e r s

WHERE TO GET HELP

There are many types of help available to stepmothers who need information, assistance and/or support in meeting the challenges of raising their stepchildren. Child guidance centers, mental health clinics, family service agencies, and groups organized around specific areas of concern may be helpful. In order to locate such groups in your area contact your local and/or state Mental Health Association, Department of Health or Department of Social Services.

Referrals for counseling services in your area may be obtained from:

Stepfamily Association of America, Inc.
National Headquarters
215 Centennial Mall South
Lincoln, NE 68508
800/735-0329
(For a Stepfamily Association chapter in your area, call or write the Stepfamily Association of America.)

Child Abuse and Maltreatment
1-800-342-3720

Drug Abuse Information Hotline
1-800-522-5353

Missing Children (KIDWATCH)
1-800-543-9282

For additional telephone numbers of groups, organizations, and agencies in your area consult your telephone directory. Most have crisis hotline numbers and government agencies under separate headings that are located either in the front or back pages of your directory. In addition to professional organizations and groups, religious leaders, teachers, school counselors, friends, magazine articles, and your children's pediatrician may be appropriate sources to turn to for guidance.

Some stepmothers just yearn for someone else with whom to share their experiences. If this is your situation, try beginning your own stepmother group: seek out interested stepmothers in your area. Place ads in your local newspaper, hang up notices in your local market, workplace, beauty shop, coffee-shop, etc. Be creative.

Bibliography

Beard, M. Ruth. *An Outline of Piaget's Developmental Psychology.* New York: Mentor, 1969.

Berman, Claire. *Making It as a Stepparent: New Roles, New Rules.* New York: Doubleday, 1980.

Bettelheim, Bruno. *The Uses of Enchantment.* New York: Knopf, 1976.

Clingempeel, Glenn W. and Eulalee Brand and Richard Ievoli. "Stepparent-Stepchild Relationships in Stepmother and Stepfather Families: A Multimethod Study." *Family Relations,* July 1984.

Coleman, Marilyn and Lawrence H. Ganong. "Effect of Family Structure on Family Attitudes and Expectations." *Family Relations,* July 1984.

Despert, J. Louise. *Children of Divorce.* New York: Doubleday, 1953.

Einstein, Elizabeth. *The Stepfamily: Living, Loving and Learning.* Boston: Shambala Publications, 1985.

Esses Lillian M. and Richard Campbell. "Challenges in Researching the Remarried." *Family Relations,* July 1984.

Fischer, Judith L. "Mothers Living Apart from Their Children." *Family Relations,* July 1983.

Francke, Linda Bird. *Growing Up Divorced.* New York: Fawcett-Crest, 1983.

Ganong, Lawrence H. and Marilyn Coleman. "Stepparent: A Pejorative Term?" *Psychological Reports,* 1983.

Ganong, Lawrence H. and Marilyn Coleman. "The Effects of Remarriage on Children: A Review of the Empirical Literature." *Family Relations,* July 1984.

Ganong, Lawrence H. and Marilyn Coleman and Jane Henry. "What Teachers Should Know About Stepfamilies." *Childhood Education,* May/June, 1984.

Ginott, G. Haim. *Between Parent and Child.* New York: Avon, 1969.

Giles-Sims, Jean and David Finkelhor. "Child Abuse in Stepfamilies." *Family Relations,* July 1984.

Glick, Paul. "Parents With Young Stepchildren and With Adult Stepchildren: A Demographic Profile." Unpublished paper delivered at 10/4/91 meeting of Stepfamily Association of America. Arizona State University: 1991.

Lutz, Patricia. "The Stepfamily: An Adolescent Perspective." *Family Relations,* July 1983.

Maddox, Brenda. *The Half-Parent: Living with Other People's Children.* New York: M. Evans, 1975.

Mills, David M. "A Model for Stepfamily Development." *Family Relations,* July 1984.

Noble, June and William Noble. *How to Live with Other People's Children.* New York: Hawthorne, 1979.

Papernow, Patricia L. "The Stepfamily Cycle: An Experiential Model of Stepfamily Development." *Family Relations,* July 1984.

Paskowicz, Patricia. *Absentee Mothers.* New York: Allanheld/ Universe, 1982.

Piaget, Jean. *The Grasp of Consciousness.* Boston: Harvard Press, 1976.

Robinson, Bryan E. "The Contemporary American Stepfather." *Family Relations,* July 1984.

Roosevelt, Ruth, and Jeannette Lofas. *Living in Step.* New York: McGrawHill, 1977.

Rosenbaum, Jean and Veryl Rosenbaum. *Stepparenting.* California: Chandler and Sharp, 1977.

Skeen, Patsy, and Bryan E. Robinson, and Carol Flake-Hobson. "Blended Families—Overcoming the Cinderella Myth." *Young Children,* January 1984.

Stone, L. Joseph and Joseph Church. *Childhood and Adolescence.* New York: Random House, 1966.

Turnbull, Sharon K. and James M. Turnbull. "To Dream the Impossible Dream: An Agenda for Discussion with Stepparents." *Family Relations,* July 1984.

Visher, Emily B., and John S. Visher. *Stepfamilies: A Guide to Working with Stepparents and Stepchildren.* New York: Brunner-Mazel, 1979.

Visher, Emily B. and John S. Visher. *Stepfamilies, Myths and Realities.* New Jersey: Citadel, 1979.

Visher, Emily B., and John S. Visher. *How to Win as a Stepfamily.* December, 1982.

Walker, Glynnis. *Second Wife, Second Best.* New York: Doubleday, 1984.

A MESSAGE FROM THE PUBLISHER

When Pearl Prilik suggested her book idea to me, she said, "Whether you know it or not, there are more stepmothers than regular mothers in America today." I started to look at our employees and friends and realized firsthand she was right. Prilik, founder of the Step-Parenting Association, did her homework. This book fills a need for its market, and we're proud to present it to our readers.

W. R. Spence, M.D.
Publisher

$\mathcal{A}$t WRS Publishing, we are only interested in producing books we can be proud of—books that focus on people and/or issues that enlighten and inspire, books that change lives for the better, either through the celebration of human achievement or the revelation of human folly. **Call us at 1-800-299-3366 for suggestions or for a free book catalog.**

WATCH FOR THESE RELATED TITLES:

I LAFFED TILL I CRIED is the story of Patti Lewis, her thirty-six years of marriage to Jerry Lewis, and the pain that lay behind the laughter.

FATHER BEHIND BARS A steel-hard story of poverty, racism, prison, reform, and responsibility—one man's struggle to try to give his family the kind of life he never had and to become the father they so much deserved.

THE GHETTO SOLUTION, an intimate portrait of Roland Gilbert, how he overcame a life of self-inflicted pain, drug-addiction, and incarceration and went on to create **Simba,** a "rites-of-passage" program designed to teach African American men and boys to break the cycle of ghetto conditions.

MILLICENT tells the story of how Millicent Collinsworth overcomes years of abuse, illness, and disability to emerge as a strong, successful, blind actress, speaker, and role model.

WRS
PUBLISHING
A Division of WRS Group, Inc.
Waco, Texas